Service-Oriented Architecture

A Planning and Implementation Guide for Business and Technology

ERIC A. MARKS

MICHAEL BELL

WILEY

For general information on our other products and services, or technical support, please contact our Customer Care Department within the United States at 800-762-2974, outside the United States at 317-572-3993 or fax 317-572-4002.

Wiley also publishes its books in a variety of electronic formats. Some content that appears in print may not be available in electronic books.

For more information about Wiley products, visit our web site at http://www.wiley.com.

Library of Congress Cataloging-in-Publication Data:
Marks, Eric A.
  Service-oriented architecture: a planning and implementation guide for business and technology / Eric A. Marks, Michael Bell.
      p. cm.
  Includes index.
  ISBN-13: 978-0-471-76894-4 (cloth)
  ISBN-10: 0-471-76894-4 (cloth)
   1. Business enterprises--Computer networks--Management. 2. Information technology--Management. 3. Computer network architectures. I. Bell, Michael II. Title.
  HD30.37.M3642 2006
  004.068--dc22
                                    2005034273

Printed in the United States of America

10 9 8 7 6 5 4 3 2

Contents

Acknowledgements

Writing a book is never accomplished in a vacuum. There are many insights and ideas that come from the valuable interactions and conversations with friends, peers, colleagues and partners. For all of those who have helped shape our ideas in this book, we thank you.

In addition, the authors would like to recognize the following individuals for their help in reviewing portions of the book and providing valuable insights and feedback to us.

Gabe Benvenuti, Dan Bertrand, Brent Carlson, David Cohn, Greg Coticchia, Christopher Crowhurst, Robert Fletcher, Major Lloyd Herbert, Alan Himler, Lt. Col. Freeman James, Jeff Kessler, Paul Leung, Lisa Nathan, Tom Pedersen, Doug Priest, Jeff Poulin, Ajaya Sahoo, Rollin Shank, Vince Snyder, Mark Stender, Sushil Taneja, Steve Witkop.

To all of you, we thank you for your time and commitment to the success of this book.

Dedications

"To Yvonne, Agamit, Lisa, and Gizela, thanks for your love and support."

-Michael Bell

"For Diane, Jessica and Jonathon, whose love, patience and support carried me through."

-Eric A. Marks

Preface

In 2002, Web services were a hot topic and the concept of *service-oriented architecture* (SOA), while not a new idea, was beginning to pick up steam. It did not take long for organizations to realize that Web services mandated the concept and organizational model of SOA to guide their selection, design, implementation, and management. SOA, we know, is a critical discipline to make Web services, or services in the general sense, work together to help organizations achieve the business goals they are seeking. SOA is an important influence on information technology (IT) strategy and enterprise architecture.

This book is unlike any other SOA book on the market today. There are no XML snippets. There are no blocks of code. We seldom mention specific technology platforms or vendors. In this book we generalize SOA. We express business and technology issues of SOA so that they will apply to all industries, technology platforms, and operating environments, and cover all use cases. This book combines two critical SOA perspectives in one volume: the business perspective and the technical perspective. We examined SOA and services from two very different and complementary perspectives, yet we feel as if we have conquered many of those very barriers that create friction for business and IT organizations.

When we began this book, we established this mission statement for our efforts:

> This book will represent the state of the art for SOA planning, business, organization, and services modeling, architecture design and implementation. This book will present a business and technology modeling approach that answers most of the critical questions asked by IT and business leaders in today's organizations: How do we get started with SOA? Where do we begin? Where should we focus our SOA efforts? What "services" should we begin with? How do we identify and expose them in our SOA? How do we measure results of our SOA efforts? This book will be a reference work for IT executives, architects, team leaders, and developers seeking to understand how to make SOA real for their organizations to enable desired business results.

As we discussed the outline, chapter ownership, and eventual integration editing, it became clear that what we were doing with this book reflected many of the organizational challenges that are spurring business interest in SOA. We became a metaphor for an organization pursuing SOA—I was the business and Michael was the IT organization. As coauthors, we were merging two distinct approaches to SOA: one from a business and strategic perspective, more top-down in nature, and the other from a technical and architectural perspective. At first our language, perspectives, goals, and approaches were difficult to reconcile, but because we were committed to the project within a tight deadline, we had to work it out. And we did.

Many organizations wrestle with the semantic and linguistic barriers between the business community and the IT community, as well as between specific disciplines within the IT community. Often the overarching goals and objectives are shared, but the approaches to meeting those goals are quite different. After all, even different sides of the same coin are distinct and unique yet inseparable. And so it is with the concept of SOA.

SOA offers the potential to create a unified language of business based on a unit of analysis known as a service. In fact, we dedicate a chapter to the concept of services because they are indeed the fundamental unit of analysis for an SOA. The first SOA challenge is to establish shared meaning for services in a given organization. Our book is about *all* possible services in an organization, a subset of which will most likely be Web services. We are building a generalized model for services, and therefore in the remainder of this book we use the term "services" to also mean Web services.

Our goals for the book are lofty. We want to:

- Represent the state-of-the-art SOA planning and modeling book in the industry.
- Address "services" in the general case as opposed to targeting only Web services.
- Create an SOA business book with the technical aspects of SOA framed with "big picture" thinking and business results in mind.
- Be relevant beyond the expected 10-year SOA time horizon. In other words, we want to be a "lasting reference guide" for SOA.

Ultimately you, the reader, will tell us how we did. To answer the questions we hear all the time, we had to attack the SOA domain in three sections.

Part 1 of the book is all about SOA business concepts: the motivating forces for SOA, the importance of a general model of services, and SOA business modeling.

Chapter 1: Introduction to the SOA Business Model

Chapter 2: General Model for Services

Chapter 3: SOA Business Modeling

These three chapters set the stage for Part 2. Part 1 is focused on business concepts and will be very useful for business and IT executives, architects, and others seeking the business context and perspectives for SOA.

Part 2 delves into the topics of services identification, analysis and design, services integration using various classes of enabling technology, and achieving services reuse.

Chapter 4: Service Identification, Analysis, and Design

Chapter 5: SOA Technology and Services Integration Model

Chapter 6: Fundamentals of SOA Asset Reuse: Service Reusability Model

Part 2 is really targeted for chief technology officers, architects, and developers. These chapters contain some great business concepts and some innovative ideas to help with identification, modeling, and implementation of services for an organization.

Part 3 of the book focuses on the concepts of SOA governance, organizational models, and enterprise architecture, and also offers a new approach for harvesting return on investment (ROI) using SOA. These chapters address the aspects of SOA that require all of the constituents of an SOA—business management, process owners, IT leaders, architects, developers, business analysts—to work together.

Chapter 7: SOA Governance, Organization, and Behavior

Chapter 8: Architecture Organization Model

Chapter 9: SOA Business Case and Return on Investment Model

Chapter 7 is very thorough; we believe it is among the most comprehensive to date on the crucial topic of SOA governance. Chapter 8 addresses architecture, a critical capability for SOA success. And Chapter 9 creates a model for the realization of business results from SOA.

We hope you enjoy the book and engage in the SOA dialog with us. We believe we have filled a need in the industry with this work. SOA is a complex topic and a complex organizational goal. Our goal is to clarify, simplify, and enable your organization to realize its business objectives and goals through judicious implementation of SOA and services. Please let us know how we did.

CHAPTER 1

Introduction to the SOA Business Model

*S*ervice-oriented architecture* (SOA) is a concept whose time has come. SOA is garnering great hype for such a simple concept, and we are here to tell you that SOA is more than hype. It is a concept with great promise for your information technology (IT) operations, for your business operations, and for your organization as a whole. We must remember, though, that SOA is a concept. Before we put our simple definition of SOA on the table, let's discuss what SOA is not.

SOA is not a product. SOA is not a solution. SOA is not a technology. SOA cannot be reduced to vendors' software products, much as they would like you to believe. SOA is not a quick fix for the IT complexity that has accumulated over 30-plus years. And finally, SOA does not address every IT challenge facing business and IT executives today. However, with proper planning and execution, SOA will deliver compelling business benefits to your organization in the short, medium, and long term. SOA is the right model for IT today, and for IT in the future. So, what is an SOA?

> *SOA is a conceptual business architecture where business functionality, or application logic, is made available to SOA users, or consumers, as shared, reusable services on an IT network. "Services" in an SOA are modules of business or application functionality with exposed interfaces, and are invoked by messages.*

ELEMENTS OF AN SOA

An SOA has many moving parts, not the least of which is the enabling technology that makes it work. The following list represents the essential ingredients of a successful SOA. Each ingredient is explained in the sections that follow.

- Conceptual SOA vision
- Services
- Enabling technology
- SOA governance and policies
- SOA metrics
- Organizational and behavioral model

Conceptual SOA Vision

An SOA is a business concept, an idea or approach, of how IT functionality can be planned, designed, and delivered as modular business services to achieve specific business benefits. The conceptual SOA vision includes clearly defined business, IT and architectural goals, and a governance model and policies to help enforce standards and technical requirements of the SOA over time. This is the definition of an SOA target state, the goal to be achieved over time.

Services

Yes, an SOA needs services, which as we said, means *all* possible services in the organization. Along with services comes a services design model to assure reusability, interoperability, and integration across all business processes and technology platforms. Services are the central artifact of an SOA. Services are the primary architectural asset of an SOA. As such, they merit significant attention throughout this book and throughout an organization's migration toward SOA through many projects and initiatives, each of which will most likely contribute services to the SOA over time.

Enabling Technology

While the technology of Web services and SOA generates lots of press, it is probably the easiest area to implement despite the vendor flux and standards volatility for various categories of technology solutions. The technology is essential to support realization of your SOA vision. However, the enabling technology is *not* your SOA. The enabling technology must be implemented to accomplish two objectives: (1) It must allow your services to operate reliably and securely in your enterprise in support of your stated business objectives; and (2) it must enable you to carry forward your existing IT architecture as well as enable your legacy systems to be leveraged to support your SOA goals. In many organizations, legacy mainframe systems and other applications are major contributors of services to an SOA.

SOA Governance and Policies

An SOA conceptual architecture cannot be realized unless it is communicated to the constituents of the SOA—business users, developers, architects, business and IT executives, and business analysts. In addition, communicating your SOA conceptual architecture to close trading partners is also advised. However, telling your SOA constituents what your conceptual architecture, vision, and goals are is one thing. Enforcing conformance to your SOA conceptual architecture, vision, and goals is another matter. SOA is not a big bang implementation model that we expect from large, packaged software applications. SOA is achieved incrementally through time at the project level by continuously defining and enforcing the standards that it will be based on. These standards are the policies that in the aggregate define your SOA conceptual architecture and, when implemented, help your organization achieve its SOA vision and business goals. An SOA governance model defines the various governance processes, organizational roles and responsibilities, standards and policies that must be adhered to in your SOA conceptual architecture.

Metrics

SOAs require a battery of metrics in order to measure the results you are achieving. These metrics include fine-grained metrics, such as service-level agreements (SLAs) for individual services, as well as usage metrics, policy conformance metrics, developer metrics, business and return on investment (ROI) metrics, and process metrics. Plan your metrics early, and don't forget them when you go live with services. You'll want the data, count on it.

Organizational and Behavioral Model

Your current IT architecture is the result of years of organizational behaviors, business decisions, and architectural choices. In order to achieve SOA, behavioral and organizational considerations must be understood and changed first; then over time will come gradual migration toward your SOA vision and goals. New organizational models and behavioral models will be essential to your SOA success.

SOA: BEHAVIOR AND CULTURE

SOAs contain a substantial amount of behavioral content because these initiatives are process-driven and span organizational boundaries. The "soft issues" of an SOA strategy must address the organizational issues and challenges that may help or inhibit SOA adoption, such as services ownership, the business and IT relationship, budgeting practices, and more. Organizational, cultural, and process issues thread through several facets of an SOA initiative. How do you organize your enterprise architecture functions and roles to support an SOA? How do you organize your developer resources to help ensure the realization of the goals and performance of your SOA initiative? What is the optimal IT structure for an SOA? Is centralized IT better? Or is a centralized enterprise architecture team optimal, supported by distributed developers embedded within specific business units? What are the skills, roles, and competencies of your architecture organization that will facilitate migration to and attainment of your SOA?

In addition, cultural and behavioral aspects are crucial to achieving SOA success. We will use a metaphor here. Imagine you're an archaeologist. You're examining the artifacts of a long-since deci-mated culture—the physical remains, artifacts, tools, cooking uten-sils, and so forth—to ultimately make inferences about the behaviors that caused these artifacts to be frozen in their earthen matrix in the way that you've discovered them. That's what archaeologists do. They attempt to derive behavior from the physical remains and arti-facts. Now, fast forward to your current IT architecture. It is com-prised of legacy mainframes, distributed systems, desktop systems, software and documentation, user manuals, data models and schemas, which are all artifacts that resulted from the accumulated behaviors of your organization through time. These behaviors were a result of business and IT strategy and the various choices and deci-sions that caused your IT architecture to develop into its current state. So, if you plan to achieve SOA, you have to begin with behav-ioral, cultural, and other organizational factors that will lead to SOA success, and then architect your way toward SOA. You must enable and reinforce the behaviors that are more likely to result in the desired architectural outcome: SOA. If you start with enabling tech-nology without changing behavior, years from now you'll end up with another layer of technology that an IT archaeologist will have to interpret.

Exhibit 1.1 depicts these elements of an SOA according to our model. As you can see, the SOA strategy drives the governance model and policies. Services are at the center of the model because they are the central asset and organizing principle of an SOA. They are the key asset of an SOA. The enabling technology surrounds the services, within the framework of the SOA governance model and policies. The SOA governance model also drives the metrics, the SOA architecture process, and finally the behavior and culture that must be addressed to ultimately realize the business and technology benefits of SOA.

Although these elements represent the essential ingredients of an SOA, there is much more to it. What most organizations will find is that they need new ways of managing various business and IT processes to meet the demands of an SOA initiative. This book represents a collection of models required to implement SOA. But why is SOA such an important concept now, and why is there so much interest in it these days? Simple. SOA offers too many business and IT benefits for business executives to ignore. Competitive advantage is at stake with SOA. First movers will have it; SOA lag-gards will not.

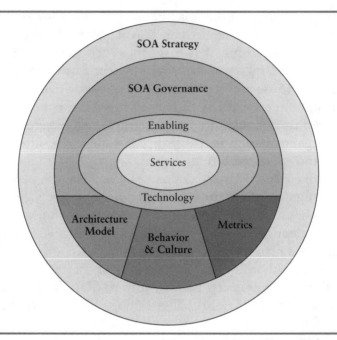

EXHIBIT 1.1   Elements of an SOA

NEW SOA CONCEPTUAL, ARCHITECTURAL, AND ORGANIZATIONAL MODELS

SOA initiatives will stress and in most cases break current operational and architectural models of IT organizations. SOA will require new ways of modeling and implementing various IT processes we have become accustomed to, such as services design models, integration models, reuse models, architecture processes, and enterprise architecture models. These other models, of course, augment the required SOA governance model.

SOA: ITS TIME HAS COME

One thing we know for sure, SOA is a concept whose time has come, and you do not need Jack Welch, Larry Ellison, Dr. Phil, or Oprah to tell you it's the right thing to do. If you are a business or IT executive and you are *not* thinking about how to implement an SOA in your organization, you have already fallen behind your competitors. Your business and IT costs are higher. Your time to market is slower for new products and services. Your ability to implement IT solutions in support of business goals lags behind your competitors. And your legacy IT architecture is like a boat anchor embedded in the seafloor. You are at the mercy of the tides with no control of your destiny because you are beholden to your existing IT architecture. You are unable shed your legacy burden: the fixed costs, the outdated technology platforms, and the skills required to sustain it.

Over the years, your IT architecture has accumulated layer upon layer of complexity. When client-server architectures dominated the IT industry, client-server applications were layered over your mainframe platforms. When the Internet era rose to ascendance, Web-centric platforms were added on top of client-server solutions. And as these evolved into *n*-tiered architectures, the layers of IT complexity built up, building more modern complexity on top of legacy complexity.

Chances are you addressed the legacy systems problem with integration middleware, such as enterprise application integration (EAI) platforms or similar solutions. And this became yet another layer of complexity, or, as Brent Carlson, chief technology officer of LogicLibrary, calls it, "YALOT" (yet another layer of technology). These middleware or integration platforms were supposed to solve the legacy system integration problem and help simplify your IT architecture, but the reverse was true. These platforms became part of the very same problem, just more expensively and equally proprietarily.

Although IT architecture through the years is accretive, and nothing seems to ever go away, there are ways to "architect" your way out of this conundrum. One approach is to rip out all the legacy applications and replace them with modern ones. This rip-and-replace model is too expensive for most organizations. In addition, often it is not worth the risk and effort of replacing these still-working legacy systems with new software that will require significant modifications to suit your business model and business processes.

Another approach is to rewrite or refactor your legacy systems for modern application server platforms, such as J2EE or .NET. Even though rewriting systems is also very expensive, at least you know they will match your business processes when you are through. Like the rip-and-replace model, this approach usually is avoided, however, not because it is not the right thing to do, but because it is expensive and difficult to cost justify to the business.

But there is a way out of this mess that avoids big bang system rewrites and expensive enterprise software projects. The way is *service-oriented architecture*. SOA is a simple concept, one that has the potential to alleviate many long-standing IT challenges and enable many coveted business goals that have until now been very elusive. SOA, by introducing a services layer into an existing IT architecture, can provide opportunities to isolate areas or elements of the architecture that are problematic, failure prone, or cost prohibitive. The services layering approach can enable the isolation, replacement, and/or potential consolidation of these architecture challenges while enabling the flexibility of reusable services. How often have business executives pronounced a desire to become more agile? When has time-to-market *not* been a mission-critical business requirement? Yet more often than not, these lofty business goals are constrained by outdated IT systems and incapable business processes that are subservient to tradition as well as to the digital concrete of today's enterprise software applications.

Why SOA Now?

SOA offers an avenue out of myriad business and IT challenges. However, before you leap into the SOA fray, you must understand a few things about it. First, SOA is not a new concept. It has, however, been refreshed with the advent of Web services, which have achieved more consensus from the vendor community than has been achieved in the history of computing.

SOA has also achieved trend status because of the degree of dissatisfaction that IT and business executives share with the current state of IT within their enterprises. Chief executives (CEOs) are fed up with hearing why they cannot expand into a new geographical location because the IT systems are not ready yet. They don't want to hear why the enterprise resource planning (ERP) system that cost $30 million will not support the new business process targeted to launch in six months. Chief financial officers (CFOs) are tired of waiting for regulatory compliance issues to be resolved, and they certainly are not pleased with an overbudget IT organization. Chief operating officers (COOs) resent being told they cannot get a report because data are spread across three different systems, all on different computing platforms. Chief technology officers (CTOs) are fed up with vendors pushing more new technology when the old technology is still underutilized and operating as islands of functionality. They are tired of the endless need to keep integrating systems when the integration models themselves become part of the problem—more legacy silos to maintain. And chief information officers (CIOs)? They are tired of explaining the same problems time and time again. They're tired of having their budgets cut. They wish they had more funding for strategic projects instead of being hamstrung by having 80 to 90% of their budget committed to maintaining legacy systems. CIOs could do much more for the business if they could shed their legacy systems and focus on forward-looking strategic solutions for the business. There has to be a way out of this quandary. SOA could well be an answer. SOA is not new, but it's here to stay. SOA is finally achievable thanks to three major factors:

1. *Standards consensus.* Microsoft and IBM agreed, and the rest fell in line.
2. *SOA enabling technology.* Finally, implementing standards-based services is possible and affordable.
3. *Integration fatigue.* There has to be a better way to achieve application and business integration.

Standards Consensus

For the first time in the history of IT, there is widespread agreement on major SOA and Web services standards by all IT vendors. This nearly unanimous agreement means that whether you move now or later, you most certainly are going to be using services in your organization. Your software and platform vendors are going to take you there whether you want to go or not. Our advice? Preempt your vendors with your own SOA strategy and roadmap. Rapidly accumulate SOA experience. And be prepared to fend off any proprietary platform-specific approaches to services. Implement industry standards in your SOA governance model and in specific policies that will govern services identification, design, and implementation. You may have to dedicate some internal resources to tracking relevant standards, but the ROI on standards will be well worth it.

SOA Tools and Infrastructure

With the advent of new tools and infrastructure solutions that enable SOA and services in a cross-platform, reusable, and interoperable fashion, SOA is real. This is perhaps the most significant departure from previous SOA implementations, such as CORBA (Common Object Request Broker Architecture), COM/DCOM (Common Object Model/Distributed Common Object Model), DCE (Distributed Computing Environment), and other proprietary schemes for reusable services. Interoperability for services is largely due to the standards for Web services, primarily SOAP for messaging and WSDL (Web services description language) for service descriptions. The variety of tools for legacy systems enablement, services development and exposure, Web services management, and multiple run-time environments for services have made the SOA industry very interesting to watch. There are as many ways to enable services and SOA as there are legacy systems and platforms in your architecture. Of course, bear in mind that we refer to the general case of "services" in this book. Some of your services will be Web services based on XML (eXtensible Markup Language), SOAP, and WSDL, as well as the extended WS-* standards. However, do not limit your SOA total value by examining and considering Web services only. Think services first, and then specific implementation models later.

Integration Fatigue: "There Has to Be a Better Way"

IT "business as usual" is over. Business and IT executives are frustrated with the lack of integration of their internal systems, with their business processes, with their trading partners, and with their customers. We call this *integration fatigue*. The business is demanding change, and IT executives know there has to be a better way. The frustration with IT as we know it is at an all-time high. IT budgets continue to be stressed, and they rarely increase. The majority of IT budgets are focused on maintaining current systems and keeping the lights on; very little IT budget is focused on strategic initiatives that may pay future dividends. It is a do-more-with-less environment.

Business continues to change while IT is saddled with maintaining the systems and architectures of the past. IT doesn't have the luxury of eliminating its legacy or underperforming assets. Those very IT assets contain business logic that is most likely running a mission-critical portion of the organization's business. Yet while the business logic is mission critical, nonetheless the logic and data are locked up within individual silos of systems and technology. You cannot afford to rewrite the application, and your integration strategy has proved to be supremely costly to implement and maintain. There has to be a better way, and there is. It's called *service-oriented architecture*.

SOA: EVOLVED ENTERPRISE INTEGRATION

A major impetus for SOA initiatives is solving the age-old problem of integration. For many executives, SOA holds the potential to eliminate, via industry standards and modern tools, the proprietary integration model they've become accustomed to. According to many analyst estimates, up to 30% of a typical IT budget is allocated to integration activities. What would business be like if there was less integration, or, rather, if the integration that was performed was directly related to process integration, enterprise integration, and mergers and acquisitions (M&A) integration? In other words, value-added integration. How would spending less money on integration change an organization's competitive advantage? Could that budget be shifted to more strategic projects?

Origins of the Integration Problem

Where did all this IT complexity come from? Why is 80 to 90% of your IT budget focused backward on maintaining the past rather than looking ahead to supporting the future? This "rearview mirror budgeting" problem is legendary among CIOs and is partly responsible for the lack of strategic IT investment by CIOs today. How backward committed is your IT budget? What percent of the IT budget is allocated to maintaining your legacy investments rather than focused on forward-facing initiatives that may move the organization ahead? This is a real challenge for both business and IT executives today. If you feel as if you're managing your IT budgets using a rearview mirror, you're not alone.

The demand for IT and process integration is driven by business requirements, such as:

- Increased M&A activity
- Corporate reorganization or restructuring
- Application and/or system consolidation
- Data integration and data warehousing initiatives
- New business strategies leveraging current systems for new processes
- Achieving regulatory compliance (e.g., Sarbanes-Oxley, or HIPAA, the Health Insurance Portability and Accountability Act of 1996)
- Streamlining of business processes to improve productivity

Addressing the business drivers for integration is a great impetus for SOA and Web services. At what point does IT complexity become an obstacle to business goals and an impediment to achieving IT's goals? We believe that complexity becomes intolerable when organizations are considering or taking these actions:

- Hiring a chief architect
- Creating a central architecture team
- Acquiring or developing your own enterprise application integration (EAI) software
- Creating an internal integration team, or a middleware organization, to help solve the integration challenges for your organization

Now, this does not mean that hiring a chief architect is a bad thing. More than likely it is a good thing. Chief architects can help address the architectural complexity and pain your organization is facing. The other actions just listed also can help address these areas. The problems are symptoms of the IT challenges that SOA could address. If you have considered or taken one or more of these actions, your organization is at the point where the integration burden is consuming IT resources, compounding the existing complexity problem, and inhibiting business and IT effectiveness. You most likely have a rearview-mirror IT budget, and you are ready to try a new approach.

Stop Integrating; Service-Enable Instead

Stop integrating now. What we mean is stop integrating the way you have been using proprietary middleware solutions, homegrown point-to-point integration techniques, and tactical integration approaches that are doomed from the outset. These techniques are almost always going to break and require a significant ongoing maintenance burden from the organization.

An organization should integrate without integrating. Eliminate all point-to-point integration projects in your enterprise and rearchitect these initiatives from an SOA point of view. Inventory the integration solutions in your organization. Identify the IT budget allocated to these solutions and projects, including support staff, maintenance, and infrastructure. Determine how many of these integration efforts can be eliminated using reusable services in an SOA. (Integration projects are very good services opportunities. Chapters 3, 4, and 5 discuss the process of identifying and modeling services opportunities for an SOA initiative.) Identify the consumers of these integrations and determine their satisfaction with the current approach. How often do these integrations break? How often must they be enhanced or modified to support changing business needs? Do the n^2 math to determine how many interfaces can be eliminated with a services approach to integration. There will be a cost savings when comparing SOA and services to your current integration strategy. A services approach will be a more flexible, reusable approach than the point-to-point model you've been using. Although service-oriented integration will require more discipline and planning than previous integration paradigms, the results will be well worth the investment. Stop integrating now. Service-enable instead.

Exploring an SOA Business Scenario Exhibit 1.2 depicts a hypothetical approach to SOA as an alternative to conventional integration. This exhibit shows a fictional insurance company with three business units—Group, Voluntary, and Individual—at the top. Corresponding to the three business units are their own collections of systems and

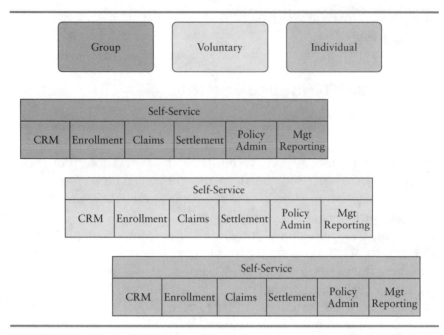

EXHIBIT 1.2   Typical IT System Silos

duplicate IT capabilities, accumulated over the years, and purportedly so unique that the business units must have their own systems to accomplish the very same business processes.

Each business unit has duplicate systems for sales and contact management, enrollment, claims, settlement, policy administration, and management reporting and controls. On top of these, all the business units have portal, intranet, and extranet capabilities to allow self-service for customers, agents, and brokers.

Identify SOA Business Opportunities   Exhibit 1.3 examines this hypothetical business from an SOA perspective, exploring the potential business value that SOA may bring to this enterprise. What if the duplicate IT systems and business processes could be integrated and united as shared services by all three business units? What if the business processes across the three business units could be simplified to take advantage of shared IT services in an SOA model?

As shown in the exhibit, SOA offers several potential business benefits to this organization, such as product and process simplification,

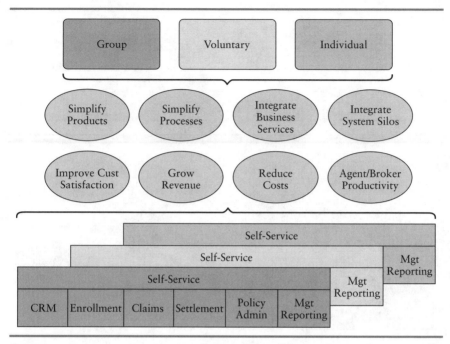

EXHIBIT 1.3 Identifying SOA Business Opportunities

integrated systems, integrated business services, better customer satisfaction, cost reductions, increased revenue and margin, and better agent and/or broker productivity. Of course, you cannot realize these potential benefits without performing proper analysis.

Examining the SOA Information Technology Potential Continuing the example, Exhibit 1.4 shows specific SOA opportunities that may apply to this insurance company. These opportunities include integration, process orchestration, better interoperability, services reuse, improved IT productivity, and achieving a real-time, event-driven enterprise.

Again, proper analysis and SOA planning of the business and SOA opportunities will determine the unique SOA value that will apply to any given organization.

Seeking Reuse Value from an SOA Initiative Let us assume that services reuse is a key SOA driver for this insurance company. Our SOA strategy, planning, and analysis will identify significant services reuse benefits in many areas of this company, across the multiple business units,

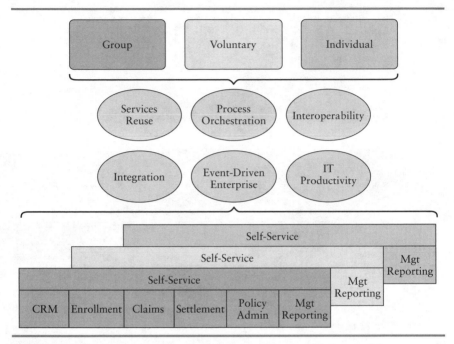

EXHIBIT 1.4   Identifying SOA Opportunities

and across the IT systems that support them. Exhibit 1.5 focuses this example on services reuse. In this insurance company, it was determined that reuse was essential to reducing costs, increasing IT productivity, and improving responsiveness to business demands.

This example shows how analysis might show that reuse of specific IT capabilities may offer tremendous business value. In this scenario, we focus on the enrollment process, which is supported by an excellent system but which can be improved by exposing its capabilities as shared reusable services in an SOA. Doing this allows reuse of a single IT service, enrollment, across three business units. This reuse eliminates IT complexity, increases IT productivity, and leads to simplified business processes in this organization. SOA applies as much to business processes and enabling better business functionality as it applies to IT systems—eliminating redundant systems, duplicate support infrastructure, and fragile and expensive integration strategies.

Service and Process Orchestration in an SOA   Furthermore, this same organization is able to leverage its reusable services by orchestrating them

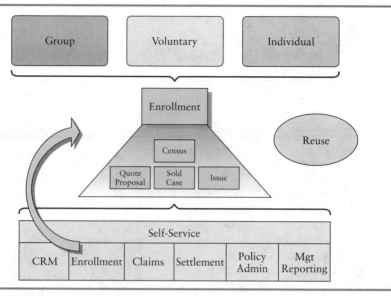

EXHIBIT 1.5 Services Reuse in an SOA

into business processes. Service and process orchestration extends reuse benefits by leveraging services as reusable composite applications and orchestrated process work flows. Exhibit 1.6 shows the enrollment process as a simplified series of services orchestrated into the business process work flow that the company decides is most reflective of how it wants to operate.

SOA allows an organization to stop integrating and instead recast its IT capabilities as shared reusable services. Once there are enough services to reuse in an SOA, further value can be harvested by orchestrating business processes based on these reusable services. In addition, the integration challenges that have historically plagued IT organizations can be avoided. Implementing the SOA scenario just described enables an organization to realize the many business benefits of SOA.

SOA: Competitive Advantage via Services

SOA is a concept that has direct business and competitive advantage implications for all organizations. For the business, SOA means increased customer satisfaction, real business agility, faster time to

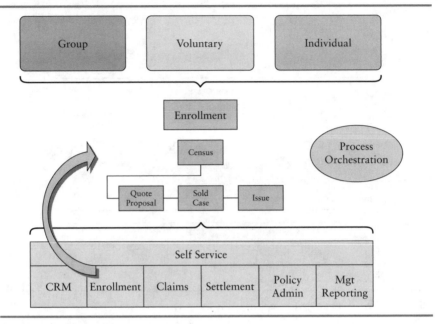

EXHIBIT 1.6   Orchestrating Processes in an SOA

market, ease of partnering, and lower business costs. Imagine that you can launch new products and services 30% faster than your competitors because you have eliminated friction within your enterprise, allowing better collaboration between your suppliers and your design engineers as well as better collaboration with your channel partners.

Your SOA has allowed you to speed up IT delivery to your business consumers. The time to implement needed system changes to support these new products has been cut by 25%, and you are able to make these changes using fewer resources: less development resources, less quality assurance resources, and less overall IT resources. Exhibit 1.7 depicts typical business benefits of SOA.

For IT organizations, SOA means greater productivity, faster time to market, greater asset reuse, agility, and lower IT costs. What if you could deliver IT services with less budget and few resources, while providing faster, higher-quality application support? SOA benefits an IT organization through faster application development, lower overall costs, greater software asset and services reuse, more

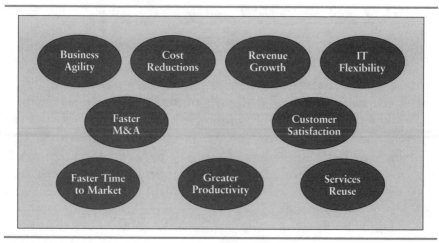

EXHIBIT 1.7 Business Benefits of SOA

repeatable software development processes, higher-quality applications via pretested components and validated Web services interfaces, and overall faster response to business customer requests for system enhancements and modifications.

SOA benefits the business through greater flexibility, faster time to market for business initiatives, faster response to business changes, and closer mapping of IT services to business needs. Many analysts see SOA as a mechanism to help finally achieve alignment of business goals and objectives with IT services and capabilities. Better alignment is partly attributable to the speed with which Web services can be developed and deployed in an SOA as well as the flexibility from leveraging proven, tested software components and Web services.

SOA also benefits an organization by abstracting business services (or Web services) from the specific technologies they were originally developed with and the platforms they were meant to run on. This twofold abstraction has two key benefits: (1) an organization can modify the technology architecture without mandating changes to the services available, and (2) the business community can change business processes without causing the ripple effect of changes to the services and underlying IT systems. Doing this leads to greater business agility and IT flexibility.

SOA MEANS "SERVICE-ORIENTED AGILITY"

SOA holds promise to finally make the word "agility" real for organizations. That's why the "A" in SOA, which stands for "architecture," could just as well stand for "agility." Service-oriented agility is one of the most oft-articulated goals of SOA. SOA enables business and IT agility along a number of dimensions. Although nearly every business and IT executive for the last 30 years has wistfully dreamed of achieving business agility, there has been little real progress toward that end save for a few exceptional firms. For most organizations, business agility is a vision without reality. Until now. SOA and services provide a means to achieving true business agility. Business agility can come from two broad forms: the ability to change business processes to meet changing market demands and customer requirements, and reduce costs; or the ability to execute business processes faster or launch new processes, products, and services faster. Agility and speed are both real and tangible benefits of migrating to SOA and reusable services.

SOA can help an organization unshackle its business processes and data from the IT systems that support or, in many cases, constrain them. Using a services approach and SOA, enterprise software systems will be decoupled from business processes through the use of business services. Business services will be defined as abstracted entities separate from the business logic that is locked within enterprise applications such as SAP, Oracle, Siebel, and other monolithic enterprise applications. When application logic is exposed as a business service, it becomes a shareable and reusable software asset, or *service*, that can be coupled with services from other applications to create new sources of business process value, completely new business processes, and even more efficient versions of existing processes using business process management (BPM) tools.

Service-Oriented Agility: Speed

One aspect of agility is speed. The ability of an organization to hasten its response to market changes or competitive threats, or to quickly preempt competitive moves from the competition, is clearly an advantage. Speed consists of two dimensions: the total elapsed time of a business action or response, and the speed of the IT component of the business action or response. Enhancing speed could require installing a new system, developing a new system, running a new report, or whatever the specific business requirement is to support of the business.

If the software development cycle of an organization is too slow for the business to respond to market changes or competitive threats, then the business does not have agility, and clearly IT doesn't have it either. SOA can create agility through speed via faster application development, which in turn will contribute to speedier business responsiveness to market conditions, competitive threats, and customer requests.

Service-Oriented Agility: Flexibility and Range of Response

Service-oriented agility can also be expressed as flexibility, or by allowing a greater range of options for a competitive response and making that response easier. An IT architecture can by its very nature limit the range of options an organization has to respond to market opportunities and customer requests. However, an SOA may offer a greater range of options by reducing the fundamental unit of IT to a business service.

Business agility and IT flexibility are always mentioned in corporate documents, in annual reports, and by business executives when they talk to analysts and customers. Agility and flexibility are among the most discussed and yet least achieved goals in corporate history. Part of the problem comes from a failure to operationalize the terms so they can be implemented and to put metrics in place to help realize them.

SOA: Agility Focal Point

SOA represents an opportunity to regain the agility and flexibility that many organizations lost in the 1990s with enterprise software applications and point-to-point home-grown and commercial integration models. SOA allows the creation of a services layer that resides between the business architecture of an organization and the IT architecture of an organization. We call this layer the agility focal point. This services layer is the decoupling abstraction layer that insulates business processes from IT changes and allows IT to change technology without changing business processes. Exhibit 1.8 depicts the concept of the agility focal point via an SOA.

An SOA implements the agility focal point concept by facilitating the flexing of the business and IT architectures—the SOA in particular—in response to business changes. SOA enables this strategic business capability, which allows an organization to compete based on agility, or *service-oriented agility*.

Competing on Service-Oriented Agility

With more IT flexibility and business agility, all organizations should be seeking faster time to market for new products and services; faster responses to business, competitive, and environmental change; and an overall better ability to quickly adapt both business processes and IT systems in support of change. In their seminal book *Competing Against Time*, Stalk and Hout discuss the notion of time-based competition and how those who are faster to market are more profitable than those who are not.[1] SOA enables many of these time-based

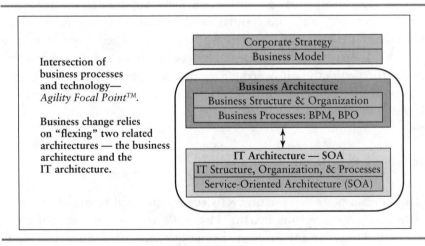

EXHIBIT 1.8   SOA and the Agility Focal Point

capabilities by eliminating many of the traditional IT and business barriers to change (e.g., inflexible business processes, business processes locked up within rigid IT systems, inflexible IT architectures with rearview-mirror commitments to legacy systems, etc.). SOA and services provide a business solution to the problem of adapting to change, and this business solution is based on both the business and IT being able to adapt and respond quickly.

Regaining IT Flexibility: Breaking the "Rearview Mirror" Paradox

Much as agility is the Holy Grail for business executives, flexibility is equally sought after and is equally elusive for IT executives. For IT executives, their continual challenge is supporting the years of accumulated legacy systems and infrastructure in the face of shrinking budgets. SOA and Services provide a pathway toward breaking free of the rearview-mirror budgeting paradox. First, in order to inject flexibility into your IT architecture, you do not have to rewrite or refactor every legacy application or enterprise application in your portfolio. You merely have to begin exposing portions of business functionality as services that match to business process requirements of the organization. Second, most of the services you will target initially in your SOA initiatives are contained within existing applications. The challenge is to expose the business functions as reusable services that can in time be combined with other services into composite applications, orchestrated processes, and BPM solutions. Third, SOA is an incremental architecture, meaning that it is not implemented or attained in a big bang model. SOA is achieved over time by defining and adhering to a body of architectural goals, standards, and design guidelines so that all services will interoperate over time within and, when necessary, outside of your enterprise. SOA is the "anti-enterprise application" in that it encourages freeing services from inflexible application architectures imposed by others, namely software vendors, and begins to define your vision of services and business processes to better match the way you want to conduct business. Finally, the concept of business services can allow the IT organization to insulate itself from the constraints imposed by both its legacy systems and its more modern applications. SOAs future-proof your IT architecture. SOAs are built to accommodate change.

Why You *Must* Begin SOA Initiatives Now

With the analyst and media buzz about SOA, you may be asking yourself why you should believe it. What's so special about SOA that you need to invest your time and resources in this concept at this time? Why now, when you survived the past technology paradigms that were nascent attempts at SOA, namely CORBA, COM/DCOM, and others?

This time, the stars and moon are aligned in SOA's favor. We've covered many of these already, such as the unanimous agreement on the core standards of SOA, the cross-platform capabilities of SOA using Web services and these core standards, and the fact that IT maturity is now more able to assimilate the concept of SOA to drive a business result. There is so much discomfort with the current state of IT that something has to give, and in this case, it's the entire process of IT architecture and services delivery that has to be reconstructed.

SOA presents an opportunity to change the rules of the game. SOA will allow firms to compete using their SOA efforts along a number of business and IT dimensions. These firms will be applying SOA to their businesses to create service-oriented business.

These advantages will characterize SOA first movers:

- *Competitive advantage.* If you beat your competitors to the SOA punch, you will have achieved competitive advantage on a number of fronts, including business speed and agility, IT cost and delivery, and customer satisfaction.
- *SOA cycles of learning.* SOA first movers will gain the experience required to fend off IT vendors partners; you may as well preempt your vendors by getting in front of the SOA wave. If you're going to end up with services anyway, you may as well be prepared and ramp up your ability to consume and provide services.
- *Break the rearview-mirror budget crisis.* There are two ways out of this situation: (1) fix your architecture process to suit an agile, changing services world and (2) stop integrating and service-enable instead.

SOA first movers will be in a better position to compete in a world of services, where vendors, customers, and business partners will all eventually transact via SOA and services. This is a world of service-oriented business, or business-oriented architecture.

SERVICE-ORIENTED BUSINESS: SOA = BUSINESS-ORIENTED ARCHITECTURE

Although many organizations are seriously considering SOA, some are doing it from a pure IT perspective while others are really looking at a new way of running their businesses. They are pursuing the concept of service-oriented business, or the idea of running all aspects of their organization from a "services" perspective. This has broad ramifications for an organization.

IT is a major budget item in many firms, especially for financial services organizations. IT affects all aspects of these organizations in profound ways. IT affects the cost of everyday business transactions, which over time equates to billions in efficiencies. IT allows interdisciplinary collaboration across a business enterprise, which means better cooperation, better sharing of information, and a more united capability to compete in your markets. IT improves many diverse business processes and increases productivity across the organization. IT amplifies the productivity and efficiency of all business processes, both internally as well as those that are exposed to trading partners and customers.

Business Impact of SOA

The potential business impact of SOA is significant to an organization, but only if the appropriate business modeling and business context are considered during the planning and implementation of SOA. The range of business benefits is broad, and includes both specific and tangible benefits as well as less tangible yet more compelling benefits. Of these, one of the most interesting concepts is the notion of the *SOA Network Effect*. This concept was first developed in a *ComputerWorld* column to describe the importance of the soft issues relating to achieving service-oriented architectures, such as cultural issues, behavioral issues, and organizational dynamics.[2] Are these as important as the technology of SOA? The answer from the field is that these soft issues are more important than the technology, and thus they are not all that "soft" as we would suppose. These soft issues are among the most difficult aspects of achieving SOA. Yet they are the key to an SOA's ultimate success or demise.

Characteristics of a Service-Oriented Business

A *service-oriented business* is an organization that has progressed with its SOA efforts such that its business really does operate using an SOA. SOA as an IT architectural strategy actually uses services as the "operating system" for the business and its business processes.

What if your CEO could acquire another firm and integrate its information and operations into the existing business and IT architecture without integration challenges? What if the acquired firm's business processes could integrate seamlessly with yours with zero latency? What if there was no integration effort required at all? What if the IT systems were "preintegrated," meaning that they could exchange information with one another without any incremental integration expenses and effort? What if business processes could be more quickly combined into new composite processes that represent the combined business entity better than those of the two individual business processes?

Imagine how business would be without two factors that have become ingrained in our expectations of IT today: the IT integration hurdles that attend every business initiative and the inevitable time lag between the need for the business initiative and the ability of the IT organization to deliver it on time and, more important, with zero time-to-market latency. This is the zero integration business enterprise.

How would this enhance the business case for a mergers-and-acquisition strategy? How would this improve the return on investment equation for any IT or business initiative? What is the value of faster time to market for any information-based initiative? That's the business case for a service-oriented business.

Exhibit 1.9 is a vision of how SOA becomes the foundation for a service-oriented business. It depicts how SOA can enable significant

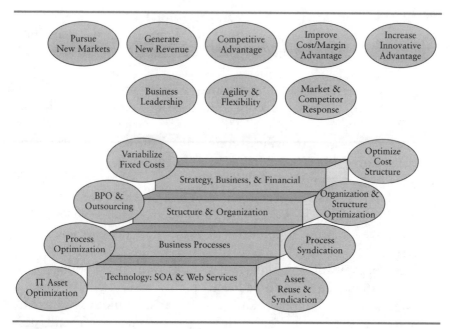

EXHIBIT 1.9   Service-Oriented Business

strategic business benefits through many tangible contributions. These include IT benefits, such as reuse and asset optimization that are often initial target benefits of most SOA efforts. However, as we progress from the IT level to business processes, organization and structure, and ultimately the strategic level where business and financial goals are critical, SOA has value to offer there as well.

CHARACTERISTICS OF A ZERO-INTEGRATION ENTERPRISE

Implementing SOA will allow tremendous reduction in integration expense and maintenance, such that we go so far as to call it the "zero-integration enterprise." A zero-integration enterprise is an organization whose business and IT teams are committed to the precepts of SOA. These organizations see the business value and strategic advantages of SOA, and are migrating their organization, processes, applications, and skills to support the concept of services, specifically Web services. This organization has eliminated traditional integration models in favor of SOA and standards-based integration. Some characteristics of a zero-integration enterprise follow.

- This organization can launch new business initiatives faster than its competitors because less IT integration is required to support various business projects. This time-to-market benefit allows faster response to business conditions, customer requirements, competitive threats, and increased innovation.
- This organization has a higher return on assets and greater IT productivity than its peer companies due to the asset-related benefits of SOA, such as software component reuse, services reuse, and extending the capabilities of existing IT systems and infrastructure.
- This organization launches new software applications 35% faster than before with reduced quality assurance and testing effort due to component and services reuse. Building on proven software and services capabilities, the organization spends less time developing new code and more time focusing on business process issues.
- This organization uses the 30% of its IT budget previously used for integration projects to solve strategic business problems, such as improving customer satisfaction, reducing time to market for new products, and increasing sales through various IT initiatives.
- This organization implements concepts of agility and flexibility through its SOA initiatives. Agility is reality, and is measured by clear unambiguous metrics.
  - This organization has an agile business model that can quickly respond to business challenges, competitive threats, and customer needs.
  - This organization has greater customer focus deriving from reduced effort spent on internal integration and more effort spent on customer satisfaction, partner communication, and efficient business processes.
  - This organization has a business-focused IT organization that no longer must concern itself with assuring interoperability issues but rather can focus on forward-looking strategic issues.

- This organization has a flexible IT architecture, based on SOA and services, that facilitates superior business performance, enables world-class business processes, and is highly efficient with all corporate resources.
- This organization integrates without integrating, both internally and externally with customers and partners. This organization does not integrate, it service-enables instead.

WHAT ARE THE CHALLENGES OF SOA?

Now, with all of these benefits, where's the catch? Simple. SOA is difficult to implement, manage, and control. Not because of the technology, mind you, but due to the organizational, cultural, and behavioral aspects of SOA that contribute to success. And technically, although there has been great progress with regard to the standards, supporting tools, and development and run-time platforms, there are still issues to be resolved. These issues include support for long-running transactions, security concerns, and many others. However, the organizational, cultural, and governance issues far outweigh the technical aspects of implementing SOA. That's not a reason to avoid trying to achieve SOA, but it certainly is a reason to pay attention to many of the softer aspects of technology initiatives to ensure you can reap the rewards. A discussion of major SOA challenges organizations will face as they migrate to SOA follows.

Enterprise Architecture Model May Need Tuning for SOA

As many organizations consider their SOA approach, they will realize that the organization, processes, and disciplines of their enterprise architecture organization may require tuning to suit the requirements of SOA. Often the process of enterprise architecture is somewhat flawed, which helps explain the current state of IT architectures today: rigid IT architectures characterized by heavy carryover legacy systems, inflexible "digital concrete" of enterprise applications, and a portfolio of applications that demand integration software to make them work together.

Perhaps architects have been too focused on building things and getting them to work as opposed to building things that are flexible, reusable, and support the business: the things that are now most important for businesses today as they grapple with change and global forces. These are the new requirements of SOA.

SOA will fail unless the process of architecture is changed from one of static advice, creation of presentations, application blueprints, and architecture road maps to one of actively shaping and implementing flexible and reusable IT assets that support business processes. In other words, SOAs. A model for tuning the enterprise architecture process is presented in Chapter 8.

SOA Is Spatially and Temporally Distributed

One of the challenges of SOA is that it is not implemented all at once. Rather, it is achieved through many discrete projects across both space and time. This temporal and spatial distribution of SOA projects makes governance all the more critical to SOA success. SOA governance and enforceable policies are the keys to managing conformance to the SOA across geographic and time horizons.

SOA Is Organizationally Complex and Behaviorally Challenging

SOA is a complex goal to achieve. It is organizationally, behaviorally, and culturally challenging for most organizations. We describe an SOA behavioral model in Chapter 7 to help you anticipate and create the behavioral pattern your SOA will require.

SOA Requires Governance to Achieve and Manage

SOA requires a robust SOA governance model, clear and enforceable policies, and a way to implement SOA governance across all the lifecycle processes of an organization: enterprise architecture, services design, publishing, discovery, and run-time. SOA governance is essential to realize the ultimate business value of SOA.

SOA Is All About Services

Implementing SOA requires new approaches to identifying, modeling, and implementing reusable, interoperable services. Repeatable processes for determining appropriate granularity, version management, and enforcing design-time policies for services are essential. In fact, even the definition of services is important for many organizations.

The fundamental architectural unit of an SOA is a "service." Services, per our definition of SOA, are units of business capabilities, processes, or functions that are delivered in a repeatable way to consumers of those services. Consumers of services in an SOA can be developers, architects, and analysts, or they can be external customers, business partners, and internal business customers.

Without services, there is no SOA, and an SOA with services is useless unless there is actual consumption of the services that are available. Therefore, an organization can deliver or realize no SOA value unless the services in an SOA have real consumers using them for business reasons.

Services Identification, Modeling, and Design Challenges

Services are critical to an SOA. However, the process of identifying the right services for your organization is challenging. And what makes these services the "right" ones? This discussion is further complicated by questions about granularity, reuse, and other related services modeling and design issues. Chapters 3, 4, and 5 address these concerns using some innovative services modeling concepts. *These chapters will help you achieve the "SOA Three Rights": Identify the "right" services; build those services the "right" way; and run them on the "right" enabling technology stack.*

Where Are We Headed?

SOA is an iterative business approach. There is no single correct path to achieving SOA. Instead, there are multiple routes to the SOA goal. It is important to recognize the fundamentally iterative approach that

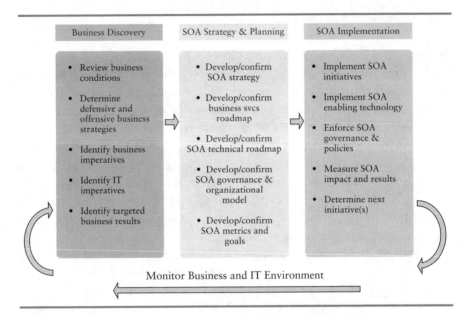

EXHIBIT 1.10 SOA Business Iteration Model
Source: AgilePath Corporation, copyright © 2005. Used with permission.

SOA requires to achieve its stated goals objectives and business results over time. This approach, which we call an SOA business iteration model, is depicted in Exhibit 1.10.

This model builds explicit business context into the SOA strategy and planning process, recognizing that SOA must be aligned to business and IT objectives as well as to the current urgencies of the organization at that particular moment in time.

Remember: SOA is a lifestyle change. It is a long-term commitment to achieving specific business objectives. That is why we wrote this book, and that presumably is why you are reading it: to learn how to plan, design, and implement SOA via reusable services to achieve clear business results.

NOTES

1. George Stalk Jr. and Thomas M. Hout, *Competing Against Time* (New York: The Free Press, 1990).
2. Eric A. Marks, "The SOA Network Effect: Technical and Cultural Issues Drive Value," ComputerWorld Online, August 16, 2004.

CHAPTER 2

General Model for Services

Services are the fundamental unit of analysis and concern in a service-oriented architecture (SOA). Services are the primary organizing principle of an SOA. In order to begin the process of implementing SOA, an organization must begin thinking about its information technology (IT) capabilities as a body of services. But what are services? How do we identify them? How do we know we have the right services? These are all common questions, which will be addressed in this chapter and in Chapters 3, 4, 5 and 6. One thing is clear: You must understand the services concept in order to implement SOA successfully.

Services are the enduring business asset in an SOA, and attention must be paid to identifying, designing, and implementing them. Implementing SOA requires new approaches to identifying, modeling, and implementing reusable interoperable services in an SOA. Repeatable processes for determining appropriate granularity, version management, and enforcing design-time policies for services are essential. In fact, even the definition of services is important for many organizations. This chapter provides an overview of services and their important role in an SOA. This will set the stage for Chapters 3, 4, and 5, the services identification, analysis, and design chapters.

SOA IS ALL ABOUT SERVICES

Service-oriented architecture is nothing without services. Services are the primary asset of an SOA. Recall our SOA definition from Chapter 1:

*SOA is a conceptual business architecture where business function-
ality, or application logic, is made available to SOA users, or
consumers, as shared, reusable services on an IT network.
"Services" in an SOA are modules of business or application functionality with exposed interfaces that are invoked by messages from
service consumers.*

The fundamental unit of an SOA is a *service*. Services, according
to our definition of SOA, are reusable modular units of business
capabilities, processes, or technical functions that are accessed and
delivered in a repeatable fashion to consumers of those services.
Consumers of services in an SOA can be developers, architects, and
analysts, or they can be external customers, business partners, and
internal business customers.

An SOA with services is useless unless those available services
actually are consumed. Therefore, an organization cannot deliver or
realize any SOA value unless the services available in an SOA have
real consumers using them.

But why are services so important to an SOA? Ronald Coase in
1937 presaged the concept of business services under another term:
transactions.

Services Concept: Ronald Coase and Transaction Theory

Why is the concept of services compelling? Services, it turns out, map
very clearly and elegantly to business processes and transactions that
occur every day, both internally to IT organizations as well as with
business users of IT services. Services are easy to understand from
both a business and an IT perspective. Consider the process of opening a new account at a bank. The activities performed by a bank teller
to provide that business service to a customer, as well as to the IT
processes executed to conduct the "new account" service on behalf
of that customer, are a simple yet profound way to understand
"services" as the fundamental unit of analysis in an SOA. Business
services, whether performed manually or in an automated fashion, or
both as in the bank teller example, represent an appropriate granularity of business process for further analysis. The IT systems that help

execute the business services are technology proxies. They essentially mirror and support the steps that are being taken by the tellers to provide service to a bank's customers.

Services at a high level can be conceptualized as things of an organization. If the term "account" is a core entity of an organization, then the phrase "open new account" would represent a potential service business process. Services are entities, and they contain service operations that actually execute the business functionality of the service. In many ways, business process analysis can elucidate the events and activities that represent these of an organization. The process of identifying the right services will use process analysis and data modeling techniques, which will unite the notion of services activities (events, processes, and transactions) with the concept of organizational core entities, attributes, and relationships.

Ronald Coase, as early as 1937, described the nature of corporations in his article entitled "The Nature of the Firm."[1] According to Coase, firms exist as long as they perform transactions more efficiently than the transactions can be done outside of the company. Relative transaction costs determine the size and configuration of the firm. In other words, as long as companies provide products and services that are valued in an efficient, affordable manner, they will continue to exist.

As transaction costs fluctuate according to supply, demand, and other market forces, an organization may change the composition of processes, activities, and ultimately the transactions that it conducts during the course of performing its business functions. As transaction costs increase or decrease, an organization will variably insource or outsource the execution of these transactions, which therefore determines the size and functional composition of that organization. In Coase's view, transaction costs exist in six basic forms: search costs, information costs, bargaining costs, decision costs, policing costs, and enforcement costs.

Coase argues that firms are created because the incremental cost of organizing and maintaining them is cheaper than the total transaction costs involved when individuals conduct business with one another using the market. A firm should perform internally only those functions that cannot be performed more cheaply in the market or by another competing firm.

Services in an SOA are a unit of business or process activity. They equate very nicely to Coase's concept of transactions. Decomposing silos of application functionality into business services helps identify the business processes and transactional context for the business services. Doing this makes the services concept a powerful analog for analysis and improvement using business process analysis and management techniques.

Services can be more easily equated to business transactions than IT applications in general. Using this type of analysis, an organization can easily recast its business processes and transactions as services, and thus assess their internal and external productivity through time. Services can be managed as atomic units of productivity for internal and external processes. In this manner, an organization will be able to manage its operations much more effectively than before using relative service transaction costs similar to the Coase approach.

Componentizing business processes into services can lead to more granular control of and management of business processes in an SOA. When business services are packaged and exposed as services, an organization can modify and optimize the fundamental composition of and execution of its business process based on the services model. Business services are the appropriate unit of transactional analysis for many reasons, including:

- Identifying business transactions and associated costs.
- Improving business processes.
- Achieving reuse of business services and supporting IT functions across systems, processes, and business units.
- Communicating with the business consumers of IT resources. Services are a granular way of describing and delivering IT services to business consumers.

Services, like transactions, are atomic components of business and process analysis. When an organization begins thinking about its capabilities as modular reuasable services, it can begin to understand how to conduct these business transactions using an SOA model. Most of Coase's transaction types can be found as services in most organizations. We must first generalize the kinds of services that will be important to an organization in order to identify and build them.

What Are "Business Services"?

We often hear the term "business services" used in discussions of SOA. Organizations will have two broad classes of services: (1) business services and (2) technical services. What exactly are business services as compared to the general model of services?

Business services reflect business concepts and events, and thus are excellent organizing principles for an SOA. They could also be called business process services, because typically they are associated with execution of business functions of an organization or business domain. They resemble our business and event-based reality. Newcomer and Lomow define services as "IT assets that correspond to real-world business activities or recognizable business functions that can be accessed according to the service policies that have been established for the services."[2]

Business services, or coarse-grained business functionality delivered as services, represent real processes or business activities of an organization. Concepts such as "open new account," "get account balance," or "get phone bill details" are real business events that can be represented as business services for broad consumption by humans (bank tellers), portals, voice response units (VRUs), and other systems and business services.

The process of identifying services in an organization often focuses on process domains or business units within a larger organization. These process domains provide a focus and scope for services identification and analysis. Think about your organization and the various process silos and business unit silos that exist. These organizational domains to some extent are responsible for the silos of IT functionality that SOA will help eliminate. Services analysis encourages horizontal cross-domain perspectives. Achieving reuse of services requires you to identify domain or process services within silos, and then to look across business units and process domains for reuse opportunities in a horizontal fashion. If you focus your initial services efforts on a single business unit or process domain, be sure that your services identification approach looks across all business units and process domains for reuse opportunities. If you do not perform this horizontal domain analysis, you may miss reuse opportunities and focus only on vertical domain services.

Business services provide the starting point for services identification and analysis for an organization. Beginning with customers and external touch points into an organization helps focus SOA efforts on areas where transactional friction can endanger customer satisfaction, revenue generation, and process efficiency. However, business services offer another critical benefit: a common business language.

Business Services as a Common Language

Business services extend very naturally into business language and thus can form the bridging terminology between IT and business users/consumers during analysis and design. As the fundamental unit of analysis for SOAs, services can provide common understanding of processes, events, transactions, and IT capabilities that underlie or implement these activities in an organization. This is a critical aspect of services in an SOA. The ability to understand and communicate within an organization using business services concepts will pave the way to a better IT and business relationship as well as provide a common language of business processes and IT functionality. This benefit of SOA and services should be front and center in all organizations.

Technical Services

Technical services are those services that are horizontal in nature or are reusable by all business processes, business units, or process domains. Technical services include security services, logging services, audit services, transformation services, and similar "IT services" that would be leveraged by and across all lines of business. In some organizations, these technical services are described as enterprise common services. They are enterprise-wide and common to all business processes. Another common model is to assign ownership of SOA technical infrastructure to an organization that also manages these enterprise common services. In this approach, the term "services" refers to the infrastructure technology as services as well as the technical services that are running on these infrastructure services. Be careful with your terminology here. The services model is meant to simplify and clarify, not confuse. Use clear services taxonomies within your organization to eliminate confusion.

Beware of allowing technical services to become the sole focus for your SOA efforts. SOA should be a business-driven initiative, beginning with business services and accommodating technical services as well. This is not to say that an IT-focused SOA initiative cannot deliver tremendous organizational value. It can. However, focusing an SOA initiative solely on the IT organization may overlook opportunities to positively impact business operations with SOA benefits of time to market, process orchestration, and agility. If SOA is reduced to "just another IT initiative" without clear support for and by the business, there may be some organizational value left on the table. If an SOA effort is an IT-driven and IT-focused activity, treat it from an IT business perspective. In other words, make sure SOA addresses the business needs of an IT organization.

Characteristics of Services

Services, in order to meet the needs of the organization, must meet certain criteria to provide the most value to the organization. These attributes are important features of services for this book:

- Coarse-grained services
- Well-defined service contracts
- Loosely coupled
- Discoverable
- Durable
- Composable
- Business aligned
- Reusable
- Interoperable

Coarse-Grained Services Services should be coarse-grained entities. By "coarse-grained," we mean that services should represent business functions, processes, or transactions and encapsulate other fine-grained components or services within them. This term is one of the most used in the rapidly evolving world of SOA. Service granularity depends on how much functionality a service encapsulates and exposes. The internal functionality of a service depends on the scope and functionality of components and transactions encapsulated in the service.

A service that is too big or too coarse-grained will suffer from performance issues and will not be reusable. A service that is too fine-grained will be too narrow in scope to meet requirements of multiple business processes. Services should encapsulate lower-level or fine-grained entities, components, transactions, and other implementation-specific details in order to abstract them from the specific physical and technical implementations they are currently instantiated in.

Fine-grained services provide a narrow scope of business and process utility. Consider software components being exposed as services one for one. These would most likely be fine-grained services. They may encompass little business functionality and hence would be too fine-grained for an SOA. Consuming such fine-grained services could potentially cause excessive messaging traffic to complete the desired business process or transaction. Good services design seeks coarse enough granularity to meet business process requirements while optimizing XML processing and messaging traffic. The art and science of services design is finding the right granularity that solves the business problem, can be reused, and can be technically implemented.

Well-Defined Service Contracts   Services must have well-defined contracts that separate the functionality of the service from its specific technical implementation. The service contract informs consumers what the service does as well as how to consume or use the service. Service contracts present the service functionality to the outside world in a standardized, interoperable fashion while hiding the specific internal technical details of the service. In the world of Web services, the service contract is defined by the WSDL document in conjunction with other metadata, such as policies, XML schema, document semantics, and more.

Loosely Coupled   The term "loosely coupled services" is another one that is clear yet ambiguous. The reason is that "loosely coupled" has implications both for services and for the enabling technology required to operate services. In the services design aspect of the term, "loosely coupled" means designing services such that specific implementations of services can be replaced, modified, and evolved over time without disrupting the current service consumers and the overall activities of an SOA. In this sense, then, loosely coupled services reduce lifecycle costs, such as development and maintenance costs, by isolating the impact of changes to the internal implementation of services and encouraging reuse of services.

Loosely coupled services are more typically associated with document-style services than remote procedure call (RPC)-style services, which sometimes have a tendency to be tightly coupled to specific technology platforms from which the services were exposed.

The fact that services are loosely coupled also implies certain aspects of the SOA enabling technology along with services design. Consider the synchronous-asynchronous dichotomy of message exchange patterns. Services designed to be asynchronous take advantage of messaging platforms supporting message queue technology, publish-subscribe (pub-sub) functionality, and related message exchange patterns (MEPs). Services that implement asynchronous messaging have a tendency to be more loosely coupled than services that are synchronous. This is a generalization, as synchronous services can be implemented using loose-coupling concepts. However, implementing loosely coupled services and taking advantage of asynchronous messaging when appropriate will allow a transition to an event-based model of SOA, where an asynchronous event-driven services paradigm replaces a synchronous tightly coupled and brittle approach.

Discoverable Services should be discoverable. This means not only that the services are designed well, but that their contracts are published and visible to an intended audience—the consumers. Discoverable services implies that the service contracts—WSDL documents in the case of Web services—are published to a location where they can be discovered, whether that location is a service registry, metadata repository, subdirectory, or some known location. Once the service contracts are published, they must be advertised to potential consumers. An important point must be made here. Services should have known consumers and reuse patterns before they are created or exposed. These intended consumers will use the services as "advertised" in the service contract. However, one of the benefits of an SOA is the unintended or *emergent* consumption of services as more of them are available for consumption. These emergent patterns of service consumption and reuse may lead to new innovations, new business processes, and other organizational value derived by creating reusable interoperable services in your SOA.

Durable   Services should be durable yet elastic. Durable services are those that map to lasting business or process themes. For example, insurance companies will always have a claims process. The claims process is thus an enduring process theme. The business services that comprise the claims processes may change, and the claims process itself may change, but there will always be a claims business process in an insurance organization. The services may change but the business or process themes will remain. We like to say that services are the lasting and enduring assets of your SOA. Design them well, pick the proper services, and make them the central asset of your SOA process.

Composable   Services should be composable. The word "composability" has as many definitions as the term "loosely coupled." Composable services are designed to be incorporated into other services as composite services as necessary. In addition, composable services can be assembled into orchestrated process flows. In this sense, composable services are stateless and atomic in nature. They stand on their own yet rely on other services or infrastructure for state and context.

The World Wide Web Consortium (W3C) defines composability in this way: "Composability of web services refers to the building, from a set of web services, of something at a higher level, typically itself exposed as a larger web service. Web services are required to be composable—you should be able to make a web service implementation by building it out of component web services."[3]

However, IBM and Microsoft have advocated another aspect of composability during the standards process for services and SOA: "Composability enables *incremental consumption* or *progressive discovery* of new concepts, tools and services. Developers only need to learn and implement what is necessary, and no more. The complexity of the solution increases only because the problem's requirements increase, and is not due to technology 'bloat.'"[4]

In many respects, composability of services is a result of Web services standards and the multipart message structure. This modular structure enables the *composition* of new functionality. New message elements supporting new services may be added to messages in a manner that does not alter the processing of existing functionality. Composability also means that incremental functionality may be added to existing services without breaking the contract with existing services consumers, and new standards may be implemented similarly without compromising the existing interoperability and functionality of the same services. In both of these contexts, composability of services is an essential requirement.

Business Aligned   Services should be business aligned. By this we mean that services identification and analysis should begin with business imperatives and business requirements, and then cascade into the other services we expect to find in most organizations, such as technical services, data services, infrastructure services, and more. Services, or business services, represent business concepts and match business needs as determined through business strategy and planning and the associated business discovery processes that should precede an SOA initiative.

Reusable   Services must be reusable. This is a function of proper services identification, analysis, and design. Spending time and effort on services that are not reusable is dangerous and wasteful. You must implement services that have clear and defined reuse across and within business processes and that have multiple consumption patterns in your current and planned business processes. Again, bear in mind that the intended reuse of services may lead to unintended or emergent reuse by other consumers who find value in a particular service. This is a good thing. However, you must have a management infrastructure in place to track actual consumption patterns in order to ensure proper performance of the services and appropriate sizing of hardware and bandwidth of your networks.

Interoperable   Services must be interoperable. This sounds obvious, but many services do not interoperate. This lack of interoperability can result from the differential application of policies, standards, and other design criteria during the services design and development process. The way to achieve interoperable services is to enforce a body of SOA policies across the services lifecycle: identification, design, and implementation.

Services First, Not Web Services First

A common misconception with SOA and services is to focus only on Web services, which are really a special case of interoperable reusable services that make use of the core SOA standards such as XML, SOAP and WSDL. We suggest taking the conceptual view of all possible reusable services first, and then implementing Web services where they make sense. Intradomain services may not require WSDL documents and SOAP messaging due to their domain-specific behavior and context. However, cross-domain services are great candidates for Web services because they will be exposed outside of a particular domain for shared usage by a diverse community of interest. Consider these four simple rules for services:

1. Focus on business services first.
2. Determine services that map to business processes.
3. Decide what services are best exposed as Web services.
4. Implement as priorities dictate.

SERVICES ADDRESS PERSISTENT CHALLENGES AND PRESENT NEW OPPORTUNITIES

The services paradigm has the potential to introduce many new opportunities to IT organizations. The organizations that embrace SOA and can capitalize on service orientation will realize a wealth of new concepts, technologies, methodologies, and development approaches that have never been practiced in their environments. Major service opportunities for enterprises include:

- Service strategies and operating models
- Abstraction and conceptualization
- Breaking silos of asset ownership
- Service reuse and asset leverage
- Business and consumer growth

Services Strategies and Operating Models

SOA and services provide new business opportunities through the ability to impact both IT and business processes in a variety of beneficial ways. For example, SOA can shorten time to market for products and services through the introduction of service identification, analysis, and design best practices that can influence product development life-cycles. These new methodologies encourage the formation of business and technology strategies that may influence management structures, business models, business processes, and software development life-cycle activities. Many organizations already had begun the migration to a services delivery model before the advent of SOA and services. However, with the industry adoption of standards for SOA and Web services, the opportunity to drive IT and business change through service delivery models is clear. Shared reusable and interoperable services offer many benefits to the organizations that embrace the opportunity.

Abstraction and Conceptualization

Service-oriented development helps elevate software abstractions and generalizations beyond the traditional software development process.[5] This higher level of abstraction based on services facilitates the establishment of discovery, analysis, and design practices that can meet business requirements much earlier in the organization's business process and software development lifecycle. These opportunities encourage a top-down conceptual analysis, services design, and architecture process that are aligned with business requirements and strategies. SOA discourages ad hoc approaches to IT and business solutions, yet it will provide a more agile approach to rapid business solutions based on reusable and interoperable services.

Breaking Silos of Asset Ownership

Services provide an opportunity to break the organizational silos of asset ownership. This problem is partly responsible for the silos of application functionality that exist today, which traditionally required the point-to-point integration solutions of the past. An SOA model of shared reusable services allows an organization to change the asset utilization model to one of shared business services instead of domain ownership, business unit ownership, or even departmental ownership. The movements toward grid computing, utility computing, and other similar trends are all based on improving return on assets (ROA) and variabilized cost structures. Services and SOA can help by recasting legacy assets and enterprise software as shared services leveraged by horizontal governance and common business processes.

Service Reuse and Asset Leverage

SOA as an iterative process of services identification, analysis, and design offers an opportunity to drive tremendous services reuse and asset leverage. This approach emphasizes modeling and analysis of services early in the service lifecycle, before they are committed as actual physical services, rather than late in the process. The service modeling approach we advocate identifies opportunities to consolidate processes and reuse services and related information assets early in the service lifecycle rather than applying such concepts after services have been implemented. Bottom-up services identification and design often results in tight coupling to specific technology platforms and usually cannot adequately surface reuse opportunities at the business level. In our model, reusability and interoperability best practices are applied to conceptual business services before they are designed, and implemented as concrete deliverables. To drive the organization's reuse strategy, services reuse analysis should be performed on candidate business services.

Business and Consumer Growth

The services opportunity may enable organizations to focus on consumer requirements by applying service consumption, utilization, and prioritization policies based on revenue, customer satisfaction, and other market-facing capabilities. These customer segmentation approaches enable an organization to concentrate on providing outstanding service to the most valued customers and thereby help grow the business and the consumer community.

Furthermore, SOA, services, and their enabling technologies facilitate measurement and tracking of services capacity, services consumption, quality of service, and related operational metrics to potentially apply charge-back approaches based on service contracts and the stipulated service-level agreements (SLAs). Service consumers and providers are connected through these service contracts and are accountable for providing the agreed-on quality of service (QoS) and complying to related SLAs and policy assertions specified in the service contracts and message metadata.

GENERAL MODEL OF SERVICES

Common Architecture Language

Business and IT organizations must communicate strategies, standards, best practices, and policies using internal terminology and language that reflects the culture and heritage of the specific organization. Often the "language" of an organization reflects the degree to which business and IT communities can interact to achieve the organization's goals. However, there is often a communications breakdown between business and IT communities due to language, performance, and other barriers. Services offer a way to bridge this gap by serving as a universal language—a language of "business services"—that is understandable by all business professionals. Services provide organizations with a common vocabulary that facilitates service lifecycle activities such as business modeling, service analysis and development, deployment, and management. Furthermore, service vocabularies can be expanded and transformed into new product and service concepts, which begins to leverage services as an innovation platform within an organization.

An Internal View of Services

Services are comprised of various elements that are vital to their operations, such as components that implement business logic and composite services. They facilitate and express service identities and behaviors that ultimately result in business and technology solutions. These elements have distinctive responsibilities, must comply with service communication protocols, and participate in routing, distribution, and dispatching of messages and transactions. Internal elements principally operate within service territories exclusively managed and controlled by their respective container services.

Service structures may require the inclusion of specific fine-grained services, which provide particular business and technological support for a services implementation. The concept of composite services accommodates this notion.

Services Are Extensible and Composable

Services, due to their composable and extensible nature, are amenable to change. As mentioned earlier, the functionality of a service's original scope does not impose a limitation on its future functionality. Services are designed and architected to handle growth and accommodate changes because they are composable. Services can easily accommodate changes as new requirements are introduced and as business and IT strategies change along with demand for services modifications, changing business services, business processes, and/or technology changes. Thus, service extensibility enables an organization to manage unexpected business threats and disruptions and to respond rapidly to the unpredictable business landscape. Time-to-market and agility strategies can be implemented using SOA and services to respond to unforeseen challenges by virtue of services extensibility.

Services Support Business and Technology Goals

Services are expressions of abstractions—for example, theories, business processes, concepts, and ideas. Services thus do not have clearly defined boundaries. They originate from a variety of sources, such as business events, concerns, challenges, business models, and strategies. Services abstractions can be manipulated to offer solutions to organizational challenges. In order for services to support business and technology goals, they must first be identified, modeled, and organized, using simple logical techniques, into potential solutions. Service abstractions must be modeled to facilitate solution design.

To clearly define and implement services to address business and IT challenges, a structured, repeatable methodology is necessary to map organizational concepts to the concrete world of physical services. These services modeling practices employ a set of logical operations on service abstractions to identify and prioritize services to meet business and technological goals. They provide analysis tools that can facilitate the inspection and the examination of abstractions and can decompose, decouple, or unify them into discovered new entities. This transformation process redefines conceptual sets, resizes their boundaries, discovers business commonalities, and focuses on organizational solutions. (See Chapters 3, 4, and 5 for more detailed treatment.) Exhibit 2.1 depicts this idea. Transformation processes operate on organization abstractions and produce entities, such as business and solution services.

Some of the skills and expertise required to perform such structural analysis on coarse entities include understanding of the business, having the big-picture perspective toward problems, being able to analyze market conditions, and generalizing private instances into more generic and holistic organizational views.

Furthermore, the ability to understand the granularity of concepts and ideas, sizing their operational range, and establishing their responsibilities can facilitate the discovery of enterprise service requirements. Doing this can reveal actual SOA organizational needs and address the motivation and justification for conducting such initiatives.

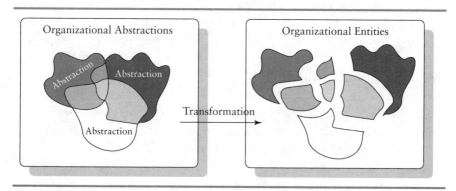

EXHIBIT 2.1   Transformation of Service Abstractions

Services Align with Business and Technological Requirements

Services offer a pathway toward business and technology alignment. Because services provide a common language for business and technology professionals, there is a better opportunity to align business goals around the concepts of services. And owing to the agile nature of SOA and services, there is an opportunity to eliminate the latency between business demand for IT support and the actual implementation of that support via services. The demand for dynamic alignment between business and technology requirements can galvanize the need for SOA and services in strategic initiatives. This may cause a reevaluation of current initiatives and the existing service inventory to analyze available services and their fit with current and future SOA initiatives.

A proactive approach to alignment of services with business conditions can better support strategic goals than reactive initiatives that often yield a tactical and potentially compromised response to organizational challenges.

Services Are Autonomous Yet Interdependent

Services are autonomous and self-contained entities, yet they depend on a wide range of operational capabilities and integrated entities, such as peer services, applications, middleware, and networks. Services, although atomic and self-contained, still require the supporting functionality provided by enabling technology, design time tools, registries, and metadata repositories, and various run-time solutions. Their operations are augmented, supported, and facilitated by external resources that make this collaboration inseparable. Services dependencies will tend to increase over time because of their organic growth, expansion of their operational bandwidth and functional coverage, increased consumer demand and business, and technological changes. Furthermore, the interdependency of services is often attributed to architecture standards and best practices that encourage decoupling of entities for the benefit of asset reuse, ease of development, publishing, discovery, distribution, integration, administration, and management. For example, a trading *account profile service* may utilize a number of external peer services, such as *account balances service, statements service, positions service,* and *customer name and address service.* This architectural style supports decoupling of customer service functionalities by establishing a finer-grained environment that is highly interdependent yet enables greater reuse of these distributed assets. Thus, while the *account profile service* does rely on the other services it is composed of, in and of itself it is self-contained and atomic in nature because of the composability of services.

SERVICES IN AN SOA CONTEXT

We have stated that an SOA is nothing without services. Services are the central artifact of an SOA and the fundamental unit of analysis. Services do not operate in a vacuum, however. They require other services, appropriate enabling infrastructure, business context to give them value, and the ever-so-critical SOA governance to provide oversight for the overall operation of services within the SOA. The services operating context includes all of these entities as well as consumers, providers, and all related constituents of the SOA.

Service Governance

SOA governance and policies provide a management structure, processes, and policies to oversee operations and management of services. Without SOA governance of all service lifecycle processes, there will be chaos. SOA and service governance are covered in detail in Chapter 7.

Service Abstractions: Three Views

Services are abstractions of technical elements, business process elements, data elements, and conceptual elements. Services encapsulate business and technological solutions. Service abstractions provide a unique logical landscape of service concepts and implementations as depicted by three abstraction views:

Conceptual view

Business process view

Technological view

Conceptual View   A service conceptual view defines services in terms of their characteristics, their logical boundaries, and the value they provide to business or to technological consumers. This view illustrates ideas, business and technology concepts, and abstractions that services are associated with. *Loan exposure* and *credit verification* can be conceived as core service abstractions that facilitate loan origination processes in a personal loans division of a financial institution. The *loan exposure* abstraction identifies loan organization needs to calculate risks that are involved with issuing credit letters and committing to loan executions. The *credit verification* service abstraction is another milestone in loan origination processes that an applicant must comply with.

Business Process View   Business processes are a different type of abstraction. The business process view depicts services as orchestrated (and potentially choreographed) sequences of business process activities that conduct day-to-day business transactions. In this scenario, services require orchestration to manage state and provide business context, as well as determine where data validation will occur in the process. For services operating outside of an organization, services choreography will be used to connect cross-firewall business processes between organizations. For example, stock trading business processes such as *order management, order routing*, and *commission calculations* can be expressed in details by depicting their activities. *Order management* tasks take place through the lifecycle of trading orders, such as capturing new orders and providing order browsing capabilities. *Order routing* processes illustrate the distribution of stock symbols for execution to various markets. *Commission calculations* processes describe various activities to compute commissions for brokers.

Technological View   Technical service abstractions encapsulate technological ideas and concepts, and specific technical details of services,
based on the platforms and applications they are exposed from or
created from. These represent a wide range of enabling technologies,
such as commercial applications, legacy systems, integration platforms, message brokers, and more. Exposing services as abstractions
from their native implementations is essential to creating reusable
interoperable services in an SOA.

SERVICE LIFECYCLE

The lifecycle of services reflects the process of identification and discovery, modeling (analysis and design), implementation, management, and portfolio management of services. These stages depict the
evolution of assets from origination to maturity and through execution. These phases are categorized into two basic service lifecycle
domains: (1) the *problem domain* and (2) the *solution domain*. The
problem domain is comprised of all service lifecycle activities that
result in the identification and analysis of organizational services
through the analysis phase. Here organizational challenges are
defined based on events, imperatives and concerns, which are the
motivating forces for SOA and services. These lead to identification
and analysis of candidate or potential business services.

Following the problem domain activities, the solution domain
activities commence. These activities accept business services as
inputs and begin the services design, implementation, and integration
activities that result in physical solution services.

The service lifecycle progresses in stages to drive the development
of services by supporting iterations of tasks and activities. It is
designed to perfect and refine its outputs, which ultimately are solution services. The five unique service lifecycle stages—*service motivation, conceptualization, service modeling, service realization*, and
lifecycle *management*—are depicted in Exhibit 2.2.

Market and organizational events such as *problems* and *concerns*
affect respective lifecycle stages, goals, and milestones. Lifecycle discipline activities such as *analysis, design,* and *realization* shape service
design and architectural outcomes for which SOA services are being

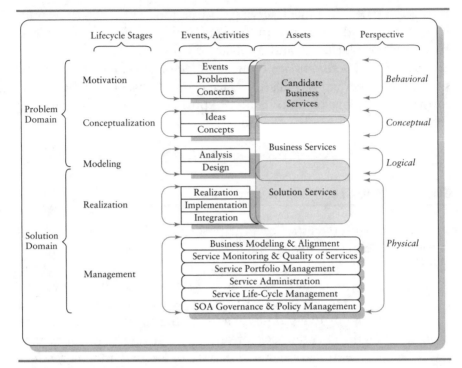

EXHIBIT 2.2 Service Lifecycle

established and developed. Service origination and subsequent lifecycle stages lead to the establishment of tangible services through the foundation of abstractions, such as *concern entities*, *core entities*, and *business services*.

Service lifecycle stages utilize different perspectives of product development practices, such as *behavioral*, *conceptual*, *logical*, and *physical*. These views constitute directions and strategies of service creation in organizations. Furthermore, they facilitate simplification and provide touch-point opportunities for bottom-up and top-down service development approaches. The bottom-up method begins service construction from the *physical* perspective and proceeds vertically where it meets the top-down approach. The top-down approach begins with the *behavioral* perspective. Once the top-down and bottom-up approaches meet, they have covered a complete service lifecycle.

Service Motivation Lifecycle Stage

The *service motivation stage* is comprised of a number of motivating forces for SOA and services. These forces include external and internal lifecycle influences such as events, challenges, business imperatives, IT imperatives, problems, and concerns:

- *Events.* Events impose an array of organizational challenges, attract immediate management attention to possible business threats, and potentially impact enterprise stability. Events can be diverse. They can originate from market trends, competition, political unrest and instability, and technological occurrences. Events can impact business activities, management structures, and migration of personnel. Events do not have to be negative in nature, or threats. There can also be positive events, such as surge in demand for goods and products, which nonetheless can apply pressures on enterprise business execution and become grounds for reassessments of business and technological strategies and business models. Motivations, reasons, and needs for services are spurred by these alterations to business directions. The *service motivation* stage provides initial substance for SOA, for services identification and service abstractions, which are founded to provide short-term comfort to obstacles and difficulties that the business is running against.
- *Business and IT Imperatives.* Business and IT imperatives are critical challenges an organization faces for which solutions must be implemented or serious negative consequences will occur. Business imperatives are critical business issues such as lower customer satisfaction, intensified competition in a market segment, or slow time to market for new products. They are central issues to an organization's core business model. IT imperatives, on the other hand, are issues within the information technology domain. Examples of IT imperatives might be excessive integration costs, inability to support business change, lack of appropriate skills to support the business, or chronically late project delivery. These IT imperatives must be addressed or there will be negative consequences in the IT organization. One more point should be made. Often IT imperatives will be surfaced from business imperatives, and so addressing IT imperatives may

contribute to solving a business imperative. These both lead to opportunities to originate services in an organization.

■ *Problems.* Enterprise problems occur because there are no preventive measures in place to halt the impact of events on the business. Business and technological strategies are unable to provide guidance, organizational standards, and best practices on how to deal with unpredictable influences and prevent or suspend crisis conditions in the enterprise. Problem domain statements can depict the background and fundamental causes for occurring circumstances, illustrate the current state of the business, classify and describe severity of problems, and provide rudimentary definition and justification for inception of services.

■ *Concerns.* Concerns galvanize organizational initiatives designed to identify the needs for solutions. They underline risks and probable business threats and depict a variety of scenarios that may occur if proper remedies are not introduced. Expressions of formalized enterprise concerns are designed to minimize and dampen extreme influences and facilitate moderation of enterprise instabilities. Concerns can be derived from occurring *problems*; yet they can be introduced by proactive activities that are driven mainly by strategies. Concerns are the motivating factors and reasoning behind the establishment of service abstractions, which are comprised of service concepts, business processes, or technological propositions.

The outputs of the service motivation lifecycle phase are candidate business services. These candidate business services will be analyzed and transformed into final business services, which will be designed and implemented following a repeatable process that we provide in Chapters 3, 4, and 5.

Conceptualization Lifecycle Stage

This lifecycle stage is dominated by the identification of candidate or potential business services. This process is all about *ideas* and *concepts* where SOA and services may benefit the organization and provide solutions that match organizational challenges and concerns. At first, these lifecycle activity outputs suggest approaches and processes, mainly tactical solutions and short-term plans that depict ways to attack problems and alleviate concerns in the form of *ideas*. Subsequently, *concept* generalization and refinement processes lead to the formation of organizational *core entities* that can provide strategic directions to the analysis, development, and construction of concrete services. Thus, the main events that occur in the conceptualization lifecycle stage are the origination of ideas and concepts.

- *Ideas*. Ideas are merely sporadic streams and flows of statements that depict immediate reactions to events that are occurring. At times, they can be conclusions of meetings or thoughts and management inspirations to address outstanding issues. Ideas are only mental and conceptual constructs. In many cases, they are simply a natural reflection of human creativity and expressions of talents. *Ideas* are not organized campaigns, institutionalized processes, or methodological procedures to solving problems and do not commit organizations to action plans or schedules. They are necessary for the creation of service abstractions because they provide generalized forms of problem analysis and introduce business proposals to address *concerns*.

- *Concepts*. Concepts are formalized and established *ideas* and components of propositions. They attempt to capture enterprise conditions and reality, conceived as organizational material storage of information and generalized snapshots of problems and concerns. *Concepts* provide strategic views and directions to business and technology organizations by introducing a common dictionary, terminology of abstractions, language, grammars, and communication protocols. *Customer-centric approach, customer household profile,* and *linked accounts* are examples of *concepts* and propositions that emphasize a shift in this particular organization's culture and the way it conducts business: Client necessities become a focal point of its *concerns* and its strategy targets.

Service Modeling Lifecycle Stage

The service modeling lifecycle stage accepts as inputs the candidate and potential business services that were identified during the conceptualization lifecycle phase. Service modeling involves *analysis* and *design* activities on the candidate business services to prioritize and select the services that will be implemented. The analysis phase consists of logical modeling operations on conceptual candidate business services in order to understand their functionality and reusability factors, their granularity, and their business impact relative to the organization.

- *Analysis.* Service *analysis* is performed on candidate business services in order to simplify complexities of service abstractions and apply logical modeling operations to better understand candidate services. *Services*, which are coarse forms of *ideas* and *concepts*, provide raw material and context to such operations. The difficulties in rationalizing and visualizing these abstractions can be alleviated by utilizing *analysis* methods and tools that can assist with decomposition or aggregation of *candidate business services*. This lifecycle stage enables visualization of abstraction boundaries—a refinement process that provides definitions and identities to enterprise assets and leads to the formation of final *business services*, which are more refined and focused on problems and concerns. Final *business services* encapsulate processes and operational logic, and later play a major role in the construction of *solution services* (physical entities).

- *Service design.* Service *design* processes and tools offer mechanisms to define the scope and coverage of *solution services*. Thus *business services* provide foundation and raw material for the design phase. They are evaluated and ranked based on their granularity level and grouped into new business formations to support or exclude lines of business or domains. Business process abstractions can be shared, borrowed, or exported to various services based on their affiliation, message exchange, and transaction models. These transformations facilitate the mapping of business objectives to technological goals and enable design of service compositions and their internal structures. The *modeling lifecycle stage* ensures the successful transition from the conceptual world to the more tangible one, and subsequently sets the stage for the recognition of concrete services.

Service Realization Lifecycle Stage

Service *realization* accepts final *business services* as inputs. At this point, candidate business services have been analyzed, designed, prioritized, and selected for services realization. These business services will now be implemented and integrated into an SOA network or service community. Finalization of services design and architecture blueprints, construction and implementation of tangible solution services, and service integration are the main activities that take place in the service *realization* phase. This stage facilitates the final transformation of service abstractions into concrete assets. The output of the services *realization* phase are *solution services*. *Solution services* become physical services when they are actually implemented in an operational SOA network.

- *Realization. Solution services* are recognized, realized, and established in the *realization process*. This is where physical services are created. Reconstructed and refined *business services*, which are the outcome of the *visualization phase*, provide context and content for establishing tangible *solution services*. This process, again, uses granularity scaling methods to facilitate the design of service structure and architecture. Service elements, such as components and processes, are positioned in the grand scheme of internal service operations. Transformation and conversion processes facilitate the assignment of roles and responsibilities of service internal and external elements.
- *Implementation.* Development and implementation of physical services occurs in the *realization* lifecycle stage. Integrated development environments (IDEs) that are provided by vendor products can offer service construction assistance, best practices, and industry standards. These packages generally support a bottom-up approach to service creation and do not engage development teams in top-down service lifecycle stages such as the *conceptualization* and *visualization*. Contemporary development tools provide support for multiple languages, frameworks, and libraries, but they do not support service strategic planning and the business architecture and service analysis approaches we advocate here. Nevertheless, some vendors plan integration of service

lifecycle stages in their offerings. Lack of service lifecycle industry standards hampers these projects.

- *Integration. Integration* initiatives take place in the *realization* lifecycle stage. They are facilitated by standards, policies, best practices, and integration patterns that are fully described in Chapter 5. Disciplines of service integration provide guidance and processes to enable service deployment and configuration, construction of service topologies, incorporation of intermediaries (i.e., hubs and gateways), and the foundation of enterprise service bus (ESB) and middleware facilities. Furthermore, the service integration model in Chapter 5 introduces formal integration modeling techniques that facilitate the construction of heterogeneous environments and the establishment of interoperability and reusability disciplines. Finally, service integration practices create opportunities for origination of service congregations, which are collaborative environments that evolve with time into service communities. These integrated service communities develop consumer-producer dependencies and influence service management practices in the enterprise.

Lifecycle Management Stage

Service management and support activities span all service lifecycle stages as depicted in Exhibit 2.2. Business, analysis, design, implementation, integration, deployment, and production events are facilitated by SOA management disciplines, best practices, and policies, all variously supported by vendor tools. There are a variety of industry standards and specifications that offer formal documentation and automation of SOA and service lifecycle management. These facilitate Web services policies, provisioning, distributed asset management, and security through standards such as WS-Policy, WS-Security—a security framework that depicts security requirements for services and their assertion format in messages[6]— Service Provisioning Markup Language (SPML)—a standard protocol that describes exchanging of provisioning requests between requesting authorities and provisioning services[7]—and Web Services Distributed Management (WSDM)—for management of services and resources through Web services protocols.

Management lifecycle stage activities are centered on the following areas:

- *SOA business modeling and alignment.* This activity provides support for the discovery and establishment of business processes, foundation of business models, and alignment of business requirements with technological initiatives that take place in the *service motivation* and *conceptualization* lifecycle stages.
- *Service operations and management.* These activities involve the management and maintenance of the services run-time, operation, and management infrastructure of an organization. They include adding new SOA capabilities as more services are realized and as solution platforms are enhanced and upgraded to meet market demands. Furthermore, service operations and management activities include SOA management, monitoring, messaging infrastructure, and all run-time and operational aspects of the SOA enabling infrastructure.
- *Service monitoring and quality of services (QoS).* Monitoring activities and QoS are concerned with reporting of service run-time capacities, capabilities, consumption rates, performance, and continuity of product offerings. Performance of service-level agreements between service consumers and producers can be tracked and registered by utilizing monitoring and alerting tools. Violation of service security can be discovered and published to participating parties.
- *Service portfolio management.* These activities include the classification and the cataloging of services (by service types or taxonomies, e.g., business or technical), characterization of service functionality, and management of the organization's services and related assets. These repositories reflect business and technological perspectives and how the services therein provide solution coverage for enterprise challenges. Portfolio management is critical for asset consolidation initiatives, discovery of business commonalities, budgeting, overall funding of development projects, maintenance, and licensing cost. The service portfolio management activities also include service administration functions, which are described next.
- *Service administration.* Essential organizational SOA governance policies influence asset administration activities. These continuous

efforts and initiatives are triggered by integration and deployment requirements; enforcement of new organizational policies, standards, and best practices; changing business rules for service transactions and message exchange; modifying service environments and communities; altering interoperability rules; and configuring and relocating services to different service environments. Furthermore, administration responsibilities can address service dependencies and interactions, such as service workload management, load balancing, failover, and prioritization of transactions and message routing.

■ *Service lifecycle management.* Service lifecycle management provides the processes and supporting tools to manage services across the service development lifecycle—from conceptualization to modeling to realization and maintenance. Service lifecycle management can interact with portfolio management, version management, and publishing and discovery processes, and also includes various design time governance processes.

■ *SOA governance and policy management.* SOA governance and policy management provides the SOA management framework for process and policies that will be enforced across all service lifecycle phases and activities: identification, analysis, design, implementation, integration, and ongoing maintenance. Policy management includes the process of defining and managing SOA policies decoupled from the services themselves as well as performing impact analysis of policy changes to the existing portfolio of services of an organization. SOA governance and policy management also includes organizational and procedural aspects of managing, budgeting, and maintaining services that are shared and reusable across business and process domains.

SUMMARY

Services are critical to the planning and implementation of SOA. They are the fundamental unit of analysis and concern for SOA planning, architecture design, and implementation. An understanding of services and their composition helps situate them in contraposition to tightly coupled application delivery models. The service lifecycle developed in this chapter provides a conceptual flow of services from the initial motivation for SOA and services to identification, analysis, design, and implementation of services. The remaining chapters work the lifecycle to help organizations implement a repeatable service lifecycle process of their own. SOA is all about the services.

NOTES

1. Ronald H. Coase, "The Nature of the Firm," in *The Firm, the Market and the Law* (Chicago: University of Chicago Press, 1988), pp. 33–56. See also Ronald H. Coase, *Essays on Economics and Economists* (Chicago: University of Chicago Press, 1995).
2. Eric Newcomer and Greg Lomow, *Understanding SOA with Web Services* (New York: Addison-Wesley, 2005).
3. www.w3.org/DesignIssues/WebServices.html.
4. Donald Ferguson et al., "Secure, Reliable, Transacted Web Services," IBM White Paper, October 23, 2004.
5. Olaf Zimmermann, Pal Krogdahl, and Clive Gee, "Elements of Service-Oriented Analysis and Design," IBM White Paper, June 2, 2004, pp. 1–2.
6. BEA Systems Inc., International Business Machines Corporation, Microsoft Corporation, SAP AG, "Web Services Policy Framework (WS Policy)," version 1.0, December 18, 2002, p. 3.
7. OASIS, "Service Provisioning Markup Language (SPML)," version 1.0, June 3, 2003, pp. 10–23.

CHAPTER 3

SOA Business Modeling

The process of achieving service-oriented architecture (SOA) is exactly that—a process. Facilitating the ongoing achievement and maintenance of SOA requires processes thinking, ongoing attention, and reinforcement to achieve the desired results. The SOA approach that we advocate is a business-focused change model where business processes are tuned, service-enabled, and optimized through the use of SOA concepts, capabilities, and enabling technologies. An SOA initiative must be business-centric, not information technology (IT)–centric. SOA must be focused on resolving pressing business challenges.

This is a crucial point. *SOA is not a big bang implementation model based on a single momentous event.* It is a conceptual IT architecture, based on reusable services, that is achieved through multiple implementations of "services" projects across an organization or enterprise. SOA also enables multiple iterations of service versions through time by virtue of the composable and flexible nature of well-designed and well-crafted services. All of these services projects must comply with the SOA vision, goals, standards, guidelines, and policies through time to retain the agility and flexibility promised by SOA. Services projects in an SOA are not implemented centrally. They are implemented through many projects over time, potentially across multiple departments, business processes, and business units, to eventually reach some critical mass of SOA benefits, or *SOA Network Effects.*[1] SOA is accomplished through continuous iterations.

It is this spatially and temporally distributed aspect of SOA that is most challenging and daunting for many organizations. How do you enforce a consistent set of design, reuse, and interoperability standards across a spatially diverse organization so that the ultimate benefits of SOA can be realized? How do you manage the temporal challenges of SOA, where services developed using one generation of Web services standards have the potential for incompatibility with a later generation of Web services standards? And how do you manage functional enhancements of services, version management, and retirement of deprecated services that no longer are supported? These are important SOA issues that are addressed by SOA governance and policies, and enforcement of those policies by a combination of decree, education, employee management, incentives, and overall enforcement during services design and publishing/discovery, and at run-time.

However, do not let these challenges frighten you from the SOA path. The organizational, cultural, and behavioral issues can be managed to help achieve SOA results. Do not forgo these fundamental changes and instead focus on a software tool to implement SOA. Doing this would be a grave mistake. Everyone knows that IT initiatives fail because organizations take the software shortcut or follow the path called *technological reductionism.* Technological reductionism is when an organization attempts to solve business or organizational problems with a piece of software or some other technological silver bullet. By reducing a business challenge to a technology solution, often the real challenge remains left behind, and the organization is now saddled with yet another layer of technology. This common approach to business problem solving has plagued IT and business organizations for years as misconceptions about the role of technology and its ability to resolve business process, organizational, and even behavioral/cultural challenges have persisted. In order to ensure an appropriate business focus for SOA, we advocate an SOA business modeling approach.

SOA BUSINESS ITERATION MODEL

SOA is realized over time through many initiatives that will individually contribute services to the SOA. Remember, the services are what make an SOA. The SOA enabling technology is there only to enable and manage services.

However, it is crucial to also bear in mind that SOA is all about the business, too. It enables an organization to be more competitive through the superior application of IT to business problems or challenges. SOA is an IT model that first and foremost addresses business requirements of an organization. In fact, even the decision that SOA is appropriate for an organization begins with a proper business analysis to determine the fit of services and SOA to a particular class of enterprise challenges.

Exhibit 3.1 is an SOA macrolevel model that depicts how SOA is implemented at a very high level by incorporating business strategy inputs into the SOA strategy and planning process, which then drives the SOA implementation projects that will follow. This high-level model shows the iterative cycle of business discovery and analysis; SOA strategy, planning, and analysis; iterative implementations of services through multiple SOA initiatives; and finally, services iterations where individual services are tuned and improved based on changing business conditions. There is a feedback loop from iterative cycles of SOA implementations back to the business analysis periodically to provide proper external and internal feedback on the SOA strategy.

SOA is realized through four types of iterations based on the SOA macrolevel model:

1. SOA business iteration
2. SOA strategy iteration
3. SOA project iteration
4. SOA services iterations

An *SOA business iteration* is a full feedback loop to determine any changes to the organization's business strategy, based on relevant business and IT conditions, in order to feed those inputs into the SOA strategy and planning process. SOA business iterations provide assurance that any new business conditions and business context are inputs into the SOA strategy and planning process. An SOA business iteration should be performed annually, during the normal business and IT strategy development processes, with perhaps quarterly or midyear reviews. Exhibit 3.1 represents an SOA business iteration feedback cycle.

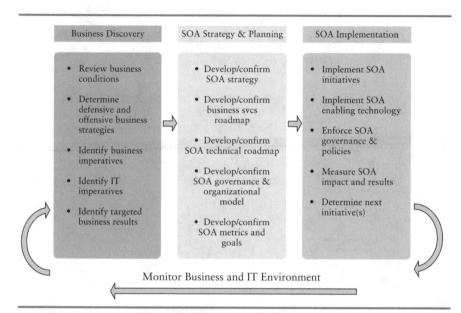

EXHIBIT 3.1 SOA Business Iteration Model
Source: AgilePath Corporation, copyright © 2005. Used with permission.

An *SOA strategy iteration* is a feedback loop between various SOA projects and the overall SOA strategy and planning process. SOA strategy iterations are performed to assess the current SOA strategy, the SOA governance model, and whether the performance objectives have been met by both the SOA strategy and the cumulative results from the various SOA projects over a given time frame. SOA strategy iterations will be performed after major projects are completed and during the annual and semiannual business and IT strategy planning process. Exhibit 3.2 represents an SOA strategy iteration feedback cycle.

An *SOA project iteration* is the process of implementing multiple SOA initiatives or projects within the framework of a current SOA strategy. An SOA project iteration is simply the iterative model used to implement various SOA projects under the guidance and oversight of a given SOA strategy and governance model. More than likely, many SOA projects will be implemented during a single iteration of an SOA strategy. These projects may include the initial services projects, installing enabling technology platforms and infrastructure, followed by more services projects. These are defined within the business

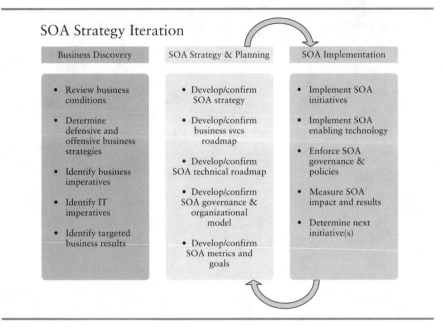

EXHIBIT 3.2 SOA Strategy Iterations
Source: AgilePath Corporation, copyright © 2005. Used with permission.

services roadmap, which in turn determines the SOA enabling technology roadmap. It is important to note that there may be multiple iterations of services projects and enabling technology projects, depending on the nature of a given organization's IT architecture. Exhibit 3.3 depicts the notion of SOA project iterations.

Finally, *SOA services iterations* should be anticipated during the course of an organization's SOA implementation strategy. SOA services implementations are scenarios where existing services are remodeled or reengineered based on new business requirements or technical requirements (or other performance-tuning issues). Implementing services modeling and design practices, along with an appropriate services development process, will facilitate rapid iterations of services within existing projects or business initiatives. Because services are composable, rapid SOA services iterations can occur, where new functionality or requirements may be implemented quickly into existing services without requiring long project lead times. This "agile" services development approach is one of the target outcomes of an SOA initiative: to be able to quickly develop

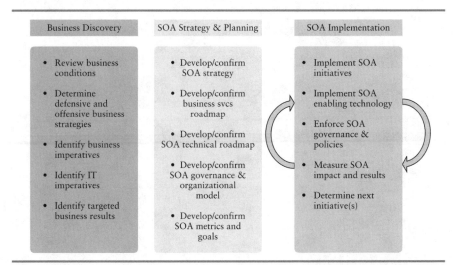

Business Discovery	SOA Strategy & Planning	SOA Implementation
• Review business conditions • Determine defensive and offensive business strategies • Identify business imperatives • Identify IT imperatives • Identify targeted business results	• Develop/confirm SOA strategy • Develop/confirm business svcs roadmap • Develop/confirm SOA technical roadmap • Develop/confirm SOA governance & organizational model • Develop/confirm SOA metrics and goals	• Implement SOA initiatives • Implement SOA enabling technology • Enforce SOA governance & policies • Measure SOA impact and results • Determine next initiative(s)

EXHIBIT 3.3   SOA Project Iterations
Source: AgilePath Corporation, copyright © 2005. Used with permission.

services and orchestrate business processes in response to changing business conditions or requirements.

SOA services iterations will occur whenever business requirements or technical requirements dictate that an existing service be updated or improved. Exhibit 3.4 shows the concept of SOA services iterations.

Exhibit 3.5 shows all four SOA iterations in an SOA macrolevel model. This "nested iteration" of services projects may occur due to many rapid implementations of SOA initiatives in a relatively short time frame. In this case, the overall business iteration feedback loop, which validates the business strategy and SOA objectives as well as confirming and/or adjusting the SOA strategy, business services, and technology roadmaps, is how business feedback is introduced into the SOA planning and implementation cycle to assure that the SOA initiatives have the proper and current business context.

The iterative approach to SOA is the only realistic way in which a multitude of projects across distributed business units and diverse development teams ultimately will converge around an organization's SOA vision, strategy, and SOA governance model. SOA requires iterations of business context, or continuous reframing of the current SOA strategy, and multiple project and services iterations. SOA is not

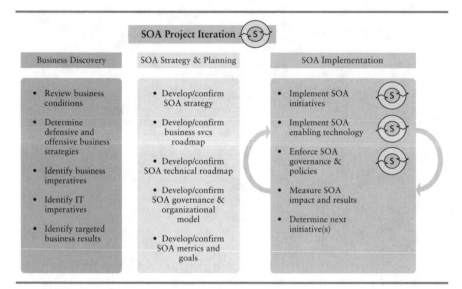

EXHIBIT 3.4 SOA Service Iteration Model
Source: AgilePath Corporation, copyright © 2005. Used with permission.

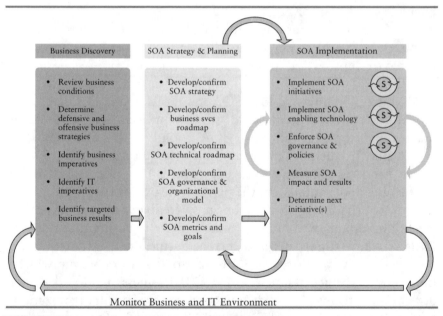

EXHIBIT 3.5 SOA Business Iteration Model
Source: AgilePath Corporation, copyright © 2005. Used with permission.

a single project. It is a lifestyle change. SOA is the goal, and it is achieved through time via many projects. The SOA macrolevel model is a useful way to describe the multiple iterations of business strategy and SOA initiatives. In the next section, we examine the process of SOA strategy and planning, or SOA business modeling.

SOA BUSINESS MODELING

SOA business modeling is the process by which an SOA initiative is pursued within the business and strategic context of an organization. Whether an organization is a commercial for-profit enterprise, a large federal government agency, or a major nonprofit, its business strategy and business imperatives must be explicitly factored into the planning for an SOA initiative. The process of SOA business modeling ensures appropriate business context for all SOA initiatives, which is the primary reason we emphasize it here. However, it also prevents an SOA initiative being reduced to a technology solution, such as an application server or an enterprise service bus (ESB), which is still a common trap for many organizations. The challenges of SOA will not be technical; they will most likely be organizational, behavioral, and cultural. However, proper business context for SOA initiatives will lead to desired business results and unmitigated SOA success.

One way to avoid reducing your SOA effort to a technology solution is to conduct SOA business modeling. Doing so will provide two benefits for an SOA initiative:

1. It will ensure that an SOA initiative is truly a business initiative rather than a technology initiative.
2. It will ensure that the SOA initiative targets clear business results.

Sometimes ensuring proper business context for IT projects is difficult. However, our experience suggests that finding a clear business context for an SOA project will have direct bearing on its relative success and its overall business value. For example, IT-focused projects have a relevant business context, even if it relates solely to the business of IT. Find that business context and factor it into your project planning process. Doing so will help ensure project success.

SOA business modeling therefore tries to determine direct relationships of SOA initiatives to customers—customer experience and satisfaction—which leads to revenue and profit, product quality, process cycle time, productivity, and other organizational success factors. The only way to do this is to force business context into the SOA planning process.

SOA Business Modeling: A Rapid Approach to SOA Strategy

The SOA business modeling approach we advocate is first and foremost a business approach that establishes business context for any SOA initiative. What do we mean by "business context"? We mean that before beginning solution framing, development, and implementation of an SOA initiative, you must analyze a number of business conditions. Business context is determined by the overall business strategy and business model, organizational structure and processes that achieve the organizational goals, and the supporting operating models that lead to realization of the organization's purpose. Finding the appropriate business context for your SOA strategy will lead to better business alignment and executive sponsorship of SOA efforts. This is the primary reason for much-needed business context.

Preparing for SOA: Business Discovery and Business Inspection Activities

Before heading into your formal SOA strategy and planning, your core SOA team should prepare by performing a business discovery and inspection process. This normal business and IT strategy planning activity will be useful in setting the stage for your SOA initiative. The business discovery and business inspection activities will help create the strategic business context for an SOA initiative. From this process the team will identify the business and IT imperatives that will serve as the motivating forces for SOA. The business discovery and inspection process is important for a few reasons:

- It creates the strategic business context for the SOA strategy and planning process that will follow.
- It aligns and informs the SOA core team with the current state of the business; this is critical if members of the team have not participated in strategic initiatives previously.
- It informs business management that there is an SOA initiative under way and that management's broad support, including highly visible executive sponsorship, will be required. Doing this will help gain managers' input and feedback on the SOA effort as well.
- It ensures alignment of the pending SOA with strategic business goals. This is critical as SOA is a long-term commitment to a services computing model, and thus the SOA effort must map to the business strategy. SOA will span a multiyear horizon to achieve its goals, so strategic alignment is crucial.

The business discovery and inspection need not be an arduous and time-consuming effort. Much of this work can be accomplished through reviews of existing documentation augmented by interviews of executive leadership and business unit executives (if there are multiple business units or divisions). Try to make this as fast and efficient as possible, because these are simply inputs into the SOA strategy and planning process. This is just a technique to ensure that current and future business strategies are incorporated into the SOA planning process so that ongoing SOA efforts will provide explicit support for the business.

The business discovery activities that follow may prove useful during your business discovery and inspection process. Again, much of this work will have been done already during your organization's normal strategic planning process. Do not attempt to conduct a corporate business strategy engagement with your SOA planning process. The business discovery and inspection assessment is performed solely to add necessary business context to the SOA strategy and planning process.

Business Discovery and Inspection Activities

- Assess external environment.
- Review current business/organization strategy and business/operating model.

- Review IT strategy and IT operating model.
- Understand market position and market segments (where appropriate).
- Understand customers and customer segments.
- Know products and services that serve customers.
- Understand current and planned business initiatives.
- Identify core business activities by business units.

Each of these activities is described next. You should find the necessary data in the current business and IT strategy documentation. Assuming this is the case, focus your business discovery and inspection efforts on the gaps, if there are any, and on potential interviews with key stakeholders to gain their input into the SOA strategy process.

Assess External Environment   Assessing your organization's external environment involves an examination of the overall operating environment of the organization. External environmental conditions include the macroeconomic and microeconomic conditions, governmental and regulatory forces, customer and market influences, competitive forces, and related external conditions that may affect the organization.

Review Current Business/Organization Strategy and Business/Operating Model   You should begin an SOA initiative with complete understanding of your organization's business strategy and business model. This knowledge will help ensure alignment of your SOA strategy to strategic goals and the operating model that helps your enterprise achieve those goals. This review of the business strategy and business model documentation does not have to lengthy. It must be thorough, and can be augmented with interviews of various business and IT executives to understand the overall business context that supports or facilitates the use of SOA and services.

Review IT Strategy and IT Operating Model   An IT strategy and operating model review will be important to help ensure an SOA initiative that is consistent with IT's goals. Understanding the IT strategy will help ensure alignment of your SOA strategy to strategic goals and the operating model of your IT organization to help your IT organization in turn support the business goals. As with the last review, this IT strategy and operating model documentation review does not have to be lengthy. It must be thorough, and can be augmented with interviews of various business and IT executives to understand the overall business context that supports or facilitates through the use of SOA and services.

Understand Market Position and Market Segments (Where Appropriate) Understanding your organization's market position and market segments will help create market context for SOA efforts. This can be important in helping prioritize various business and IT initiatives where SOA principles can be leveraged to increase the overall benefit or impact of these initiatives. For example, knowing that your organization performs many of its business transactions with other businesses may increase the relevance of SOA and services to conducting these business transactions faster and less expensively. Perhaps there are areas in the customer interaction process where time and effort can be removed to create an overall better customer experience. Knowing what your market position is relative to that of your competitors across all of your market segments will help identify opportunities for SOA to drive real tangible value.

Understand Customers and Customer Segments Knowing your organization's target customers, current customers, and the various customer segments within market segments will help ensure there is customer value from SOA efforts, even if the SOA initiative is initially targeted to solve an internal integration IT challenge. Establishing a direct link to customers is always an important exercise for a business or IT initiative.

Know Products and Services That Serve Customers Continuing the business inspection process, an additional step is to develop insights into the products and services your organization provides to its customers. This analysis, along with the previous business inspection steps, may help identify other sources of business value that an SOA initiative may support. Again, do not belabor this analysis; the documentation may already exist. You are creating context for SOA, not reinventing the product development process (unless developing new products and services is a business imperative that emerges from your analysis).

Understand Current and Planned Business Initiatives   In any organization, there will be a set of current and planned business initiatives. These initiatives can include IT projects that relate to these business initiatives or are major programs in their own right.   Current initiatives are usually major business programs that are already under way. Planned initiatives are business programs that are budgeted and planned for implementation at some future time in the current calendar or fiscal year. These business initiatives are primary candidates for establishing relevance of SOA to business goals and strategic plans. They are also good for another reason: It is often easier to find an SOA business case for a planned and budgeted business initiative than it is to plan and obtain budget a new SOA initiative. Budgeting processes and funding models for SOA projects are among the more challenging issues faced during the beginning phases of SOA initiatives.

Understanding the current and planned business initiatives will help focus your attention on areas of the business that are receiving attention from executive management. These major business initiatives are being conducted for a reason: to grow market share, increase revenue, cut costs, increase competitive advantage, or for a variety of other business reasons. Bottom line: They are not being pursued just for fun. There are very good business reasons for undertaking these initiatives, and those reasons will not be trivial in nature. If there is a way to improve the effectiveness of one of these initiatives, or improve its timeliness, or change its cost equation, you can jump-start your SOA planning process in this fashion. In addition, understanding the specific business programs that are in progress will help you focus your SOA efforts on areas of the business that are receiving attention from senior management. Doing this helps focus SOA energy on areas of business urgency.

Identify Core Business Activities by Business Units   It will be useful to identify and model the core business activities within each major business unit. This work may already have been done by a process improvement team in your organization. If such documentation exists, review it. This information will be useful during the services identification and modeling process in the next chapter. We suggest modeling processes to a level 0 process map or a simple high-level overview of major business processes. Deeper process documentation, if desired, can be performed during services modeling and design.

SOA Business Context Summary

The business discovery and inspection activity is preparatory for the identification of SOA imperatives. There are two types of imperatives: business imperatives and IT imperatives. Both can and will serve as the motivating forces for an SOA initiative. And both help explicitly map SOA efforts to the business context we have developed with the business discovery and inspection activities.

Ensure Business Context for SOA Planning

Business context helps ensure that any initiative, whether it is an IT or a business initiative, has business value and relevance. In other words, there is a resulting positive business impact that occurs because the initiative is consistent with or helps enable the desired organizational goals and outcomes.

We urge you to build the business foundation for SOA early in the planning process for these initiatives. The business context for SOA comes from explicitly understanding, documenting, and linking SOA initiatives to business goals. The high-level steps that follow are suggestions for helping your SOA team identify and build the necessary business context into the SOA planning process.

You must choose the challenges your organization faces based on your current situation. Many of the business context steps are simply elements of good business strategy and planning. In fact, most of this information may already be current for your organization. If so, you can work with business executives to obtain this information and tailor it to the SOA imperatives and drivers you are trying to establish.

From this business inspection process, you are trying to extract a few key areas of business context that must be supported by your SOA efforts and can be linked to business imperatives, IT imperatives, and SOA drivers. These will form the foundation for implementing SOA over time. They will also help build business support and sponsorship for your SOA efforts, which is critical to SOA success.

SOA business modeling translates business context into SOA value. This translation occurs through the flow of steps depicted in Exhibit 3.6.

IDENTIFY MAJOR BUSINESS CHALLENGES: IMPERATIVE ANALYSIS

Business context creates an understanding of the organization's vision, goals, strategy, and overall operating environment. This comprehension leads to identification of the necessary *business and IT imperatives* that are ultimately the incentives for SOA. These imperatives will become the levers for considering an SOA initiative, and they will also be used to derive the appropriate business focus for SOA efforts. It is important to note that *business imperatives* should be the primary driving force for an SOA initiative. These imperatives will extend into the IT organization to identify *IT imperatives* or IT challenges that may be obstacles to business change. There may be enough impetus for change within the IT organization to drive a very effective SOA initiative. This initiative must be focused not on technical aspects of the IT organization, but the business aspects of IT. In this case IT imperatives are enough to lead to an SOA initiative. When the SOA is driven by IT imperatives, it is essential to map these

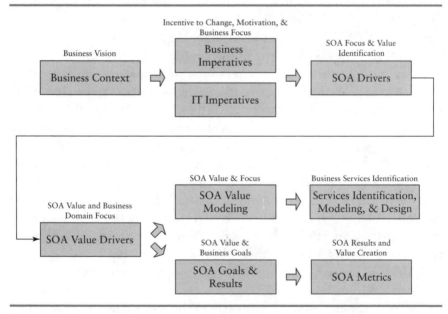

EXHIBIT 3.6   Translating Business Context into SOA Value

IT imperatives to business factors, or business imperatives, so there is explicit linkage of the two.

Once the business and IT imperatives are identified, you can begin to identify the *SOA drivers*. SOA drivers are used to focus the SOA initiative on specific areas of the business value chain where there is great potential for an SOA initiative to deliver business results. SOA focus is accomplished by using the SOA drivers to hone in on major aspects of the business value chain where there are known challenges or perceived wins from implementing SOA in a specific business domain. SOA drivers are the business or IT challenges that are forcing you to act. They are based on and derived from business and IT imperatives.

Identify Business and IT Imperatives

We like to see business imperatives for SOA initiatives or, for that matter, any project. This "imperative-driven SOA" is mapped to specific business challenges to help those challenges.

What is a business imperative? A business imperative is an organizational challenge of such gravity that failing to change or improve it may imperil the organization. Business imperatives are serious enough to cause board-level and executive action, and often will spur immediate action in the form of budgeted initiatives with funding and executive oversight. In addition to executive oversight, often there will be executive sponsorship and leadership of the initiative, with a champion whose goals and responsibilities reflect spearheading this new initiative.

Business Imperatives Drive SOA Initiatives

What factors have made SOA and services so compelling? Nearly unanimous vendor agreement on a set of core standards has helped. Web services cross-platform interoperability with SOA is finally attainable. However, we believe there are other bigger forces at work here. There is a major demand for change, both from a business and from an IT perspective. There are enough business demands for change that SOA is getting the kind of support required for success.

These business demands are what we call *business imperatives*. Business imperatives are what motivate the business to seek a new way of achieving business agility and IT flexibility via SOA. Business imperatives help galvanize the demand for a different model of IT delivery based on business services—in other words, SOA. In our view, business imperatives are *business preconditions* that will help make adoption of SOA easier and more ingrained in an organization for both the IT and the business. Those preconditions must include a number of business imperatives that demand a change in the way the business operates. Some examples of business imperatives might include:

- *Our business processes are manual and error-prone.* Our total cycle time for processing new business applications is three times longer than that of our competitors. This costs us between $5 to $10 million per year in new revenue, as well as an additional $4 to $8 million per year in renewal business. Automating the new business process can help us streamline portions of the process, and using external services providers for part of the process will reduce the total cycle time another 10 to 20%. These external service providers will collaborate with us using services that are reusable such that we can change service providers over time as they serve our needs better.

- *We are very difficult to do business with.* Our systems require months of costly integration to add new distribution partners to our channels, and the time to market costs us an additional $10 to $15 million per year. Our processes are very complex, labor inten-sive, and require heavy IT integration to modify for our customers.

- *Our business customers are increasingly frustrated with IT's abil-ity to support their fast-changing requirements.* When we make changes to our business processes that impact many of the under-lying business systems, IT can never make the requested changes without painful requirements sessions, long development lead times, and rigorous testing and debugging. By the time the sys-tems have been modified correctly, the time-to-market advantage we initially were seeking has disappeared.

- *Our integration strategy is a failure.* Our application silos inhibit our ability to deliver a coherent customer experience. Customers have multiple logon IDs and passwords to access our systems, they receive three monthly statements in the mail, and when they call our call center, they get passed from representative to representative in each department, with each one asking for the customer's account number, social security number, and mother's maiden name before they can answer an inquiry. This internal integration problem can be eliminated by SOA and services.

■ *We are aggressively pursuing a merger and acquisition (M&A) strategy.* Our M&A model calls for multiple acquisitions over the next three to five years, yet we realize that the time and energy to absorb these acquisitions will eat into their profitability. We have to find a better way to integrate our acquisitions, faster and without disrupting existing operations, while achieving the payback and synergies that are targeted. We need a new architectural model and IT competency based on integration of external entities.

Business imperatives have urgency behind them and "or else" consequences, and thus they tend to be galvanizing events around which an SOA initiative can be structured.

It is also important to note that business and IT imperatives can be offensive or defensive in nature. In other words, a business imperative may support an attacking strategy based on a series of offensive business tactics that weaken a competitor or increase competitive advantage along a number of dimensions. However, business and IT imperatives also can be defensive in nature, for example, focused on limiting effectiveness of attacking tactics by competitors or defending a market segment or class of customers. Business and IT imperatives ultimately will support corporate strategy and the IT strategy, where the broad initiatives of the organization are defined. Whether these strategies or tactics are offensive, defensive, or maintenance, the imperatives will support them.

IT Imperatives

IT imperatives, much like business imperatives, are challenges or issues that command the chief information officer's attention and require immediate resolution. These are high-priority issues, challenges, or roadblocks that have a deleterious effect on the organization as a whole and on the IT function in supporting the business.

IT imperatives can be examined from two perspectives, a positive forward-looking perspective and a fix-it-or-else perspective. One recognizes a need or an opportunity to improve; the other is focused on survival or problem resolution. Examples of IT imperatives could be:

- Lower IT costs
- Implement an M&A integration strategy
- Upgrade IT skills and disciplines
- Modernize IT architecture

Often IT imperatives are surfaced through business imperatives. For example, a recent client articulated a business imperative of "become easy to do business with." That high-level business imperative has implications along a number of business and IT dimensions. A number of IT imperatives can be deduced from the business imperative of "become easy to do business with."

Business Imperative: "Become Easy to Do Business With"
- IT Imperatives Derived from a Business Imperative
  - Improve partner integration process for information exchange and ease of process integration.
  - Implement a flexible integration architecture for ease of partner collaboration and information access across technology silos.
  - Improve time to market for business and integration initiative in support of business goals.
  - Simplify the process of connecting partners into our business processes and systems via our partner portal.

This simple example shows how a business imperative can trigger IT imperatives that help resolve or meet the needs of the business imperative. The IT imperatives will thus become high-priority fix-it-or-else initiatives that are similar to the business imperatives. They are linked in their support of the stated business strategy and are also aligned with one another.

Again, though, IT imperatives can be critical enough to drive management attention and motivation for an SOA initiative. IT imperatives do not necessarily have to map to business imperatives,

although we suggest in all cases seeking to align or link IT imperatives and SOA goals to stated business imperatives and other budgeted business initiatives of the organization.

Business and IT imperatives are important motivating forces for
change. Business inspection and discovery will identify a few key
business and IT imperatives that can galvanize support for an SOA
initiative. Both business executives and IT executives must agree to
these imperatives and support them. And the imperatives must be
translated into explicit reasons for planning and implementing SOA.
These translated imperatives are called SOA drivers.

Imperative-Driven SOA Strategy

Business and IT imperatives provide the motivation to embark on an
SOA initiative. You must begin your SOA initiatives by establishing
the SOA business context, which will be documented in your SOA
strategy. In other words, you have to begin by knowing how SOA
will create a positive outcome for your business. Once you have
established the proper business context for your SOA initiative, you
must develop your SOA strategy.

Your SOA strategy will begin with the vision, goals, and high-
level objectives for your SOA initiative. Doing this will be easier once
you've delivered a quick win via SOA pilots and proof of concepts
(PoCs) and have some organizational momentum behind you. These
topics should be part of your SOA strategy, although most likely you
will add other information as well.

- Define your SOA mission, vision, and high-level goals.
- Document your SOA imperatives, drivers, and value drivers.
- Identify a high-level business services roadmap that documents
  the initial services opportunities for your organization mapped to
  business and IT imperatives.
- Perform an IT architecture assessment and gap analysis. Conduct
  a SWOT (Strengths, Weaknesses, Opportunities, and Threats)
  analysis of your IT architecture, if needed, to illustrate the challenges you face.

- Identify the SOA technology roadmap, which will enable the transition toward SOA based on the targeted business services.
- Develop a high-level SOA governance model, documenting the organization and processes required for SOA success.
- Develop an organizational model that identifies organizational, cultural, and skills challenges for your organization.
- Define SOA metrics to be used to monitor progress and track success; align these into a federated metrics approach similar the balanced scorecard but tailored to SOA.
- Develop the SOA business case, capturing hard dollar benefits as well as cost avoidances and soft benefits. Tie the business case to the metrics model.
- Develop a change management plan, which will document education, awareness, and ongoing SOA assimilation activities to help ensure SOA success.
- Identify risks and dependencies inherent in the SOA initiative. Be sure to capture the risks of not implementing SOA as well.
- Map out the implementation roadmap, in phases or releases of services capabilities, based on alignment of the SOA strategy to business and IT initiatives.

Each organization will document its SOA strategy based on its particular internal process and policies. Regardless of the exact composition of the SOA strategy, focus on how SOA will alleviate known business pain as well as present new business value to the organization. Make sure there are quick wins in the early implementation phases. This will help accelerate SOA's flywheel effect.

A strategy and planning process is essential to help understand and document how SOA will address the identified business and IT imperatives. Exhibit 3.7 depicts the relationship of business and IT imperatives to an SOA strategy.

Often the need for an SOA strategy becomes apparent after an organization has performed an SOA or services pilot project. Perhaps some preliminary services have been developed as an experiment or a PoC. In conjunction with services pilots, it is common to implement smaller pilot projects using modern SOA enabling technology such as Web services management (WSM) platforms, SOA run-time solutions, Enterprise Service Buses, and even service registries.

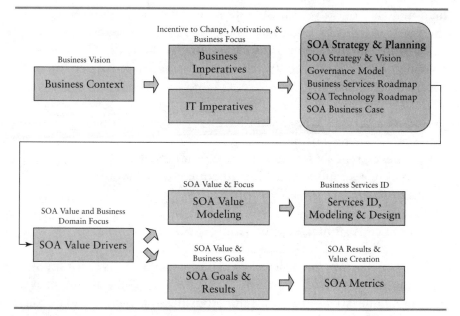

EXHIBIT 3.7 Translating Business Context into SOA Value

These services pilot projects or PoCs can help create organizational momentum and deliver a quick win to show the value of SOA and services to IT management and to business executives. However, they also serve to identify strategy, organizational, technological, and process gaps in an organization, which then spur the need for an SOA strategy. Without an SOA strategy and an actionable SOA roadmap, how can strategic business value be identified and delivered from an SOA initiative? The answer is, it cannot.

Business and IT Imperatives Lead to SOA Drivers

What are SOA drivers? SOA drivers are the specific motivations for embarking on SOA. The SOA initiative must address the business and IT imperatives by being broken down into finer-grained goals or objectives for an SOA initiative. Although business imperatives identify what must be done for the business or organization to be effective, SOA drivers begin to identify the ways that SOA initiatives may help alleviate or solve a business or IT imperative. Business and IT imperatives identify *what* must be done. SOA drivers identify how SOA can implement or positively impact those *whats*. The next list presents some high-level strategic drivers that may trigger the need for an SOA initiative.

- Begin a services transformation process.
- Achieve better business agility.
- Achieve greater IT efficiency and productivity.
- Quickly respond to market and competitive threats.
- Devise new business opportunities.
- Improve time to market goals.
- Enhance customer, supplier, and partner collaboration.

As you can see, SOA drivers are high-level objectives for an SOA that should map to and support business and/or IT imperatives. Business imperatives are overarching business problems or challenges with high urgency that must be fixed quickly. SOA drivers are more specific; they identify ways in which an SOA initiative can meet some or all of the requirements of a business or IT imperative or can positively affect some facet thereof.

Exhibit 3.8 depicts some examples of SOA drivers in an insurance context. This exhibit lists the business units or product families of a hypothetical insurance company on top. At the bottom are a series of business processes supported by various silos of IT solutions. In the middle, in the ovals, are a series of SOA drivers that support a potential SOA initiative at this organization.

These SOA drivers will serve as the basis for identifying specific SOA value that will be delivered via specific SOA initiatives over time. Note that these SOA drivers are very business oriented: grow revenue, simplify products, improve agent/broker productivity. These are desired business goals or business results to be derived from an SOA initiative.

This same visual model can be used to identify more specific IT goals that should be achieved through SOA. Exhibit 3.9 shows some targeted SOA opportunities based on the same hypothetical insurance company.

Improving integration, process orchestration, and services reuse are SOA benefits that should be achieved via an SOA initiative, and

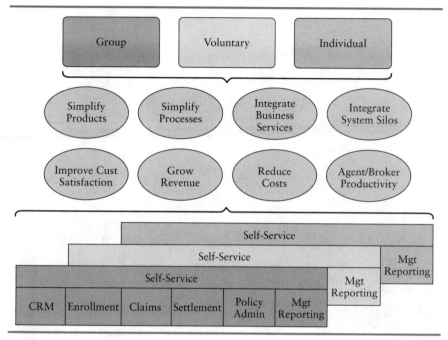

EXHIBIT 3.8 SOA Business Goals

these should support the business goals identified in Exhibit 3.10. Some examples of SOA drivers that are commonly identified during SOA strategy and planning discussions include:

- Greater asset reuse (e.g., components and services)
- Business agility
- IT productivity
- Faster application development
- Transformation from silos of technology to IT services delivery model
- Improving IT flexibility and reducing on vendor lock in
- Implementing business process management (BPM)
- Better partner integration
- Improving an integration strategy (e.g., middleware initiative)

SOA drivers should be high-level goals of an SOA initiative and can be broken down or refined into SOA value drivers.

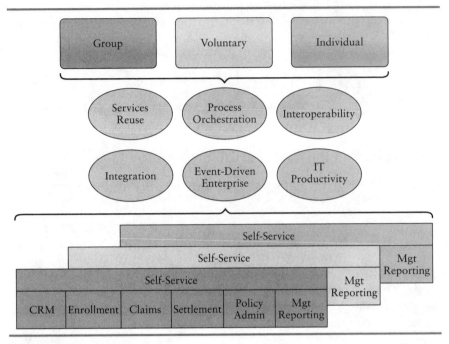

EXHIBIT 3.9   SOA IT Goals

Difference Between SOA Drivers and SOA Value Drivers

SOA drivers can be used to derive SOA value drivers. The difference between SOA drivers and SOA *value* drivers is a simple yet significant one: SOA drivers are motivating forces for SOA, while SOA value drivers are measurable and can be tracked using a series of metrics. SOA drivers help make the case for an SOA to address business and IT imperatives. SOA value drivers help identify the specific value that can be attained by applying SOA concepts to specific business or IT challenges.

SOA Drivers Lead to SOA Value Drivers

SOA drivers have a strong relationship to the concept of SOA value drivers. SOA drivers are specific business conditions that help galvanize the support for launching an SOA initiative. SOA drivers are derived from SOA imperatives—the business and IT imperatives that are critical enough to merit specific action with budget and executive sponsorship. SOA value drivers, however, are high-level business benefits or value proposition statements that will be translated into metrics before implementing the SOA initiative. These value drivers are used to help focus SOA efforts on areas of the business where SOA can be implemented via planned business initiatives to achieve the desired goals. SOA value drivers are determined based on the business context, business and IT imperatives, and SOA drivers.

Many "typical" SOA value drivers can help galvanize business and IT support for an SOA initiative. Some examples follow.

- Grow the business.
- Reduce costs.
- Increase asset reuse.
- Improve business agility.
- Achieve IT flexibility.
- Improve time to market.
- Improve the business process.
- Increase process visibility and control.

These SOA value drivers can be operationalized and translated into metrics that can and must be measured to assess the success of specific projects that help implement the SOA strategy and contribute to its overall success. An example of operationalizing SOA value drivers follows.

SOA Value Driver: Improve Business Agility

Operational Definition. Increase time to market for business initiatives that rely on IT systems development, enhancements, or modifications. Agility is defined as the relative speed with which IT can provide support for business initiatives.

Measurement. Time difference between an established baseline metric based on past projects and services-based projects, based on total elapsed calendar time.

This example highlights the importance of two features of operationalizing SOA value drivers:

1. Developing an operational definition that is concrete and has clear meaning
2. Defining a way to measure the operational definition so that progress can be determined

Metrics are revisited in Chapter 9.

Summary of Imperatives, SOA Drivers, and Value Drivers

From this analysis process should come a thorough understanding of the business context in which your enterprise is operating, its strategy, goals, and objectives, its business model, markets and customers served, and more. This analysis sets the stage for understanding the business value that an SOA initiative may provide to your organization.

- *Business and IT imperatives* point to what needs to be fixed in order to remain a viable business entity. If the organization is a government agency or a nonprofit, business imperatives are necessary for organizational survival or for accomplishing the overarching mission.
- *SOA drivers* are benefits or capabilities of SOA and services that address some or all of the needs of a business or IT imperative. Most likely several SOA drivers will support various aspects of a business imperative.
- *SOA value drivers* are *measurable* aspects of SOA drivers that can be used to build a business case for your SOA efforts. SOA value drivers also help to focus SOA efforts on areas of an organization's value chain where they can be mapped, or linked, to major business processes and areas in which there are known challenges. SOA efforts thus can be focused on these business and process hot spots. Potential metrics and business case data can be assigned to them as well.

Business and IT imperatives provide motivation and an initial focus for SOA initiatives. SOA drivers focus the motivation on addressing more specific elements of business and IT imperatives. SOA drivers drill down into the imperatives to identify the SOA threads that may apply. SOA value drivers help to operationalize the drivers into measurable entities such that you can apply metrics and track progress.

The process of identifying your SOA drivers and SOA value drivers will serve two very important purposes:

1. Focusing SOA energies on appropriate business challenges, business domains, and process domains, and using these focus areas to begin services identification and modeling process
2. Identifying SOA business goals and appropriate metrics to measure success

FOCUSING YOUR SOA EFFORTS

The discussions about business and IT imperatives, SOA drivers, and SOA value drivers really are about establishing business context and SOA motivation. However, another output of this process is focus. Focusing SOA efforts, especially in the early phases, will increase the odds of success. A tool that may prove useful for focusing SOA energies is SOA value analysis.

SOA Value Analysis

SOA value analysis is a technique that applies value chain thinking to SOA value drivers. SOA value analysis facilitates mapping of SOA value drivers to an organization's value chain and key business process. This analysis helps identify likely business and process domains that offer great potential for achieving SOA value and also helps prioritize those business and process domains using a simple scoring mechanism.

SOA value modeling makes use of the SOA value drivers identified earlier. SOA value drivers can help to identify the business case of SOA initiatives and focus SOA efforts on specific business hot spots. SOA value modeling is a visual prioritization scheme that employs value chain analysis combined with value driver analysis to help provide focus. SOA value analysis provides several benefits.

- This analysis helps identify specific SOA value propositions in specific areas of the business by business process.
- SOA value analysis can help determine what areas of the business really are SOA hot spots and how these hot spots map to or relate to business and IT imperatives.
- SOA value analysis helps prioritize business processes where SOA can contribute to improvements. If the process analysis is more detailed than a level 0 process map, even specific process activities can be targeted as service as the SOA initiative is expanded over time.

SOA value analysis proceeds using a simple matrix structure as depicted in Exhibit 3.10.

Using the matrix in Exhibit 3.10, list the SOA value drivers identified earlier down the right side of the matrix. Along the top of the matrix, lay out your organization's value chain and high-level business processes. Process details are necessary only if there is not enough detail to identify whether there is SOA value to be gained from this analysis. We suggest using a simple three-tier analysis of SOA value: high, medium, and low. For this analysis, a high value

Business Value Chain								
Perform Marketing	Develop Products	Perform Sales	Manage Custom Orders	Procure Materials/ Services	Produce Products	Manage Logistics/ Distribution	Manage Customer Service	SOA Value Drivers
H	H	H	H	M	M	H	H	Grow the Business
M	M	M	M	H	M	H	L	Reduce Costs
L	M	L	L	L	M	L	L	Asset Reuse
L	M	L	M	M	H	H	?	Business Agility
L	L	L	L	L	L	L	L	IT Flexibility
H	H	M	H	H	H	M	L	Time to Market
M	H	M	H	H	H	M	M	Business Processes
M	M	H	H	M	L	H	H	Process Visibility

KEY H M L ?

EXHIBIT 3.10 SOA Value Analysis Matrix

rating would mean that there is a high probability of realizing the particular dimension of SOA value being considered for those areas in the value chain or for those high-level business processes. A medium value rating would mean that a particular process area holds a medium probability of achieving the particular value driver being evaluated. A low value rating means that the opportunity to achieve SOA value on that particular SOA value driver is poor. These areas of the business should not be a primary focus for your SOA efforts, at least at this time. They can be revisited once some initial value has been achieved in the high-SOA-value categories.

You can also assign numerical values to each of the criteria. A high could be worth five SOA value points, for example, while a medium might be assigned three points and a low one SOA value point. Regardless of the ranking scheme, be consistent in applying it.

SOA value modeling does not have to be a time-consuming process. Its sole purpose is to help apply a logical prioritization scheme to your SOA initiatives and to focus your efforts on business process areas of high potential. These high-value segments of your value chain can be validated by comparing them to business imperatives and to the hot spots identified in the hot spot assessment. One or both of these tools may be used, depending on your situation. These assessments will result in identification of appropriate business opportunities for SOA, prioritized by business processes, and ranked according to SOA value drivers. Now you are set to identify the specific results and outcomes of your SOA efforts.

You can perform the same analysis on the IT processes of an organization. Follow the steps just given to create an SOA value analysis matrix. Exhibit 3.11 presents an example of an IT SOA value analysis applied to a generic IT value chain.

Based on SOA value analysis, it becomes easier to focus efforts on critical areas of an organization and its value chain based on the SOA value drivers.

Applying SOA Value Analysis: SOA Hot Spots

SOA value analysis provides a simple technique for mapping SOA value drivers to your organization's value chain and business processes to help identify areas where SOA offers high business value

IT Value Chain

Perform Marketing	Dev. IT Strategy	Procure IT Infra-structure	Procure or Develop IT Apps	Operate IT Processes	Measure Business Value	Maintain Infrastr. & App Portfolio	Manage Bus. & Tech. Change	Manage Bus. Cust. Service	
M	H	H	H	L	M	M	L		Grow the Business
L	L	H	M	M	H	H	H		Reduce Costs
M	M	H	H	H	H	H	M		Asset Reuse
L	L	H	H	L	H	H	H		Business Agility
H	H	H	H	M	M	H	H		IT Flexibility
H	H	M	H	H	H	M	L		Time to Market
M	M	M	H	M	L	H	H		Business Processes
M	M	H	H	M	L	H	H		Process Visibility

KEY   (H)   (M)   (L)   (?)

EXHIBIT 3.11   SOA IT Value Matrix

potential. Applying this tool is a straightforward exercise. Visually, you will quickly identify areas of your business where clusters of high- and medium-value SOA opportunities exist. Exhibit 3.12 shows two circled areas where there are several high-priority SOA hot spots in this hypothetical business.

Based on your analysis of business and IT imperatives, SOA drivers and value drivers, and the in-flight projects and initiatives in your organization, you should have a feel for where and how SOA may be able to add tremendous value. SOA hot spot analysis can offer two benefits: (1) It can validate or confirm areas of your business where SOA initiatives can add value; and (2) it may help identify new, overlooked areas of emphasis where SOA can add value. In other words, new SOA opportunities can be surfaced by SOA value analysis and the identification of SOA hot spots. In summary, SOA Hot Spot Analysis offers the following benefits:

- Imperatives point to business and process hot spots that must be fixed or else. Imperatives point to what needs to be addressed, not how to do it.
- Hot spot assessments can quickly determine areas of focus for SOA initiatives or validate areas that are already known to be problematic in your organization.

Business Value Chain

Perform Marketing	Develop Products	Perform Sales	Manage Custom Orders	Procure Materials/ Services	Produce Products	Manage Logistics/ Distribution	Manage Customer Service	SOA Value Drivers
H	H	H	H	M	M	H	H	Grow the Business
M	M	M	M	H	M	H	L	Reduce Costs
L	M	L	L	L	M	L	L	Asset Reuse
L	M	L	M	M	H	H	?	Business Agility
L	L	L	L	M	L	L	L	IT Flexibility
H	H	M	H	H	H	M	L	Time to Market
M	H	M	H	H	H	M	M	Business Processes
M	M	H	H	M	L	H	H	Process Visibility

KEY (H) (M) (L) (?)

EXHIBIT 3.12   SOA Hot Spots

■ Hot spot assessments also help align SOA initiatives to trouble areas in the business and to business and IT imperatives. This "validation" exercise helps ensure SOA initiatives match up with fund initiatives and recognized business pain.

SOA value analysis and SOA hot spot analysis are simple tools that provide focus for your SOA efforts. Matching SOA initiatives to business challenges, by business and process domain and by key in-flight projects, helps ensure alignment of SOA efforts to business needs. This is critical for garnering business and executive sponsorship for your SOA efforts and for ensuring that your SOA efforts support the needs of the business.

SOA Business Modeling Reset: Where Are We?

Exhibit 3.13 maps out the SOA business modeling activities described so far, beginning with business and IT imperatives and leading to services identification, modeling, and design.

The SOA business modeling analysis process we have described helps ensure proper alignment of SOA efforts to known business and IT pain, and it also helps speed up the process of delivering SOA business

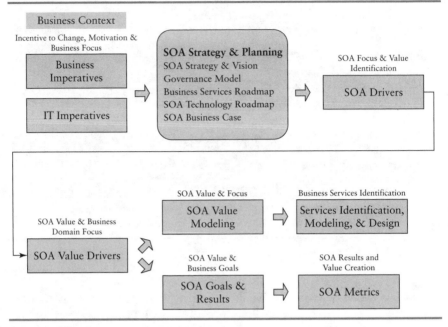

EXHIBIT 3.13 Translating Context into SOA Value

value. Some of the SOA focus and prioritization techniques may make sense for your organization. Use them if they help. Skip them if they do not. But make sure your SOA efforts match acknowledged business challenges, and continually validate your SOA business context. Make sure the results you are seeking from your SOA initiatives support the business and IT imperatives you began this process with.

Defining SOA Goals and Business Results

The SOA business context analysis performed so far will help identify specific goals for an SOA initiative. You should identify clear business results measurable and have a direct relationship to the SOA drivers, address business and IT imperatives, and lead to organizational success. The desired business outcomes must be granular enough to put metrics around and have close alignment to resolving the business imperatives previously identified.

The analysis of your organization's business context, or operating context for government or nonprofit organizations, will clearly help ensure the opportunity for adding value to your particular organization. However, this is not sufficient. Clear business outcomes must be defined, supported by specific results from supporting activities, so that you can declare victory. Business imperatives will provide a great starting point for the identification of business outcomes. However, business imperatives are probably too high level for setting specific measurable goals. Most likely you will have to break your SOA drivers and SOA value drivers down into specific tracks of value you can deliver via targeted business initiatives and projects. The identification and use of metrics for the SOA business case and determining SOA business value are discussed in great detail in Chapter 9.

Finding the SOA Sweet Spots

Performing these SOA business context analysis steps will help identify sweet spots where SOA initiatives have a better chance of success than not. What is an SOA sweet spot? An SOA sweet spot occurs when these conditions are present:

- At least one business or IT imperative has been identified that directly relates to an SOA initiative. There may be multiple imperatives.
- There is executive sponsorship for the SOA initiative, preferably a business leader. The SOA initiative addresses an area of business pain for which the sponsor has responsibility.
- You have achieved a level of cultural, organizational, and behavioral readiness for the SOA change. It has been achieved partially through the proper motivation and planning for an SOA initiative.
- You have identified clear business outcomes and SOA goals. These map to the business and IT imperatives you began the SOA strategy and planning process with.
- You have devised preliminary metrics to gauge success of the SOA initiative. These metrics can be assembled into an SOA scorecard—a "balanced scorecard" for SOA.

Business imperatives are essential, as we know, to ensure relevance of an SOA initiative to recognized business urgencies. If an SOA initiative is definitely linked to a business imperative, or to multiple business imperatives, then the chances of business success, business support, and budget are enhanced significantly.

SUMMARY

SOA value analysis helps identify focus areas for SOA initiatives by identifying business and process domains of particular interest for business improvement efforts. These target business and process domains, as prioritized by SOA value drivers and other business criteria, will help scope and constrain the universe of services for the initial SOA projects. Once there is some definition of scope for the initial SOA efforts, the process of services identification can proceed.

NOTE

1. Eric A. Marks, "The SOA Network Effect: Technical and Cultural Issues Drive Value," ComputerWorld Online, August 16, 2004.

CHAPTER **4**

Services Identification, Analysis, and Design

The process of identifying services and then analyzing and designing them for implementation is poorly understood in current service-oriented architecture (SOA) thinking. Service modeling is perhaps one of the most common discussions with information technology (IT) executives and architects, and it goes to the heart of some of the challenges of SOA. The questions typical of this phase of SOA planning and analysis are:

- What services do we start with? How do we identify appropriate services for our SOA?
- What are "services" in our environment? How should business services be identified?
- How do we model and implement services that are optimal for our business?
- How do we establish criteria for reuse and granularity?
- How do we prioritize the candidate services we have identified?
- How should service analysis and design be conducted?

There are more. The point is that determining the initial services to expose within your SOA can be a challenge, but it doesn't have to be. Exhibit 4.1 depicts the process of transitioning from SOA business modeling to services identification, analysis, and design.

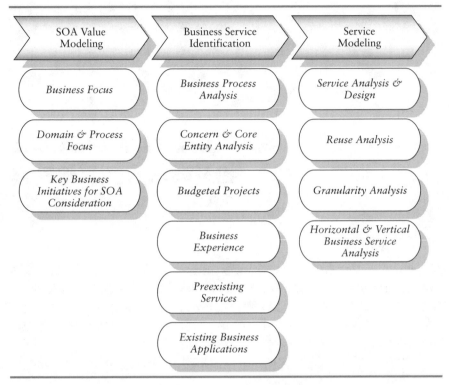

EXHIBIT 4.1   Identifying Candidate Business Services

SOA business modeling and value analysis help focus SOA initiatives by identifying business and process domains of particular interest for business improvement efforts. These target business and process domains, as prioritized by SOA value drivers and other business criteria, will help scope and constrain the universe of services for the initial SOA projects. Once there is some definition of scope for the initial SOA efforts, the process of services identification can proceed.

The methodology proposed here advocates a top-down and bottom-up model in an iterative cycle. Identifying services from a bottom-up-only perspective can tie services to their originating technology environments, which leads to tight coupling and limits reuse. However, top-down-only perspectives can achieve services reuse and conceptual agreement on the appropriateness of the candidate services, but the target services may be difficult to implement due to lack of concrete design principles from the technology perspective. In our approach, both perspectives are needed—top-down and bottom-up, and in an iterative fashion. Top-down analysis techniques focus on conceptual services analysis techniques, whereby candidate services are analyzed to evaluate and prioritize their potential before proceeding into more formal design processes and ultimately to physical solution services. When the analysis segues to services design from a bottom-up perspective, the conceptual analysis transitions the candidate business services into physical solution services.

This services modeling process is critical to identifying, analyzing, designing, and implementing the "right" services for your organization. These services will map to business and IT imperatives, support your SOA strategy, and be the critical assets of your SOA.

Business services are the lifeblood of your SOA initiative. They are the enduring asset in an SOA. Your services are what will last beyond any specific enabling technology you implement to operate and manage them. The services in your business services roadmap will determine subsequent decisions about the enabling technology, the SOA governance model and policies, the metrics used to measure SOA results, and more. We call this a services-driven SOA. The business services drive all other downstream decisions.

Candidate business services are potential services that offer value to your organization. Identifying the SOA opportunity for your organization begins with services and how reusable interoperable services can benefit projects, business units, departments, customers, and the organization as a whole. Candidate services are just that: services that may have potential value for the organization. They still must be evaluated based on reuse, business impact, and organizational value, and then analyzed and designed in order to implement them.

Examples of candidate business services could include:

- *Banking:* "name and address service," "account opening service," "account balance service," "funds withdrawal service," or "deposit funds service"
- *Life insurance:* "policy service" or "policy terms service"
- *Manufacturing:* "order status service" or "inventory service"
- *Health insurance:* "newborn service" or "insurance program service"

These are all candidate services for various industries and business processes within these industries. But how do we know if these are appropriate services? There are three broad areas of concern with services identification, analysis, and design:

1. Business Impact

   Does the service have business value? Does it offer cost savings, revenue growth, productivity, customer satisfaction, or other business benefits?

   Is it reusable within and across business or process domains?

   What are the reusing organizations, processes, or applications?

   What are the consumption patterns for the service candidate?

   Does the service address current and future business needs?

   What functionality does the service provide?

   Does the service make you more agile?

2. Service Feasibility

   What is the service granularity vis-à-vis reusability?

   How will adjusting service granularity impact targeted reuse?

   How complex is the service?

   What is the risk of building or not building the service?

   Can the service be modeled to meet desired reuse and consumption patterns?

   Does the service support agility?

3. Technical Feasibility

   What are technical requirements for the service? Will these limit reuse?

   Are there technical constraints that may limit service reuse?

   Are there technical constraints that impact granularity?

   Are there technical risks? How do they impact service feasibility?

   Does the physical service still meet business goals? Is it still feasible? Is the service more agile and flexible than otherwise?

Use these criteria to evaluate service candidates for subsequent decisions around analysis, design, and implementation. The business services roadmap is ultimately a prioritized sequence of services based on their value to your organization. The priorities assigned to various services must consider these criteria, and most likely more.

BEGIN WITH CANDIDATE BUSINESS SERVICES

Determining the initial services to expose within your SOA can be a challenge, but it doesn't have to be. The services identification process should be conducted in top-down fashion initially, with a focus on *candidate business services*. In other words, focus your identification of business services on the actual or potential business services that support your operating model, either as it is now or the future state process model. In this exercise, you should not consider the actual physical or technical environment that your business relies on. *Do not get bogged down in the constraints of your current IT architecture.* This will come later. The initial challenge is to identify the business services in your enterprise within some initial scope, such as a business or process domain, so that you can begin to prioritize, model, and design those services in support of various SOA and business initiatives.

There are six possible ways to identify candidate business services:

1. Business process analysis
2. Core entity analysis
3. Opportunistically via budgeted initiatives
4. Business or domain expertise
5. Preexisting services
6. Existing business applications

You can and probably will need to use all of these approaches to identify and model your business services. There is no right approach. The differences relate to how organizations prefer to operate. Using business and IT imperatives will help focus and prioritize your SOA efforts and help to identify the services opportunities of your organization. Keep these imperatives in mind as you identify candidate services.

BUSINESS PROCESS ANALYSIS

Some organizations prefer process modeling approaches. These organizations have invested in process analysis and documentation, and probably have completed detailed analyses of all business units and the major business and process domains within them. In this case, a process-driven approach to identifying business services may make sense. Your services—or, more appropriately, your "candidate business services"—should derive from business and process analysis initially, based on the business context and business imperatives identified earlier. The four steps of a process-driven analysis of business services might be:

1. Perform a value chain analysis of your organization.
2. Develop a high-level process map of your enterprise.
3. From this process map, identify candidate business services that relate to these major business processes.
4. Based on these candidate business services, either:

    Prioritize these services first before continuing on to services modeling; or

    Begin modeling for all of these services at once.

At this point, the identification of services transitions into *services design*.

CORE ENTITY ANALYSIS

Some organizations approach SOA and business services from a data modeling perspective. These organizations may prefer to work from documented data models, entity relationship diagrams constructed in tools such as ERwin, or business and core entities to begin their business services identification process.

Core entity analysis begins with the identification of business entities for your organization. What are the important entities or elements of your business? Customers, products, events, artifacts, business units may all be business entities. Core entities are more granular than business entities, and answer questions such as: who, what, when, where, and why? They become the unit of analysis in data modeling activities and can form the basis for identifying services.

The use of core entities as a starting point for services identification can be helpful because it may accelerate your efforts. The time and effort required to model business processes prior to identifying business services is not attractive for some organizations. In this case, identifying business services by analyzing core entities can be a very expedient method.

Core entity analysis begins with a series of facilitated brainstorming sessions focused on identifying the core entities of your business. What are the major "nouns" of your business? What services are involved in supporting these core entities? What processes and events cut across these core entities in repeatable ways such that they represent business service opportunities? What are the "verbs" that act on these nouns in support of your business processes and events? "Client" is a core entity; a service would potentially be "client information service."

OPPORTUNISTIC APPROACH VIA ALREADY-BUDGETED PROJECTS

Many firms use in-flight projects, or already-budged projects, to focus their initial business services efforts. This is an opportunistic approach to identifying business services, as it relies on a set of business priorities established by the current IT governance process. However, what if those project priorities changed based on performing services analysis? Would that change the priorities of the current in-flight business initiatives? Although this approach often is used to identify projects where services and SOA makes sense, it is not an ideal process. A more robust approach would be to identify the services first, then relate these to planned and budgeted initiatives, and then reassess the prioritization scheme. Perhaps the projects would change, perhaps the sequence would change, or both.

BUSINESS AND DOMAIN EXPERTISE

You can always leverage domain experience as a way to identify candidate business services in an enterprise. A claims expert in an insurance company will always have deep domain expertise to bring to bear in identifying appropriate business services. Similarly, other deep industry or process experience is useful in identifying business services, even in conjunction with the process and core entity approaches just listed. One must use one's experience in determining the appropriate business services for an SOA initiative, but that experience must be applied to the services problem in a systematic fashion, using process analysis and/or core entity analysis. The approach we propose is such that deep domain expertise is not mandatory to identify the right services, but certainly experience helps.

PREEXISTING SERVICES

Many organizations have preexisting services in production that have been built as pilots or prototypes, or were built with early generations of tools. Some of these services will be known and sponsored by the organization, while some may be rogue services that may have been developed without organizational knowledge or oversight. Any SOA initiative must take into consideration existing services and application capabilities in order to optimize past and future investments in services. One of the first acts for rogue services is to make them visible to the rest of the organization. Publishing them to a registry or repository often is an early priority for SOA efforts. From there, they can be reused or redesigned to meet the standards and policies of the SOA strategy.

EXISTING BUSINESS APPLICATIONS

Potential services can also be identified from existing business applications, legacy systems, and other technology platforms. In these scenarios, existing capabilities and business functionality can be targeted as services, either by closely replicating existing functionality or by aggregating or fragmenting existing functionality to facilitate more reuse and more flexible process capabilities. It is very likely that a high percentage of services will be exposed from existing business applications, depending on the organization, industry and the existing technology architecture.

TOP-DOWN OR BOTTOM-UP? BOTH, THEN ITERATE

The process of identifying and modeling services is an iterative process. There is no one way to achieve services in support of your SOA. All of the above business services identification techniques can be used very effectively as long as the process is iterative.

Often we are asked whether the appropriate analysis technique is top-down or bottom-up. We say that the answer is emphatically "Yes." Initially you have to perform a top-down analysis of candidate business services. When you are ready to begin exposing or creating actual physical services, you approach the problem from a bottom-up perspective.

A top-down, bottom-up, iterative process recognizes an iterative cycle of services identification and services modeling, which is primarily a top-down process. When those identified and modeled services are ready to be implemented, the model is bottom-up. Finally, the entire cycle must be iterative. Existing services will continue to be improved and changed to reflect changing business requirements, and new services will be identified and implemented as well.

FOCUS ON CANDIDATE BUSINESS SERVICES

We advocate the identification of business services from a conceptual and business perspective without any association to the technical implementation of those services. In other words, start with candidate business services that represent your business yet have no affiliation to your platforms or applications. When you are ready to expand your SOA efforts and expose or enable more services, the top-down approach probably will use the services identification techniques just described. Once you have identified your candidate business services, perform these five steps:

1. Identify your potential business services using the techniques described above.
2. Identify business services that relate to business events, entities, processes, and roles within your organization.
3. Based on these candidate business services, begin identifying service reuse by consumers, high-level granularity, high-level functional requirements across business channels, processes, and organizational boundaries. Often reuse is identified, high-level services scope and functionality is described, and granularity can be estimated at the candidate business services level.
4. Prioritize these business services based on your business imperatives and SOA drivers. Remember, this is an iterative process, so this initial list will not be all of your services. This is the starting point for the SOA journey.
5. Begin services analysis and design.

Throughout the services modeling process, you should prioritize candidate business services to ensure they are appropriate for your business. Consider these criteria in prioritizing your service candidates:

- The services have business benefit.
- The services support business imperatives, address business hot spots, and map to your SOA drivers.
- The services are reusable by multiple consumer communities — business processes, business units, developers, and analysts.
- The services are achievable in a reasonable time frame as compared to traditional development.
- The services help build toward your SOA strategy, goals, and objectives. Remember, these services must have relevant business context and appropriate value for your organization.

SERVICE ANALYSIS AND DESIGN

Once you have identified candidate business services based on these techniques, they must be analyzed and designed for implementation.

Service analysis and design is a logical process of determining reuse, high-level functionality, and granularity, and ultimately results in a refined and prioritized list of services that will be implemented as physical solution services.

CANDIDATE SERVICE ANALYSIS

Analysis of potential services is a top-down process consisting of logical operations and transformation mechanisms to study and inspect enterprise core entities, ascertain business ideas and concepts, and lead to the formation of final business services. Service analysis on candidate business services can address consolidation, decomposition, reuse, simplification, and refactoring of legacy assets as dictated by organizational imperatives. These activities present opportunities to transition to shared reusable services in a loosely coupled architecture.

The service analysis model that follows is based on set theory concepts that treat abstractions as related members in collections and provide a theoretical model based on *membership*.[1] This method treats aggregations as encapsulations of associated concepts. The service analysis process is driven by studying candidate service similarities and characteristics. By applying decomposition and fragmentation operations on these potential services, you can generate business, logical, and process decompositions.[2] Exhibit 4.2 illustrates various logical operations that can be employed during the *service* abstraction analysis process to derive *business services*.

Service Granularity Analysis

The granularity of services can be determined by their encapsulated business functionality, their conceptual value and abstraction level, and the scope of business processes they represent or affect. We recommend categorizing these assets based on granularity to facilitate the derivation of final business services.

Coarse-grained services encapsulate a broad scope of business activities and processes, and they also encompass a larger portion of the problem domain. Coarse-grained services will contain more process

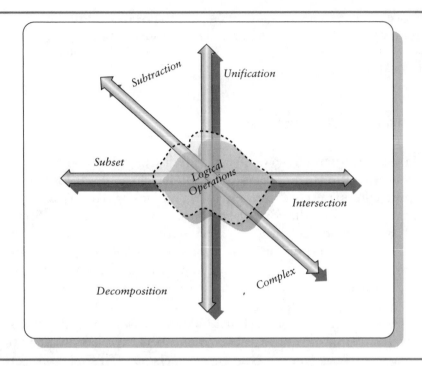

EXHIBIT 4.2 Service Analysis Toolbox

steps, more function points, and more business operations than fine-grained services.

Fine-grained services, on the other hand, provide narrower scope of business activities and processes and encompass a smaller portion of the problem domain. Fine-grained services may represent only one business operation, a few function points, or one basic process step.

The following factors are determinants of candidate business service granularity:

- Encapsulated functionality
- Business logic, number of business operations
- Business processes, business activities
- Organizational influences

In the analysis and design model that follows, granularity of services can be adjusted and modified at all levels of analysis, from services identification to services analysis to services design. This is an iterative model. You must construct a service granularity map prior to establishing your *final business services. We urge this* because the recommended service analysis operations require prior knowledge about service granularity based on the granularity matrix depicted in Exhibit 4.3. Coarse-grained services, such as *account* and *checking account,* are positioned higher on the granularity scale than fine-grained services, such as *account lookup* and *account statement.*

Unification Operation

The set of identified *candidate business services* will be a list of coarse- and fine-grained services that must be refined to meet appropriate business granularity requirements. The rule of thumb suggests that coarse-grained entities provide broader solution coverage than fine-grained services. Furthermore, fine-grained *business services* may not be useful in solving business problems due to their lack of

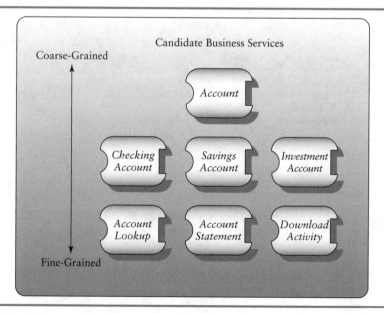

EXHIBIT 4.3   Services Granularity Matrix

reuse or business relevance. Thus, logical *unification* operations can be used when services are too fine-grained or do not provide adequate business value.

The unification operation on services encourages identification of common business context and abstractions[3] for potential consolidation. In the context of *business services*, the generalization process results in unification or aggregation of services into a larger service that provides a superior services solution. Unification raises the service abstraction level and establishes a more coarse-grained *business service* located higher on the granularity matrix.

Exhibit 4.4 depicts a unification operation that results in the creation of a final *business service*. Services that provide various account statements can be unified and consolidated into an *account statement business service*, which is a more generalized version of the statements service.

The unification process of *services* does not eliminate their original identity or functionality. They are combined because of their

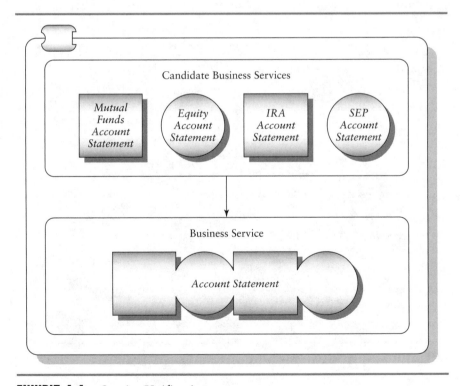

EXHIBIT 4.4   Service Unification

business similarities, yet their characteristics are preserved in the aggregated *business services*. It is conceivable that during further analysis and design, these elements might be decoupled or even promoted into individual services if business needs require the disaggregation of unified services or if technical issues dictate such a change.

Intersection Operation

The *intersection* logical operation identifies shared *services* from existing services by analyzing overlapping capabilities or shared requirements, which may result in new *business services*. New candidate services can be discovered from two or more different *services* with overlapping functionality based on their mutual business goals. The overlap lines typical of a Venn diagram help identify reusable aspects of the candidate service functionality. Reusability of these intersecting services may be increased by aggregating related intersecting services that may arise from this operation. Nevertheless, overusing intersection operations on services can increase dependency on their peer services, reduce reusability, and negatively impact manageability and interoperability.

Applying intersection operations to coarse-grained services breaks them into more manageable scopes and contexts. Intersection should not be used on very fine-grained services. Remember, the intersection logical operation is not designed for service decomposition purposes. The decomposition operation below is used for that purpose.

Exhibit 4.5 depicts a final *account lookup business service* that emerges from the intersection between two major banking account candidate services: *checking* and *savings* accounts. The *account lookup business service* can become more reusable if its functionality can be expanded to searching a wider range of banking accounts. Additionally, *checking account* and *savings account* candidate services can later become final business services themselves if there is a business justification and motivation behind the decision.

Sound architecture policies and accepted best practices should encourage reusability and endorse identification and discovery of asset commonality. These best practices will shape and influence approaches to building reusable services. Grassroots analysis and

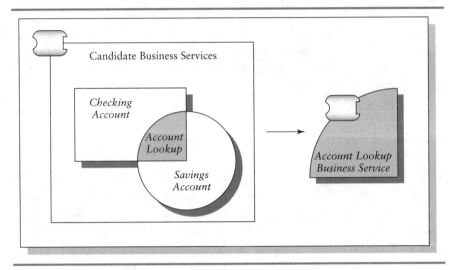

EXHIBIT 4.5   Service Intersection

design policies for services reuse and asset consolidation can have an immense effect on IT operations, efficiency, and profitability. Such grassroots decisions must become shared governance guidelines and enforceable policies to drive services design toward conformance to shared interoperability standards.

Decomposition Operation

Some candidate services will be very large and coarse-grained upon initial analysis. Decomposition analysis is an operation that breaks apart large, unwieldy, and very coarse-grained candidate services. Decomposition of candidate business services should occur early in the service analysis phase through logical decoupling or fragmentation operations. As discussed, coarse-grained services encapsulate a greater number of business operations and business process steps. Therefore, they should be partitioned into smaller modules of logic or functionality through decomposition operations, which result in a number of smaller, self-contained final business services. When using decomposition analysis, the resulting finer-grained business services should be atomic, composable, reusable, and maintainable. In other words, they should comply with the fundamental properties of services described in Chapter 2. Note that reusability of derived business services may be decreased if decomposition operations are overused. Careful balance will help identify acceptable limits of decomposition operations on large, very coarse-grained candidate services. Appropriate use of decomposition operations, though, will facilitate future customizations and enhancements of these business services.

Exhibit 4.6 illustrates a *service* decomposition logical operation. The *bank account service,* which is comprised of various candidate business concepts and processes, is fragmented into several independent

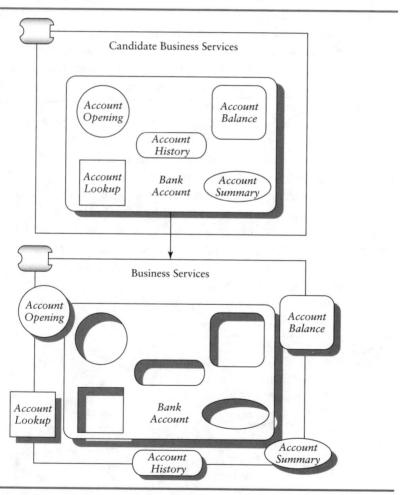

EXHIBIT 4.6 Service Decomposition Operation

business services. The newly created services and elements retain their original identities in this scenario.

Subset Operation

The subset operation aggregates individual services into more coarse-grained services by adding them into an existing candidate service. While the previously discussed unification operation aggregated multiple services into a new service, subset operations aggregate multiple services into another already identified candidate service. This operation is performed on independent and decoupled services. Subset operations treat individual business services as subsets of larger services and combine them into larger services as part of an existing service concept. In this sense, subset operations result in composite services. They are similar to composite services because the resulting service is composed from other preexisting atomic candidate services.

Exhibit 4.7 illustrates a subset operation. Individual services are transformed into an existing container service, which is a composite service. They become part of a larger service called *customer*. The new final composite service establishes *customer* as the container business service; the others, *statement provider*, *branch finder*, and *password maintainer*, are supporting services that support internal processes of the *customer* composite business service.

Services analysis best practices do not recommend extensive subset operations. Although composite services within orchestration

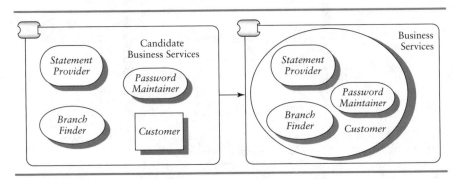

EXHIBIT 4.7 Subset

and choreography scenarios are not only desired but recommended best practices, excessive use of subset, much like unification operations, can reduce reusability and derail integration initiatives. It is best to maintain a fine balance between subset operations and decomposition operations by evaluating service granularity, business context, reuse and consumption patterns, and overall architectural value.

Subtraction Operation

Subtraction operations apply to candidate business services where unnecessary functionality of a service may hamper its business relevance, reuse, and desired SOA fit. Subtraction is necessary when entities are required to focus on specific business functions rather than providing a more diverse set of capabilities. Subtraction operations remove unnecessary functionality, processes, and business logic from both more coarse- and fine-grained services. Subtraction operations alter the characteristics of the resulting services, often resulting in a completely new service rather than a new version of a service. It is also possible that the subtracted service functionality could remain a separate atomic service, depending on the value of the functionality as a service to the organization. Alternatively, subtraction may eliminate the removed service functionality completely. In both cases, the resulting business services are new services and provide a focused solution for the problem they address.

Exhibit 4.8 depicts a *money transfer service* that is being subtracted from a *customer service service*. In this case, *money transfer* activities are no longer supported by customer service operations. Thus, the elimination of this functionality enables *customer service business service* to focus on its remaining responsibilities.

Service analysis best practices recommend eliminating service functionality that does not contribute to the business, that is ambiguous, or that encapsulates hybrid or contradicting business logic. Furthermore, subtraction operations can be used on coarse-grained entities that do not focus on high-priority business problems. Subtraction operations are encouraged when services do not provide focused support for business processes and concerns.

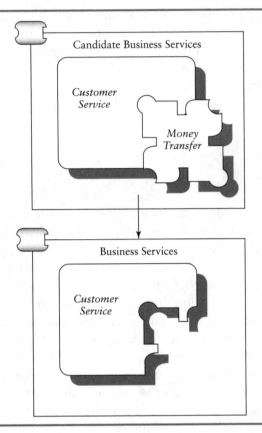

EXHIBIT 4.8 Subtraction

Complex Operations

Logical operations on services provide a top-down conceptual framework for service analysis. In many cases, due to the iterative nature of services identification and analysis, combinations of logical operations will be employed in the form of complex operations. This practice is encouraged to help increase services value, prioritize the services, and facilitate services design. The goal, of course, is to select and implement the right services for your organization.

The following example is a logical operation that is performed on the *checking account* and *savings account services* to combine their critical functionality and eliminate the *account lookup service*, which is not required. This goal can be accomplished by a three-step logical operation:

Step 1. Decompose and fragment *checking account, savings account*, and *account lookup* services. This operation separates these services and creates three independent elements, as depicted in Exhibit 4.9.

Step 2. Subtract the *account lookup* service. Exhibit 4.10 illustrates this subtraction operation. The *checking account* and *savings account* services remain after the subtraction operation.

Step 3. Unify the *checking account* and *savings account* services to create a unified *business service—account*. Exhibit 4.11 depicts the unification operation on checking account and savings account services.

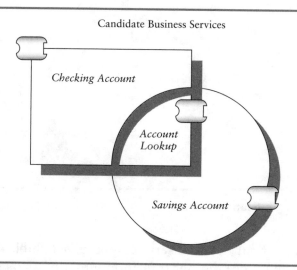

Candidate Business Services

Checking Account

Account Lookup

Savings Account

EXHIBIT 4.9   Decompose Operation

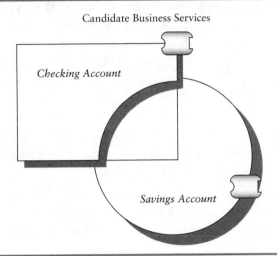

Candidate Business Services

Checking Account

Savings Account

EXHIBIT 4.10   Subtraction Operation

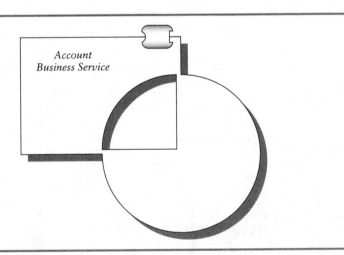

*Account
Business Service*

EXHIBIT 4.11   Unification Operation

The derived final business service appear in Exhibit 4.12. The *account lookup* service did not transform into a business service as expected. Yet the *checking account* and the *savings account* services were unified under *account* business services.

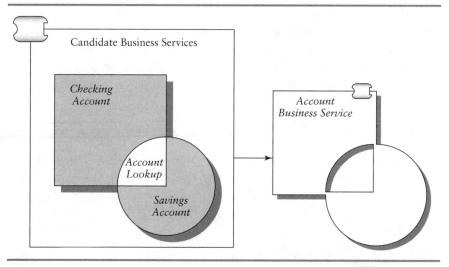

EXHIBIT 4.12   Final Goal

Impact of Logical Operations on Service Granularity

Organizations tend to have three classic asset granularity concerns:

1. What should the balance between coarse- and fine-grained assets in organizations be?
2. What should the balance between decomposition and unification operations in the service analysis phase be?
3. What is the best granularity scale that fits an organization, a business unit or a particular business process?

The answers to these challenges can be found largely in the service design phase, in which final business services are designed to be implemented as physical *solution services*.[4] Service analysis using the just-defined logical operations helps determine and adjust service granularity, as well as establish an overall approach to services granularity. As you may expect, the granularity maps will change as new services are identified, modeled, and selected for implementation.

Exhibit 4.13 depicts effective approaches to applying logical operations on services. In general, decomposition operations should be performed on medium- to coarse-grain services, while unification operations should be performed on fine- to medium-grained services. Subtraction operations, as shown, are effective on all granularity levels. Subset operations are recommended for fine- and medium-grained services. And finally, intersection operations can yield best results when they are applied to medium- and coarse-grained services.

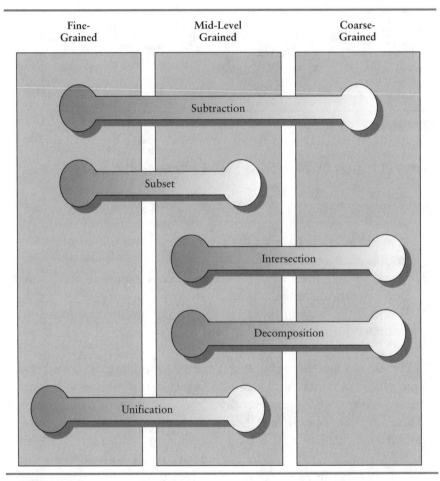

EXHIBIT 4.13   Impact of Logical Operations on Service Granularity

Service Analysis Summary

The service analysis phase helps identify and prioritize final business services for possible implementation. This iterative process (depicted in Exhibit 4.14) helps an organization focus its SOA efforts on high-value services as ranked by criteria related to business value and impact, reuse and high consumption, feasibility and technical viability. From these prioritized final business services, a set of services will be selected for implementation based on project needs, business imperatives, and other organizational requirements. The service analysis techniques are top-down logical operations to help analyze and select final business services for implementation. These logical operations provide great value in understanding functionality, scope, reuse, and granularity of candidate business services. In the next section we design the selected final business services and transform them from conceptual entities and abstractions into physical solution services.

SERVICE DESIGN

The service design phase enables the implementation of physical services through a series of design activities. The service design process

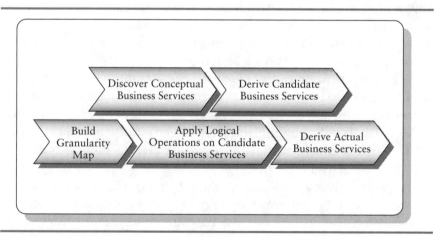

EXHIBIT 4.14 Service Analysis and Identification Process

transforms final business services into physical solution services. Inputs into service design are a set of target services that meet organization needs and have been prioritized and selected from the list of final candidate business services.

Service design begins with a final *business services* granularity map that facilitates the visualization of encapsulated business processes, their desired business value, and their potential as physical solution services. The relative granularity of services helps determine their viability and appropriateness as part of the SOA strategy.

The service design phase is not focused on the underlying technology or implementation details of service components. Source code is irrelevant to physical service structure design because service design activities tackle conceptual, logical, and physical compositions of services, examine their encapsulated business processes, and facilitate establishing reliable and reusable physical services.

Building Business Services Granularity Maps

The outputs of services analysis are a group of target final business services, prioritized according to business and technical criteria, and ready for service design. The first step in service design is to create a business services granularity map. Services analysis can provide an initial granularity assessment based on the top-down logical analysis of services functionality and scope. The various analysis operations were performed precisely to adjust granularity of candidate services prior to beginning the service design process.

The classification of final *business services* into various granularity levels is based on business and technological factors, or the same prioritization scheme used during services analysis to select candidate services that will be implemented as physical solution services. Technological considerations are a major driving force behind such an initiative. Diverse technological parameters such as integration, interoperability, and reusability, should be examined. Services positioned higher on the granularity map are more reusable than services positioned lower. This is because they are more generalized and can provide wider solution and technological coverage. However, services that are too coarse-grained will not be as useful or reusable due to their unwieldy nature, cumbersome size, and likely performance challenges. Seek the middle ground and avoid "megaservices" that are too coarse-grained. For example, a *statement* business service can provide a broad view of all customer account statements, such as *checking account statement, savings account statement,* and *investments account statement.* Fine-grained services are located lower on the granularity map. While not as business oriented as coarse-gained services, they still can play important roles as atomic services during the implementation of composite services.

Furthermore, technological factors such as capacity, performance, and complexity, can influence positioning of services on the granularity map. Services that will serve a wider range of consumers and have higher consumption should be positioned as coarse-grained services on the granularity map. Finally, technological strategies, resource allocation plans, organizational policies, standards, and best practices can influence granularity. For example, SOA policies may disqualify fine-grained services because their business value and functional scope are insignificant.

Exhibit 4.15 depicts business services on a granularity map with four levels of granularity. Services located on the top, such as *online banking service, bill payment service, money transfer service,* and *account service,* are coarse-grained and represent a holistic banking solution coverage via services. On the bottom, fine-grained services

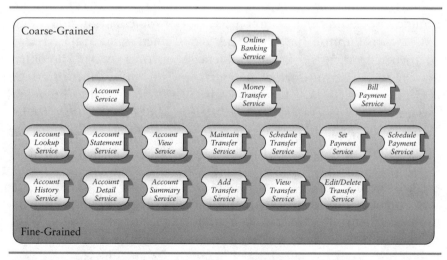

EXHIBIT 4.15 Business Services Granularity Map

such as *view transfer service* and *account lookup service* represent detailed implementations of banking product offerings.

Using the granularity map, it is visually easy to classify services according to their relative granularity in order to determine which services have more value and technical merit than others.

Building Demarcation Maps

The service analysis process results in the selection of services that meet prioritization schemes for the organization. These target services should be more coarse-grained and meet business imperatives. That said, the selected services still will vary by granularity. From the granularity mapping exercise, the services will be assembled into solution groups that will lead to the creation of contextually demarcated service groups that may be transformed later into physical services.

The demarcation process is conceptual in nature. This process should be a top-down exercise beginning with coarse-grained generalized *business services*. Begin by identifying common contextual relationships of business services. Group them accordingly. Also look for a common technology context, which will be important when services are finally exposed as physical services.

Exhibit 4.16 depicts a contextual business service demarcation activity. Services that comprise *online banking* product offerings are grouped based on their common context—business affiliation, anticipated consumption patterns, SLA requirements, and related environment parameters that can influence their operations. The *online trading* service group, which supports investment product offerings, is grouped similarly. At this stage, discovery of common context and service reuse is essential to service design. As depicted, overlapping demarcation boundaries suggest that some services are common to both solution groups and should be considered as valuable reusable organizational assets.

Continue the top-down demarcation process for all target services, including the more fine-grained services on the granularity map, grouping them by business context and technological affinity. When you have finished, there will be overlapping demarcation lines similar to Venn diagrams. Typically, the inner circles encompass more fine-grain services while more coarse-grained services are contained in

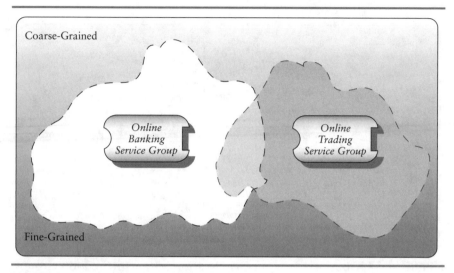

EXHIBIT 4.16   Business Services Demarcation Activity

outer circles. The demarcation process can reveal common functional, technological, and relationship features of *business services*, which will help identify high-value services as core assets of your SOA.

For example, the demarcation diagram in Exhibit 4.17 depicts *online banking* business service offerings, which encapsulate a number of subgroups that provide a granular identity for the online banking product. Overlapping demarcation groups reveal potential service reusability: The *money transfer service* uses the *account view service* to augment its business processes. Customers now have the option to view their account detail, history, and summary as a part of the *money transfer service*. The *account view service* is exposed as a reusable service that can serve multiple service solution groups as a crucial element of the online banking product.

Service Design Process

Upon completion of the granularity and demarcation maps, you can transition to service design and the realization of physical *solution services*. The services modeling ingredients are in place and ready for the creation of physical, tangible and concrete services that can execute required missions, resolve problems, and address business

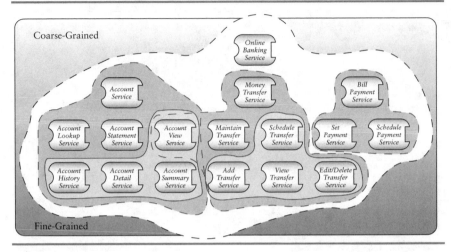

EXHIBIT 4.17   Business Services Demarcation Map with Solution Groups

concerns. Yet this realization process should follow a number of necessary service design activities. The demarcation map that is constructed from the granularity map is a good starting point. Discovered *business service* solution groups serve as raw material for constructing concrete service structures, establishing their final granularity, associating service internal elements and components, and assigning their internal collaborative responsibilities. Again, business and technological considerations are applied to each construction step and provide guidance to achieving the final outcome: physical *solution services*. Exhibit 4.18 illustrates a transition from the logical to the physical phase of this service design model.

Service Design in Practice

The actual service design process is comprised of various tasks that are performed on *business services*, which are positioned on the granularity map, grouped and depicted by demarcation lines. These design activities stabilize *business services* granularity levels, enable generalization of these assets to a more coarse-grained status, or demote others to a more fine-grained category. Some operations facilitate the expansion of

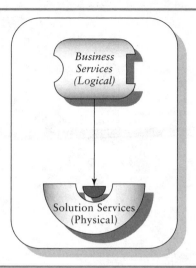

EXHIBIT 4.18 From Logical to Physical Services

business processes by importing or sharing functionalities, or narrowing down *business services* views and perspectives by exporting some of their activities. This section focuses on achieving business goals and technological objectives through alignment of business service groups rather than individual processes, and facilitates adjustment of the SOA big picture in an overall SOA initiative. Exhibit 4.19 illustrates a service design toolbox that comprises design operations on *business services*.

Service design activities consist of:

■ *Business service relationships*. Establishing relationship and identifying affiliations among *business services* can facilitate a base foundation for service structures. Business association, technological capability, capacity, and environmental parameters are inputs to the relationship matching process of business services. The affinity of business services can span one or more demarcation lines and include as many assets as required. This activity simplifies the concept of services grouping by forming service-to-service relationships that cross their original context group in the demarcation map. The recommended approach is to illustrate such *business service* relationships in a domain model diagram,

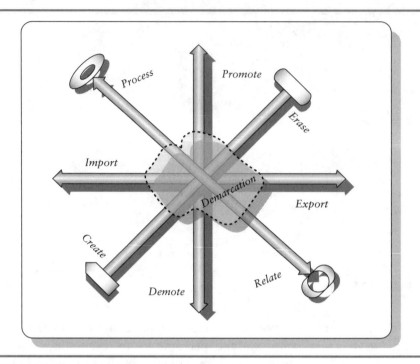

EXHIBIT 4.19   Service Design Toolbox

which in this case depicts process abstraction affiliations—specifying the number of instances of one *business service* that can be associated with each instance of any other *business services*. For example, Exhibit 4.20 depicts the affinity relationship formed between *business services through this process*. The *money transfer service* uses a maximum of three offered services by the *account view service*.

- *Demarcation.* At this step, the demarcation process continues to capture the newly established relationship between *business services*. Affiliated assets should be assembled again into solution groups to reflect the latest findings. Exhibit 4.21 illustrates an additional discovered group, which comprises *account lookup service* and *account detail service*.
- *Dynamic behavior[5] and process.* Business processes, messages, or transactions can span across multiple *business services* and business solution groups. Thus, expressing such interactions can

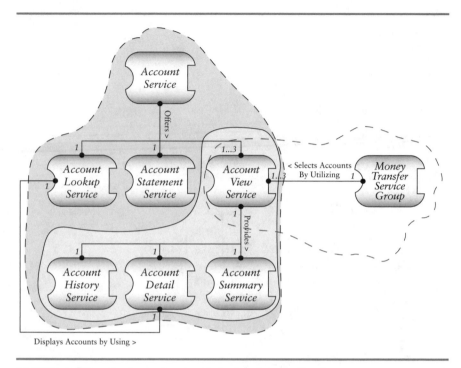

Displays Accounts by Using >

EXHIBIT 4.20   Business Service Relationship Defined

elaborate more on their relationships, dependencies, and mutual activities. Furthermore, message exchange and logical business transactions can be uncovered and documented at this early stage and then later be translated to physical implementations.

A state chart diagram or a sequence diagram can depict behavior and work flow of business processes. And again, this step can be concluded with the modification of the demarcation diagram to reflect the newly discovered business relationship that is observed in the process flow.

■ *Promotion.* A promotion may be needed to augment or broaden the operational range of existing services in the enterprise. Service promotions facilitate the containment of subordinate and related finer-grained services. Furthermore, from an organizational perspective, this activity can increase reusability of services, facilitate consolidation of assets in light of budgetary constraints or

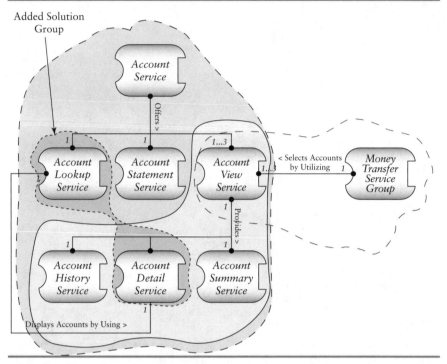

EXHIBIT 4.21   Applied Demarcation on Related Business Services

architectural considerations, and even eliminate services that do not contribute to the overall solution strategy. Business service granularity is usually increased through promotion.

Exhibit 4.22 depicts a promotion scenario of an *employee benefits service*. It is raised to the same granularity level as its peer—*employee lookup service*. The *profit-sharing service* and the *401 contribution service* are being promoted along as well.

■ *Demotion.* Demotion of *business services* means moving assets down to finer-grained levels on the granularity map. Demotion is required when there is neither business nor technological justification for maintaining the current granularity status of the services, and their solution coverage and process spectrum is too narrow. Furthermore, demotion activities can be applied to services that have limited solution coverage or that can be replaced by more generalized services that may already exist in production.

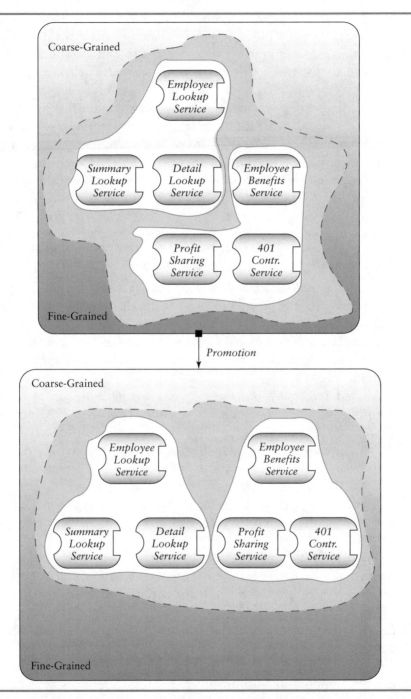

EXHIBIT 4.22 Promotion of Employee Benefits Business Services

Exhibit 4.23 depicts a demotion activity of *business services* and a creation of a more generalized service. After the demotion, the *employee service* group was inserted to contain the *employee lookup service* and *employee benefits service*. Both were pushed down to finer-grained levels on the granularity scale.

■ *Import.* Importing services is a cross–demarcation line horizontal function, similar to recent innovations of aspect-oriented programming (AOP), which pay attention to horizontal crosscutting lines of business. Importing services enables the expansion of service scope, increases their functionality, and facilitates the diversification and augmentation of their business functionalities. Business services can be imported from other service solution groups by joining the importing party's services. The granularity level of the imported services can be altered if they are moved from different levels on the granularity map. After import operations, a revised demarcation map should reflect the newly created solution group relationship. There are two variations of import activities:

  ● *Exclusive import.* A *business service* is permanently moved from one service solution group to another. The contributing solution group does not have the ability to share that service anymore.

  ● *Shared import.* A *business service* is made available to the importing solution group, and it continues to serve the original solution group owners.

For example, an *employee service* group that provides employee-specific functionality, such as *employee benefits service* and *employee profit-sharing service*, can expand its business services by importing the *continuing education service*. This act can expand the employee offerings service to provide education services to its consumers.

Exhibit 4.24 illustrates another example of a shared import operation. The *account lookup service* is imported into the *fixed income service group*, yet it still continues to serve the *mutual funds service group*.

■ *Export.* Exporting *business services* by moving them across demarcation lines to different business service solution groups will narrow the exporters' business range and solution coverage. Like the import operation, this operation resembles features of AOP. It is performed to achieve decoupling of responsibilities and

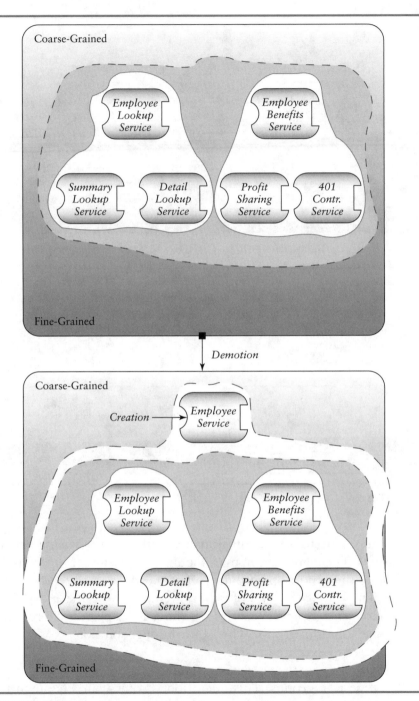

EXHIBIT 4.23 Demotion and Creation Activities

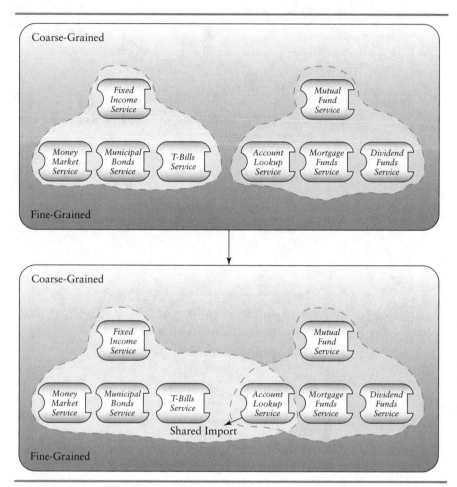

EXHIBIT 4.24   Shared Import

processes or to share functionality with other business service groups. The demarcation map should be revised with the completion of the export operation to reflect newly created relationship.

There are two types of export architecture styles:

- *Exclusive export.* A service is removed and placed in a requesting solution group. The contributing solution group loses access to exported assets.
- *Shared export.* A business service is made available to other requesting groups. This operation is somewhat similar to the shared import operation, but in this case, the exporting group owns the exported business service.

■ *Erase and create.* Erase and create operations enable flexibility in design and architecture of services. The *erase* operation facilitates the total elimination of *business services* from the demarcation map. The *create* activity enables the insertion of new *business services* and positions them in various service solution groups.

Physical Solution Service Composition

Before we move on to the service realization phase, we should take a look at a typical physical solution service composition. From service analysis and design, the next step is to generate physical solution services that correlate to the services designs. *Solution services* are physical implementations of service abstractions. They consist of components, which are comprised of business logic, and business processes. Solution services may also contain other services. They should provide access and exposure to external consumers, yet they have a distinct internal architecture that comprises business and technological ingredients. The construction of the service internals requires design disciplines that are affiliated with service internal operations, processes, and constituent associations. Shaping service structures and forming element compositions and relationships can facilitate collaborative harmony of the inner workings of services.

A physical solution service consists of internal or external physically located elements, such as components or other services (see Exhibit 4.25). These distributed element end points and locations information are irrelevant to the solution service and its operations. Yet they must work together to achieve business and technological goals. Element coexistence and collaboration requirements underline the need for design and architecture of the service structures.

Service main constituents are:

■ *Service controller.* The *service controller* is a type of an internal router, workload manager, or dispatcher that knows how to distribute requests to internal and external service elements. It enables conversations with service consumers, via service exposure management, and control of message and transaction routing. Yet this service element does not provide work flow engines or rules to manage and choreograph service activities. Typically, *service controllers* employ *service facade* patterns to provide back-end message distribution mechanisms.[6]

Solution services need to exchange messages with three major communication channels: service-affiliated and owned elements, peer services and applications, and subscribed consumers. The *service controller* has the ability to converse with its consumers by utilizing its published exposure mechanisms, such as public interfaces and remote procedure calls. Internal elements can be invoked via internal interfaces. Communication with peer services and applications can be enabled by customized adapters and interfaces.

- *Service components. Service components* are elements, which are comprised of underlying code that expresses related business logic,[7] and business processes. Components are mainly mid- to coarse-grained reusable[8] constituents that are contained and controlled by service governing rules. The main responsibilities of service components are to collaborate with other service elements and take part in service work flow activities, message exchanges, or business transactions.

  Source code platform and language types, such as procedural and object-oriented COBOL, PL1, C/C++, or Java, are irrelevant to the overall component and service composition and design. Hence, components should comply with interoperability standards, and be portable, reusable, customizable, and adjustable. Physically they can reside in close proximity to the service main logic or be distributed anywhere on the services network.

  Components do not make use of external service exposure mechanisms, yet they must comply with service internal communication protocols and governance policies.

- *Internal adapters.* These are service internal adapters ("glue code") or interface mechanisms that facilitate the communication and the transmission of information between service constituents. Service elements and component logic should employ such adapters to enable seamless internal work flow and business processes.

  Because service elements can span various heterogeneous environments, internal adapters should have the capability and the capacity to provide data transformation and protocol translation when applicable.

- *Security and trust components.* Protecting organizational assets is a major concern in integrated environments. Security measures should be applied to external and internal service environments to ensure the integrity and the reliability of service operations. Trust relationships should be applied to service constituents that often communicate and exchange messages, either to remotely distributed components or to internally contained service entities. Services security is a complex topic, and includes perimeter and infrastructure security capabilities, such as firewalls, single sign-on and access control, as well as WS-Security, and related policies, and the overall implementation of SOA security models. Achieving appropriate security will require analysis of all services and enabling technology elements of an SOA, as well as service design approaches, to adequately secure services.
- *Agents.* *Agents* are a type of listener component that provides SLA enforcement, monitoring, audit trail, and traceability. They do not participate in ongoing business transactions or internal message exchanges. They merely act on behalf of their external requesters and remain neutral with respect to service internal operations.
- *Composite services.* Services can be composed from other services, which is an increasingly common service design goal. Composite services will first require determining appropriate granularity of services utilizing granularity maps to enable composite service design and architectural flexibility. Design practices that support composite services paradigms greatly increase inter-service communication and collaboration capabilities. It introduces different kinds of utility services that do not necessarily process business logic, but they can assist with service internal operations, enforce governance policies, provide accounting facilities to accommodate service consumption chargeback to consumers, and support service publishing and advertising initiatives.
- *Internal work flow managers.* Process flow management entities provide internal governance services and assist with job coordination, prioritization, and labor distribution scheduling among service elements and components. Furthermore, these types of service elements provide assistance with logic and business activity flow, manage internal events, furnish process monitoring capabilities, enable the creation and the customization

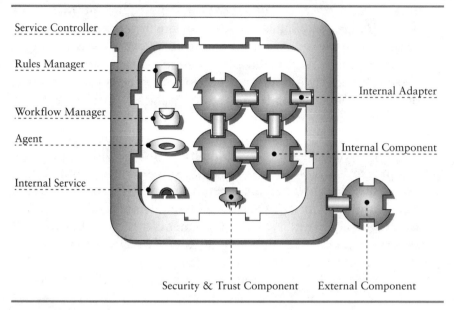

EXHIBIT 4.25   Service Elements

of business process rules, and contribute immensely to the orchestration of internal components and elements.

■ *Internal rule managers.* These services provide internal business rule management and run-time facilities. Internal service components employ these features to resolve complex algorithms and simplify business logic. Internal rule management facilities should provide sophisticated user interface capabilities to graphically create and manage business rules that can be altered and enhanced during run-time conditions.

Service Realization: The Final Step

The realization phase is concerned with the transformation of business services into tangible and concrete physical assets, or *solution services.* This process shifts the focus from conceptual services modeling to physical modeling and architecture of solution services. Service realization activities assist with the identification, recognition, and construction of service internal elements, establishment of their structures, and formation of service internal protocols that can enable element coexistence and interactions. The service realization process should result in a final blueprint of service internal composition, a granularity classification of services, specifications of service element associations, and collaboration schemes for service constituents.

The service realization process offers three major transitioning approaches and principles.

1. *Transitioning of business services to solution services.* This approach offers a service-to-service conversion of concepts, ideas, and processes that are contained in *business services* to tangible *solutions services.* If the transformation activity does not alter their position on the granularity scale, their granularity level is preserved and maintained. Transformation of these assets to lower granularity levels can be considered as demotions and vice versa. Logical elements can be promoted to higher granularity levels if they are transformed into physical services that are positioned higher on this scale.

2. *Transitioning of business services to physical components.* This method offers transformation of *business service* concepts, functionalities, and processes into physical *service* components. Finer-grained *business services* typically are converted to physical components because they are centered on narrower business functionality ranges and are not as generalized as coarse-grained assets. Such operations may demote these elements to a lower granularity level by locating them on the fine-grained segment of the service granularity map.

3. *Transitioning of business services to service processes.* This approach advocates the transformation of business services into processes, which are embedded and contained in physical *solution service* components because they are too granular to serve as components or independent services.

Logical-to-physical transitioning decisions should be based on a wide array of business, technological, and enterprise parameters. Typically, an organization's service granularity paradigms are driving forces behind the construction of service internal structures and their realization. This school of thought recognizes that transformations of business assets to physical entities are based on containment and aggregation principles that lead to hierarchical service structures. Thus, abstractions of concepts and business processes can be transitioned to various granularity levels and finally form holistic views of service identities. Furthermore, environmental factors, such as integrated service communities, middleware, and infrastructure, can contribute immensely to these decisions because of existing organizational deployment perspectives that have already defined these related service landscapes. Exhibit 4.26 depicts these transformation principles.

Service granularity maps and demarcation diagrams are prerequisites and base-level requirements for transformation processes. These artifacts serve as solid foundations for any conversion activity in the service realization phase. As illustrated in Exhibit 4.27, the *account service* solution group offers three major services: *account lookup service*, *account statement service*, and *account view service*. This exhibit defines and expresses their relationship and demarcation lines.

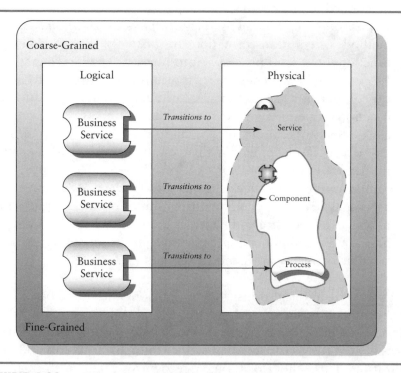

EXHIBIT 4.26   Three Major Realization Principles

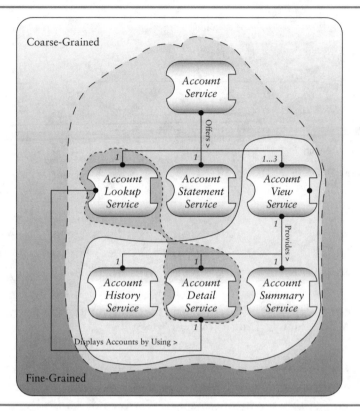

EXHIBIT 4.27   Business Services State Before Transformation to Physical Entities

Three transformation types support the transition from *business services* to physical *solution services*. These priciples apply to constructing single, composite and multiple solution services:

1. *Simple transformation.* A simple transformation takes place when the end result comprises one major coarse-grained *solution service* that contains one or more components and their affiliated internal processes.

   Exhibit 4.28 depicts a simple *business service* transformation to physical and concrete elements. The *account business service* is realized as a physical *solution service account service.* The *account lookup, account statement,* and *account view* business services are recognized as tangible components of the *account*

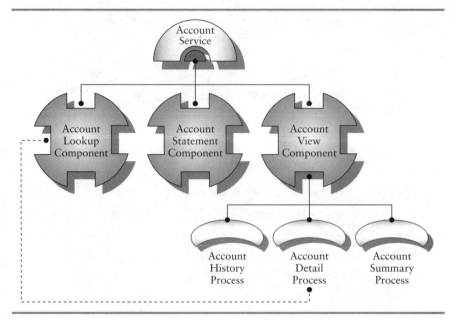

EXHIBIT 4.28 Simple Transformation

service, do not maintain their service identity, and are demoted to a finer-grained level. The *account history, account detail,* and *account summary* business services are folded into the *account view* component and serve as its internal processes.

2. *Combined transformation.* A combined transformation supports the service containment architectural style, which facilitates the inclusion of services within services, or composites. Typically, this approach encourages transitions of *most business services* to service components. Exhibit 4.29 illustrates a combined transformation of business services. In this case, the *account view service* is contained and operates in the *account service* space and is established as one of its structural elements. In addition, the exhibit depicts the transitioning of *account lookup* and *account statement* business services into service components.

3. *Complex transformation.* And finally, the example in Exhibit 4.30 depicts a complex transformation scenario: Multiple physical

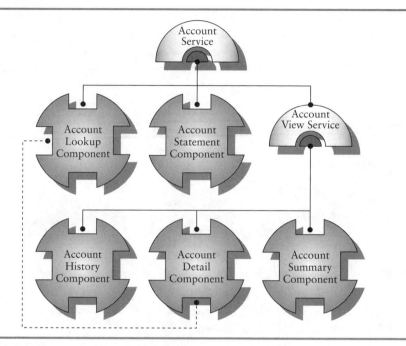

EXHIBIT 4.29 Combined Transformation

services are contained in the *account service*—the *account lookup service*, *account statement service*, and *account view service*. This configuration preserves the identity of these major coarse-grained *business services* and transforms them directly into physical *solution services*. *Account history service*, *account detail service*, and the *account summary service* are transitioned into service components which are contained in the internal *Account view services* yet their granularity level is preserved.

Architecture standards and best practices should provide guidance in designing containment and accessibility aspects of service structures. Policies should indicate how service consumers should access internal services and what their interface signatures would be. To simplify design and architectural complexities, we recommend that contained services should not be exposed to consumers, but they should be available to their internal peers.

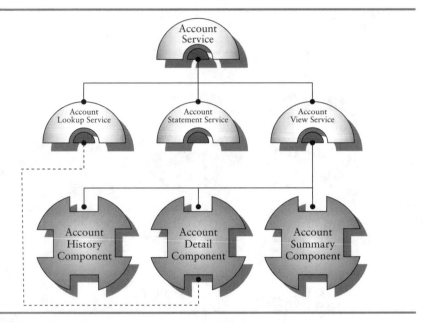

EXHIBIT 4.30   Complex Transformation

Service Design Process Summary

As depicted in Exhibit 4.31 the service design phase comprises five steps in which *business services* are examined and processed through the construction of granularity and demarcation maps. Design operations are applied to refine their positions and discover business and technological associations. Finally, the service realization phase facilitates the generation of physical *solution services*. This outline depicts the process:

Examine. Examine the state of *business services*. Explore their composition, and inspect their business processes and associations.

Design. Design *business services* granularity maps. Rank and position services on a granularity scale appropriate for your organization.

Build. Build demarcation maps. Find business commonalities and discover *business service* associations and affinities.

Apply. Apply design operations on *business services*.

Realize. Realize and expose physical *solution services*.

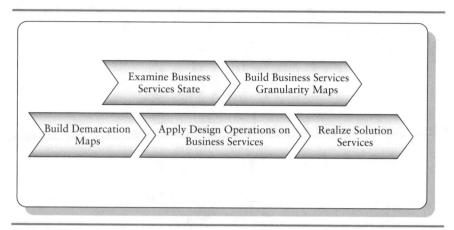

EXHIBIT 4.31   Service Design Process

BOTTOM-UP DESIGN AND ANALYSIS APPROACH

Bottom-Up Process

The bottom-up design method recognizes the importance of the evolutionary approach to software architecture and development. It is a progressive process of building services or assembling existing technologies to provide business solutions. A bottom-up approach to designing and constructing services consists of six steps:

1. Study business problems and concerns.
2. Analyze business requirements and business processes.
3. Construct granular entities, such as source code and libraries, centered on software algorithm perfection and modular design practices.
4. Establish source code modules that are founded on business context and processes.
5. Design and construct software components.
6. Group components into physical *solution services*.

Exhibit 4.32 illustrates the bottom-up approach to service design and implementation.

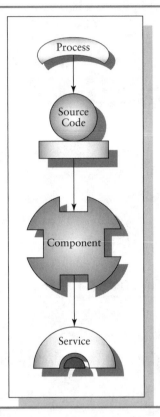

EXHIBIT 4.32   Bottom-Up Service Design and Implementation

What Is Next?

Realistically, the bottom-up and top-down approaches do not individually offer an ideal service design and architecture methodology. The top-down approach disregards the underlying technology, while the bottom-up approach lacks conceptual and analysis processes. In combination, as we advocate, they are very powerful tools.

In iterative design, architecture, and development environments, a hybrid solution can be most compelling. Such an approach would support both methods and encourage integration of design processes that would enable the top-down and the bottom-up methods to meet midway. We encourage organizations to develop a services identification, analysis, and design process that is tailored to their business and technological environments.

SUMMARY

This chapter presents a hands-on approach to services identification, analysis, and design. It provides mechanisms and tools to establish business abstractions through the discovery of *candidate business services* and to facilitate the formation of organizational assets, such as final business and tangible *solution services*.

This iterative process is driven by business necessities and IT imperatives. This progressive approach to identifying and establishing organization services can be accomplished during numerous service development lifecycles. It can enable business and technology growth, provide efficient reactive solutions to enterprise concerns, and facilitate a proactive strategy to minimize or eliminate business problems.

NOTES

1. plato.stanford.edu/entries/set-theory, Stanford Encyclopedia of Philosophy, "Set Theory."
2. Philippe Kruchten, "Architectural Blueprints—The '4+1' View Model of Software Architecture," Rational Software Corp., November 1995, pp. 2, 3.
3. Grady Booch, Object Oriented Analysis and Design with Application (Benjamin/Cummings Publishing Company, 1994), p. 13.
4. LogicLibrary Inc., "Best Practices for Reuse of Software Development Assets (SDAs)," 2005, p. 5.
5. Terry Quatrani, *Visual Modeling with Rational Rose 2000 and UML* (Addison-Wesley, 2000), p. 131.
6. Erich Gamma, Richard Helm, Ralph Johnson, and John Vlissides, *Design Patterns Elements of Reusable Object-Oriented Software* (Addison-Wesley, 1995), p. 185.
7. Graig Larman, *Applying UML and Patterns: An Introduction to Object-Oriented Analysis and Design and Iterative Development*, 3rd ed. (Pearson Education, 2005), p. 624.
8. Peter Coad with David North and Mark Mayfield, *Object Models: Strategies, Patterns, and Applications* (Prentice Hall, 1995), p. 163.

CHAPTER 5

SOA Technology and Services Integration Model

Services integration, which is also known as service-oriented integration (SOI), is an evolutionary and incremental process of enabling services relationships. It involves analysis of business strategies and business processes, requires knowledge of an organization's technology environment, and mandates an understanding of service capabilities, characteristics, and capacity. The understanding of services communities and the interaction between service consumers and providers is crucial for successful SOA integration initiatives in all computing environments. Services reusability, process and data integration, consolidation of properties, utilization of resources, time to market, and return on investment (ROI) are the motivating factors behind integration projects.

In today's integrated environments, service producers and consumers are usually connected via rigid point-to-point interfaces. Chapter 1 described the typical integration challenges that most organizations are faced with and why SOA and services present a more agile and reusable model as an alternative. Integration is still largely a manual process in these environments. Integration design and the resultant architecture are carved in stone from the first deployment, and subsequent integration initiatives continue to rely on the already established rigid concepts that inhibit business agility. Human intervention is always needed when planning and implementing services integration and deployment projects. Lifecycle management and operation of services, consumers, and providers is a demanding endeavor, made even more challenging due to their dynamic nature in rapidly evolving market conditions. Even so, service-oriented integration is a far more agile and flexible model than rigid integration paradigms of the past, such as custom tightly coupled point-to-point solutions and enterprise application integration (EAI).

Modern SOA enabling technologies provide a wide array of facilities to administer deployment and integration of services. These services include messaging platforms, services middleware, integration brokers, registries and metadata repositories, services monitoring, management and diagnostic platforms, and more. Increasingly, organizations must layer new services design, SOA integration, run-time, and management solutions over legacy integration and messaging platforms. Often only portions of a complete SOA enabling technology stack will be required as SOA is incrementally achieved through multiple services projects over time, and the sequencing of the appropriate run-time and integration solutions can vary by the nature, volume, and consumption patterns of desired services in the SOA.

The services integration model provides a dynamic integration structure that facilitates the planning, design, and implementation of your integration strategy. It simplifies the complexities of the SOA integration landscape and proposes approaches and solutions to achieve service integration in the context of your SOA.

The suggested service integration model enables SOA integration planning and deployment strategies. It proposes repeatable steps to identify service consumer and producer relationships in the context of their environment, elaborates on transportation modes for messages and transactions, facilitates discovery and determination of message dispatching and distribution mechanisms, and establishes an overall service integration process flow. Data integration principles are applied to all phases to ensure information integrity and one version of the truth for organizational data.

Service integration model categorizes various SOA enabling technology solutions based on their contribution to SOA and services integration requirements. The modeling process introduces various integration architecture steps that facilitate the creation of a services integration architecture blueprint, which consists of collaborative service environments, enabling middleware, and physical networks.

And finally, this model provides product mapping best practices and standards to be considered during product evaluation and selection phases. The product mapping section recommends product selection policies to help match vendor products to organizational and technology environments, support product interaction with peer applications, and establish requirements for agility certifications you should require your vendors to provide along with their products.

SERVICE INTEGRATION MODEL FRAMEWORK

The *service integration model* facilitates service integration strategy development, formalization of concepts, and standardization of service integration best practices. These strategies will include policies and standards that are created through multiple SOA activities, including SOA governance, policies, service design models, and organizational and industry best practices and conventions. Furthermore, this framework is a centralized service integration knowledge base that unifies and joins various experiences and expertise to provide integration solutions, integration processes, and proposed modeling techniques.[1] In addition, the reusability model is a major contributor to the service integration model based on its asset reuse and asset consolidation concepts, policies, best practices, and standards. Exhibit 5.1 depicts this relationship.

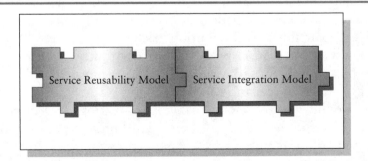

EXHIBIT 5.1   Integration Model:Model View

SERVICE INTEGRATION GENERIC NOTATION

The service integration generic notation, as depicted in Exhibit 5.2, is used throughout this model. It represents four different symbols that describe integration entities:

1. *Consumers or producers.* Physical service consumers or producers
2. *Service bus.* Messaging middleware
3. *Intermediary.* Message interceptors and manipulators, such as hubs and gateways
4. *Connector.* Logical symbol used to express various relationship and workflow types between entities

SERVICE INTEGRATION PRINCIPLES

The rapid rise of SOA adoption and reusable interoperable services in heterogeneous information technology (IT) architectures can complicate services integration and impose great challenges on the incorporation of services in an SOA. The *service integration strategy component* furnishes a simplified and generalized view of service integration environments and where they fit as layers of the technology stack.[2] This simplified view of service integration facilitates the interaction between integrated parties, the services, and their enabling technologies. These features include service consumer and producer relationships, transportation and delivery modes for messages, message integration, and service orchestration and process work flow aspects.

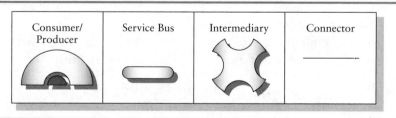

EXHIBIT 5.2 Service Integration Generic Notation

Abstraction and generalization of service integration are characterized by SOA principle integration patterns, which provide reuse of integration approaches and form the foundation for structured service integration design disciplines.[3]

Service integration aspects such as collaborations, activities, environments, and service consumer and producer relationships should be abstracted into elementary levels to simplify complexities that arise from the growth of the number of services, their dependencies, and the number of consumers and providers in an SOA network. These service integration abstractions are comprised of basic principles that should be followed during design and architecture of integration initiatives.

Relationship Principle

Services relationships are founded in business processes and in related technical solutions. The relationship of service consumers and producers should be defined during service design and during the design and architecting of the service integration environment. Doing this creates explicit understanding of required integration between services in the context of their business and technical environments, transaction and message affiliations, consumption patterns, and resource allocation. Documenting the service consumer and provider relationships facilitates the design of integration, messaging, and conversational paths between the participating parties and simplifies the complexities that can arise from emerging integrated SOA environments. Service integration relationships largely depend on two fundamental concepts:

1. *Message exchange.* Services that exchange messages and transactions are related. For example, a *loan service* has relationships with *loan* and *credit* consumers.
2. *Link dependencies.* Business and technological links between service consumers and producers define their relationship.

Relationships between services are identified by these conceptual connectivity patterns that describe their affiliation:

One-to-one relationship pattern. Service consumers and producers have a *one-to-one* integration relationship if the two participating parties exchange messages; leverage service integration, run-time, and management infrastructure available in their operating environment; and have business affiliations. An example of this could be a service consumer request for equity trading history from a *trading history service* or a service producer periodically feeding a service consumer with *trading history data*. Exhibit 5.3 depicts this concept.

One-to-many relationship pattern. This relationship defines a single service consumer or producer that exchanges messages with two or more consumers and/or producers. They all leverage service integration, run-time, and management infrastructure available in their operating environment. Exhibit 5.4 depicts a consumer that obtains *account information* from *account balances service* and *account trading information service*.

Many-to-one relationship pattern. This scenario is identical to the *one-to-many* relationship. However, in the context of services integration, it would be useful to identify this type of relationship in junction with the *process flow principle*, which is discussed later. This relationship identifies multiple assets that depend on message exchange with a single asset. In the big picture of integration planning, this type of arrangement may make a difference from a resource

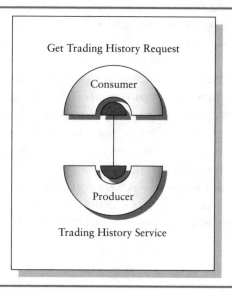

EXHIBIT 5.3 One-to-One Relationship

EXHIBIT 5.4   One-to-Many Relationship

consumption and allocation perspective, and it also depends on particular needs of the service consumers and producers involved.

Many-to-many relationship pattern. Integration relationships that are comprised of multiple producers and consumers that participate in the same transactions can be characterized as *many-to-many* entity relationships—often called ecosystems. They are complex in nature and impose management challenges because of their high dependency on their environments, peers, and service communities. Exhibit 5.5 illustrates an *employee profile* transaction that is shared among four different services: *employee retirement service, employee benefits service, employee compensation service,* and *IRA accounts service*. The *employee retirement service* retrieves its underlying information from the *employee compensation service* and from the *employee IRA accounts service*. The same two providers—*employee compensation service* and *IRA Account service*—are serving the *employee benefits service* and the *employee retirement service*.

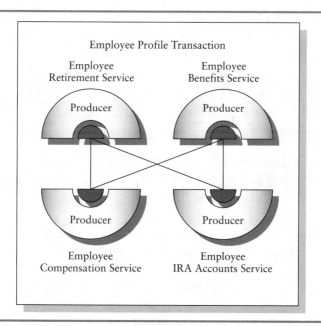

EXHIBIT 5.5   Many-to-Many Relationship

Transportation Principle

The most important aspects of message and transaction transportation facilities are message brokers and interceptors that typically are located between service producers and consumers. Service integration activities such as design, architecture, and deployment should employ transportation patterns to outline and express service integration. However, prior to identifying these message exchange patterns, additional business, technical, and service knowledge will be required:

- Characteristics of the deployed services and an understanding of their business context and their technical implementation, including their exposure mechanisms, interfaces, adaptability, portability, interoperability attributes, and any dependencies on other services
- Target integration environment, mainly physical network architecture and configurations, hardware dependencies, and operating systems

- Employed middleware and third-party products that provide message transport services; this can include message queuing products, message and integration brokers, and hubs
- Capability and functionality of intermediaries and message interceptors that can carry out functions such as routing, data transformations, security enforcement, and policy enforcement for SOA governance
- SOA monitoring, management, and diagnostic tools that can intercept messages and provide visibility, traceability, security, and enforcement of service-level agreements (SLAs) and other related policies that must be enforced

Three main SOA message transportation patterns can be utilized when designing and architecting service-oriented integration:

1. *Direct access pattern.* This pattern does not include intermediaries. Rather, service consumers and producers communicate directly with one another and do not employ intermediaries or interceptors, which are normally required to handle a wide array of functions (i.e., business rules, message routing and dispatching mechanisms, security implementations, SLA monitoring and enforcement, policy enforcement, and capacity and consumption monitoring). As illustrated in Exhibit 5.6, this overall tightly coupled implementation is suited for homogeneous environments, or for small-scale service-oriented integration requirements.
2. *Broker interception pattern.* This transportation model supports the use of one or more intermediaries that reside between consumers and providers and provide a number of architectural benefits for services (i.e., policy enforcement, security enforcement, decoupling of consumers and providers, etc.). This loosely coupled service integration architecture supports modularization and logic subdivision to reduce implementation redundancy and encourage service consolidations. Intermediaries provide a variety of features and message handling capabilities, such as routing, load balancing, workload management, data and protocol transformation, and implementation of common business logic. Exhibit 5.7 depicts a broker-oriented integration scenario in which three intermediaries provide the intermediary services just mentioned.

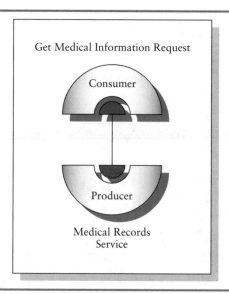

EXHIBIT 5.6   Direct Connection Pattern

3. *Service bus pattern.* This pattern is based on a messaging back-bone that provides guaranteed message delivery, message queu-ing, and publish/subscribe capabilities. The service bus pattern supports long-running transactions, enables loose coupling, and accommodates increased requirements for high-volume message transportation.

   The *service bus pattern* suggests offloading complex schedul-ing and message delivering tasks from services or, in effect, designing services in anticipation of a messaging backbone that takes care of these transport details. Implementations that sup-port this approach are capable of serving a large number of ser-vice producers and consumers and of processing a wide variety of message formats and protocols. The enterprise service bus (ESB) pattern is often used in heterogeneous computing environments, including legacy systems, commercial applications, and home-grown proprietary applications on diverse application platforms and operating systems where integration-centric requirements are a dominant feature of the SOA requirements. In many cases, enterprise application integration (EAI) solutions are imple-mented in lieu of ESBs. Although these solutions do accomplish

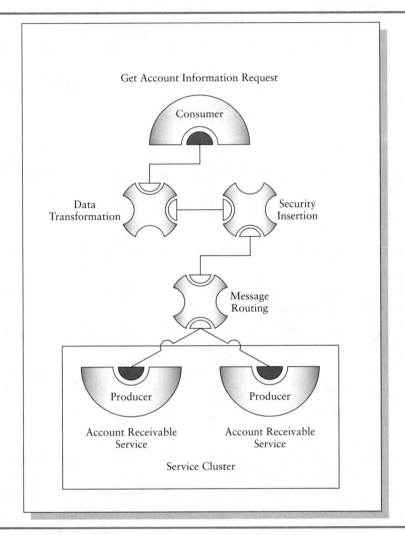

EXHIBIT 5.7   Broker Interception Pattern

some of the integration requirements presented by heterogeneous IT architectures, most of them are hub-and-spoke integration platforms that are not truly bus topologies. Furthermore, forcing the processing to the hub can impose performance penalties in service networks where XML traffic is heavy due to services volume.

Exhibit 5.8 illustrates a service bus pattern that is applied to service operations that handle and process insurance claims. Service consumers and producers utilize a central service bus

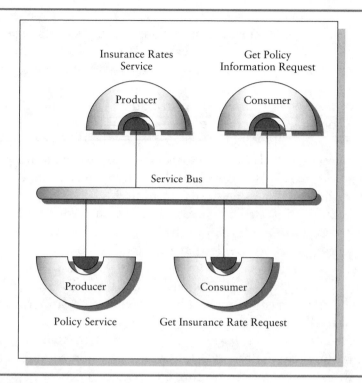

EXHIBIT 5.8   Service Bus Pattern

that provides communication means and message transportation mechanisms.

These transportation patterns can be combined to simplify integration projects and enable flexibility and agility in product, middleware, and service deployments. For example, the broker interception pattern can coexist with the service bus pattern. The question becomes one of how to allocate the intermediary functions across diverse integration and services run-time platforms. Intermediaries can augment and provide additional functionality to service bus products and vice versa.

Delivery Principle

The delivery principle describes the mechanisms in which intermediaries, consumers, and producers deliver messages to various end points. The order and sequence of message delivery depends on transaction types, business requirements, and technical specifications. The delivery principle generalizes these approaches and offers three methods and patterns to simplify delivery complexities.

1. *In-order delivery pattern.* In distributed SOA environments, service consumers may need to invoke a number of service producers to accomplish single transactions. Thus, this pattern depicts sequential delivery of messages between participating parties. Business processes and technical requirements can influence the order in which messages are transmitted.

   Exhibit 5.9 depicts a consumer that requests complete *customer profile* information by sequentially invoking multiple services that can provide that information collaboratively. The first step retrieves customer trading account information. Subsequently, customer savings account details are requested. And finally, customer checking account data are transmitted back to the requester.

2. *Same-time delivery pattern.* Simultaneous message routing is suited for parallel broadcasting of information to multiple subscribers and can match routing scenarios that do not require particular sequences of message transmissions. Additionally, this pattern supports process and service orchestrations and work flows where there are no dependencies between successive message and transaction invocations.

   Exhibit 5.10 illustrates the *same-time delivery pattern.* Market news and events are transmitted by the *market news service* to three different subscribers: a portal consumer that periodically publishes stock market events to its clients; a consumer that services other producers; and a pervasive wireless facility that feeds market news to its cellular phone consumer community. This example utilizes the *service bus transportation pattern* to implement this parallel message delivery pattern efficiently.

3. *Synchronous and asynchronous delivery patterns.* These patterns are concerned with the manner in which messages are distributed and returned to the requester.

   The *synchronous delivery pattern* describes a messaging model where the requestor must wait until a response is received. This blocking mode ensures an orderly sequence of

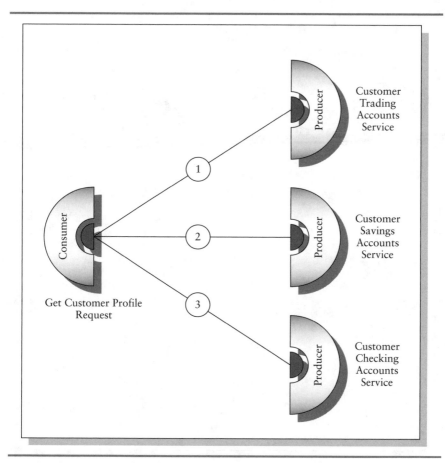

EXHIBIT 5.9 In-Order Delivery Pattern

transaction exchange and provides a schedule for returned messages. Blocking operations associated with synchronous delivery patterns may result in service delinquencies and degradation in performance.

The *asynchronous delivery pattern* enables consumers to exchange messages with their producers without halting their operations until responses are accepted and with no disturbance to their normal operations. This pattern reduces dependency on services and enhances their performance. Because the received messages do not correspond to the sequence of the transmitted ones, consumers and producers must ensure the proper content matching. Message

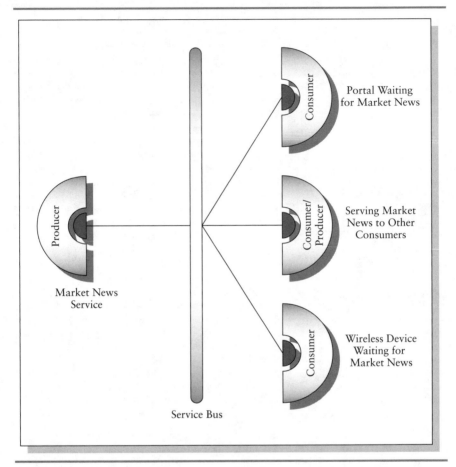

EXHIBIT 5.10   Same-Time Delivery Pattern

correlation features of messaging platforms address this requirement transparently for consumers and providers. Asynchronous messaging provides another level of loose coupling in the SOA. When combined with intermediaries and document-style services, more agility is introduced into the services architecture.

Process Flow Principle

Business processes, business affiliation, interaction and collaboration of the participating parties, technical requirements, and environmental configurations (e.g., network and security implementations) influence the process flow of service integration. Integration process flow is denoted by conversation and behavioral activities that service producers and consumers are engaged in. Conversations between participating parties are usually bidirectional in nature. In some instances, the design of services does not permit replies to consumers. Other forms of processes can be manifested in direct or indirect communication styles.

Four main patterns illustrate the *process flow principle*:

1. *Direct conversation pattern.* This pattern describes a conversation path and process flow between two assets. The *direct conversation pattern* is the simplest process form in which messages and transactions are exchanged directly between service producers and consumers. Exhibit 5.11 depicts a car information request that is being extended by a *car consumer* to a *car service*. The response is then directed back to the requester without being transmitted to other participants for further processing.
2. *Indirect conversation pattern.* This pattern depicts transaction and message redirection to a number of service consumers or producers to complete a single transaction. Exhibit 5.12 illustrates a

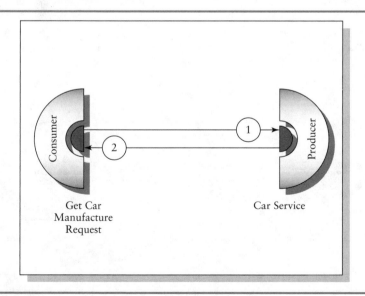

EXHIBIT 5.11   Direct Conversation Pattern

single transaction that is being processed and completed by three different services: *name and address service, open new account service,* and a *credit verification service.* A final notification will be received from the last service that was involved in this transaction.

3. *One-way message transmission pattern.* One-way message transmissions occur when receiving parties do not reply to transmitted requests for the purpose of reducing unnecessary round-trip conversations, saving network resources, avoiding unwanted acknowledgments, or complying with specific message and transaction design standards. This is a fire-and-forget model. Exhibit 5.13 illustrates this idea. A producer sends alerts to its subscribed consumer, yet the listener party terminates.

4. *Two-way conversation pattern.* A two-way service conversation is the most common communication pattern. Returning transaction values or acknowledgments that are designed to indicate

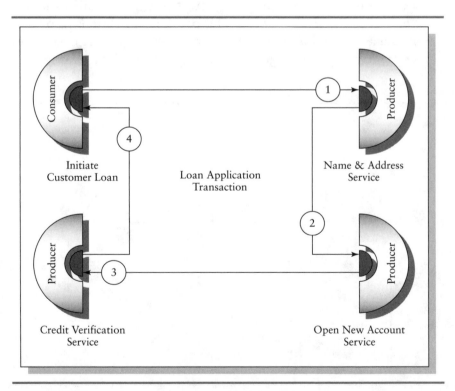

EXHIBIT 5.12   Indirect Conversation Pattern

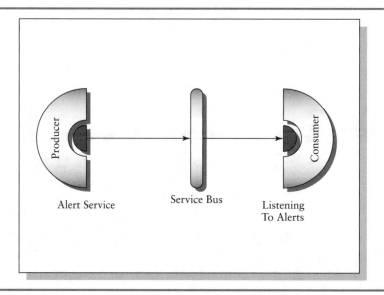

EXHIBIT 5.13   One-Way Conversation Pattern, Utilizing Service Bus

success or failure status always follows transmissions of messages. Exhibit 5.14 illustrates a *security profile service* that returns users' security information upon consumer request.

Data and Transformation Principles

Concepts such as customized treatment of data types, template-driven approaches, metadata-driven and rule-based frameworks can be found in intermediary products such as hubs and gateways that provide data transformation and transportation facilities.[4] A variety of integration capabilities define the nature of integration, transformation, and conversion of data that are exchanged between service consumers and producers:

- *Data integration offloading.* Data integration and transformation tasks should be assigned to intermediaries such as hubs, gateways, service buses, and supporting middleware. Service producers and consumers should be concerned only with business

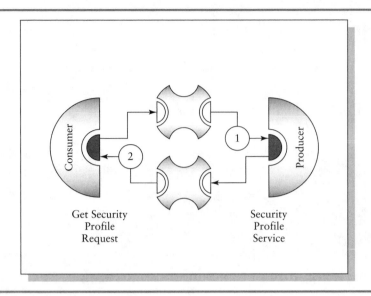

EXHIBIT 5.14   Two-Way Conversation Pattern, Utilizing Intermediaries

logic and process execution, and should be exempted from data
and protocol transformation responsibilities.

■ *Template-driven data model.* Intermediaries, integration brokers,
and messaging buses should provide design-time tools to enable
the creation of canonical data models and schemas that comply
with specific data transformation requirements and integration
needs. Organizations should generalize and abstract these models
to a reusable extent and establish an organizational base model
for future integration initiatives.

■ *Customized treatment of data types.* Integration tools, data conversion, and transformation facilities provided by intermediaries,
brokers, and message buses should support separation of data
types and recognize their characteristics and their specific formats. Data types should not be treated generically.

■ *Metadata-driven and rules-based framework.* Metadata frameworks should be used to enable the configuration, administration, and customization of data integration, transformation,
and translation. Rules and declarative approaches should facilitate integration automation and control data merging and
conversions.

■ *Data integration integrity*. Data that are exchanged between service consumers and producers should be reliable, complete, and agreed on. The data should reflect the single version of the truth.

SERVICE INTEGRATION DESIGN

The *service integration design* provides methods, guidance, and processes to facilitate service integration design and architecture. It is a step-by-step approach to combining services and enabling their interaction in an SOA network. It encourages analysis of the problem domain, organizational concerns, and business abstractions (i.e., concepts and processes) that are embedded in services. Furthermore, successful integration design should be based on knowledge of the business and technology operating environments as well as awareness of the solution domain milestones, goals, technical specifications, and roadmaps. Characteristics of service producers and consumers, and their functionality and technological composition, should be examined prior to integration design activities.

Design of service integration is based on establishing relationships between services in the SOA. This is an evolutionary approach to combining and executing business processes in the form of services connected via messages exchanged during service producer and consumer conversations. Thus, consumption capacity, resource planning, dependency, and asset reusability are all important parameters and necessary inputs into the integration design process.

A service integration design blueprint is the target outcome of this exercise. The participating parties will be accommodated on this integration map, in which consumer-provider relationships and message transportation patterns will provide a baseline for subsequent modeling activities.

Service Integration Design Process

The service integration design process is comprised of four major initiatives, which are based on the *service integration* principles. This process is iterative. The design process ends when the architecture solution is completely expressed and validated against technological specifications. The first phase, the *service integration relationship,* identifies service associations in SOA environments. The *service integration transportation definition* phase identifies message transmitters and conversation enablers. The *service integration delivery definition* follows connectivity and message distribution patterns, and finally, the *service integration process flow definition* phase identifies message paths and directions of message traffic. Data integration principles should be applied throughout all phases. Exhibit 5.15 describes the service integration design process.

Define Service Integration Relationship

Relationships among services, consumers, and providers are based on their combined functionality and the business processes that they execute. Other service integration considerations contribute to the consumer-provider relationship discovery process, such as IT architecture considerations, enabling middleware and related service infrastructure, and SOA network collaboration requirements. Exhibit 5.16 illustrates an integration relationship process, which starts with the integration analysis step, continues with a transaction identification activity, and ends with the establishment of integration

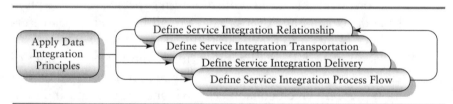

EXHIBIT 5.15   Service Integration Design Process

EXHIBIT 5.16   Service Integration Relationship Establishment Process

asset relationships. Integration relationships should follow the next three steps:

1. *Perform integration analysis.* These analysis tasks examine business transactions and strategic business processes and explore services offered to consumers via published public or private service interfaces, service descriptions, and service capacity and consumption capabilities. Additional design and architecture artifacts, such as underlying code, sequence diagrams, state charts, and collaboration diagrams, may augment the integration analysis phase.
2. *Identify transaction ownership and partnership.* Identify message and transaction exchange participants. Transactions ownership should be classified based on service provider and consumer responsibilities as well as business and technological requirements.
3. *Establish integration asset relationship.* An integration association diagram should be provided to illustrate transaction relationships that take place between service consumers and producers by employing the *service integration strategy* principle patterns discussed earlier. This diagram resembles a basic UML domain model diagram that expresses business relationships by cardinality or multiplicity notations. However, the intention here is to elaborate on aspects of integration relationships that depict physical service associations in the context of transaction ownership and sharing of responsibilities in the actual integration environment. Exhibit 5.17 represents an integration relationship diagram that illustrates a loan processing transaction. *One-to-one* and *one-to-many service integration strategy* integration patterns are employed. The owners of this transaction are:

- *Loan administrator portal.* Portal to be used by loan requesting consumers
- *Loan originator service.* Responsible for managing this transaction
- *New account service.* Responsible for opening new loan accounts
- *Loan application service.* Responsible for processing new loan applications
- *Credit verifier service.* Authenticates customers
- *Letter of credit processor service.* Responsible for issuing customers with credit commitment documents

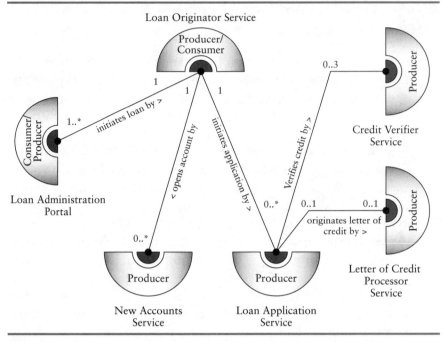

EXHIBIT 5.17 Loan Processing Transaction Relationship Diagram

Define Service Integration Transportation Mechanisms

This phase is concerned with baseline services infrastructure and middleware facilities that enable message transmission and conversations. The participating parties are assigned integration transportation duties. Intermediary-based platforms augment services with additional capabilities such as security, data transformation, message routing, and other policy enforcement tasks. Additionally, data integration principles should be utilized when planning and defining transportation utilization. Exhibit 5.18 depicts the service integration transportation mechanism process. It first suggests determining service responsibilities, next, assigning duties to intermediaries, and finally, providing a transportation integration map.

Three steps should be followed to define the transport requirements for services in your SOA:

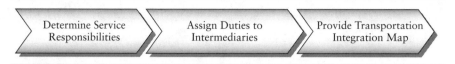

EXHIBIT 5.18   Service Integration Transportation Mechanisms Process

1. *Determine service responsibilities.* Assign individual and collaborative responsibilities to participating service providers and consumers in transactions or message exchanges. These duties identify services requirements in the context of the integration map, their relative weighting and importance in the context of message transmissions, resource allocation, access and security, and related factors. Furthermore, this step enables the discovery and incorporation of utility services, such as security providers, broadcasters, and other commercial services and products.

2. *Assign duties to intermediaries.* Determine responsibilities of integration intermediaries such as hubs, brokers, and gateways. Identify their ability to perform and facilitate message interception and manipulation activities, such as data transformation, load balancing and workload management, security enablement, and policy enforcement. Additionally, establish the intermediaries' positions and their interface touch points with service consumers and producers, along with other integration facilitators.

3. *Provide a transportation integration map.* Furnish an integration transportation map by utilizing the service integration strategy principle patterns. This artifact should be comprised of collaborating services and their enabling message and transaction transportation mechanisms. Exhibit 5.19 depicts a service transportation integration map employing two transportation patterns—*service bus* and *broker interceptor.* These patterns serve a *loan origination* transaction that is requested by a *loan administration* portal consumer. In this scenario, intermediaries perform authentication and authorization, SLA enforcement, data transformation, and message routing. The *service bus pattern* is used twice to conceptualize the broadcasting of loan rates by the *loan rates service* and depict credit processing by the credit *verifier service* and the *Letter of Credit processor service.*

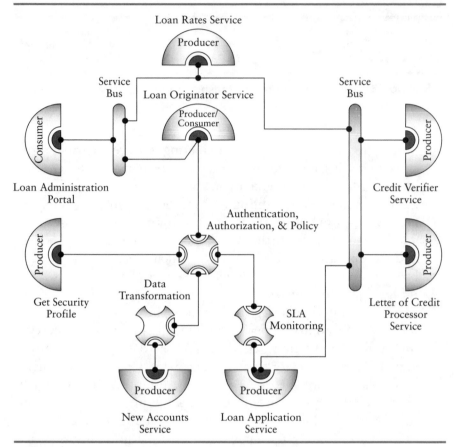

EXHIBIT 5.19   Service Integration Transportation Map

Define Service Integration Delivery

The *integration delivery* phase is mainly concerned with the mechanisms of workload management, load balancing and failover, and message distribution and routing. Messages can be delivered sequentially, in parallel, synchronously, or asynchronously. Message delivery methods depend on particular implementation needs and requirements, network configurations that enable routing mechanisms, and message distribution capabilities of services or intermediaries. Exhibit 5.20 describes a service integration delivery process that facilitates the definition of message distribution in the organization and identifies

EXHIBIT 5.20 Integration Delivery Definition Process

the parties that participate in message distribution. This process requires an integration delivery map.

Three steps should be followed in determining the service integration delivery requirements for your SOA:

1. *Determine message distribution needs.* This step requires inspection of service producers', consumers', and intermediaries' (e.g. brokers, hubs, gateways) delivery requirements. Technological requirements and specifications help identify and depict delivery characteristics of transactions and messages and match them against sequential, parallel, asynchronous, or synchronous delivery patterns. Subsequently, these templates can assist with creation of service integration delivery maps.

2. *Determine delivery responsible parties.* Assign delivery duties to service consumers, producers, and their intermediaries. The recommended approach is to shift delivery and distribution of message responsibilities from service producers or consumers to intermediaries such as hubs, gateways, or service bus middleware.

3. *Provide a delivery map.* Work with the *service integration strategy* principle integration patterns to plan the overall delivery method of services. A delivery map can be combined with the service transportation map to illustrate services and intermediary capabilities, and depict a more generic view of intended, integrated, and distributed environments. Exhibit 5.19 depicts integration delivery patterns based on transaction activities and their characteristics. *Same-time delivery* pattern is employed by the *loan rates* service, which places loan rates in two different service bus middleware installations. The *in-order delivery* pattern is used by the *loan originator service*, which employs an intermediary to first authenticate and authorize this transaction by routing requests to the security service, then engage the *new accounts service* and the *loan application service*, respectively.

Define Service Integration Process Flow

This phase is concerned with message and process orchestration and choreography utilizing transportation mechanisms. Efficient approaches to message and transaction flows should employ *service integration strategy* work flow patterns. Design of integration process flows and establishment of messages paths should be centered on distribution effectiveness of data, discovering best routes between service producers and consumers, and leveraging reusability of messaging facilities such as intermediaries and other related middleware infrastructure. Exhibit 5.21 illustrates definition activities of integration process flow by identifying proper network routes, verifying network environment support, and employing integration work flow patterns.

Follow these three steps in determining the service integration flow requirements for your SOA:

1. *Establish network routes.* Provide the best possible message paths in service topology environments, leveraging reusability of transportation facilities. This step will assist with in-depth analysis of security mechanisms and configurations, proxies, monitoring agents, and potential intercepting applications. Furthermore, identify and examine technology barriers to facilitate better consumer access and improved visibility of services.
2. *Verify network and environment support.* Validate network topology and environmental capacity as well as routing capabilities that support required network traffic and message exchange bandwidth. Outputs of this step should be service topology resource allocation, service capacity, and consumption planning.
3. *Employ integration work flow patterns.* Utilize *service integration strategy* deployment and integration patterns to facilitate process flow of messages and transactions. Exhibit 5.22 depicts service integration process flow of a *loan origination* transaction.

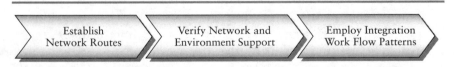

EXHIBIT 5.21   Definition of Integration Process Flow

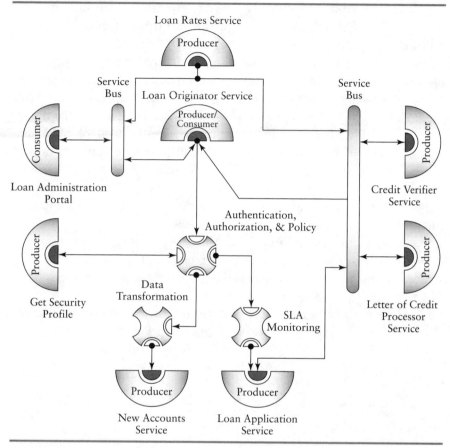

EXHIBIT 5.22   Service Integration Process Flow

The illustrated routes reflect network capabilities and consumption rates of services, intermediaries, and service bus middleware products.

SERVICE INTEGRATION MODELING

The *service integration modeling component* is a conceptual model that supports integration techniques through the introduction of backbone messaging infrastructure facilities. Various integration tools and capabilities simplify service integration initiatives since they can be acquired, assembled, installed, and configured to satisfy all integration design requirements.

Six different types of service integration enablement mechanisms facilitate message routing and conversational mechanisms: *transporters, connectors, governors, transformers, dispatchers,* and *service facilitators.* They provide the backbone and integration instrumentation to assist with the assembly and the construction of SOA networks. Integrating services and creating efficient consumer-producer interaction depends on a variety of SOA environmental factors, such as supporting network infrastructure, consumption capacity of exposed services, and enabling service infrastructure, which includes intermediaries, and transportation facilities.

As depicted in Exhibit 5.23, the *service integration modeling component* provides two major base facilities to assist with the construction of integrated and collaborative service communities:

1. *Integration backbone.* The integration backbone is comprised of governing rules and work flow instrumentation, messaging and transaction transportation platforms, transmission devices, and message delivery and distribution mechanisms.

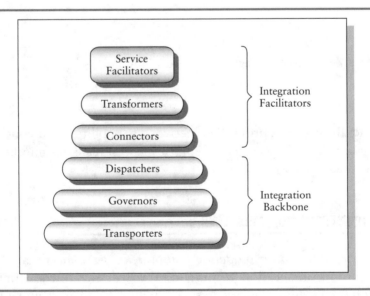

EXHIBIT 5.23   Service Integration Backbone and Facilitators

2. *Integration facilitators.* Integration facilitators provide connectivity mechanisms, data transformation and conversion aids, and SOA enablement solutions such as service registries and metadata repositories.

Service Integration Modeling Notation

Exhibit 5.24 illustrates *assets,* *integration backbone,* and *integration facilitator* symbols that are employed during service integration modeling initiatives. They identify integration construction elements that are employed to express formal service deployment diagrams and maps.

Service Integration Backbone Builders

Backbone integration elements enable efficient transportation of messages, management and distribution of transactions, governing rules, and message-handling policies. They are the driving engines

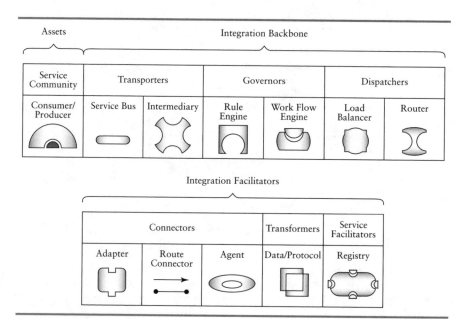

EXHIBIT 5.24   Service Integration Notation

behind the dynamic flow of messages and conversations between service consumers and producers, and also provide orchestration and choreography support by coordinating activities and maintaining service and process coexistence and harmony.

Transporters There are two major types of transporters, which provide message interception, transmission, and manipulation facilities: service bus and intermediaries. These are illustrated in Exhibit 5.25.

A *service bus* (often referred as an enterprise service bus, or ESB[5]) is a middleware transportation enabler that provides a variety of features to manage message and transaction traffic. Service buses support loose-coupling architectural concepts by offloading service consumer and producer interaction functions such as routing, service orchestration, security, data transformation, and protocol conversion. To attain maximum service reusability, service bus solutions reduce service dependencies and encourage efficient distribution of services. Service bus facilities can handle high volumes of transactions and support guaranteed delivery and durability of messages. They can support a variety of communication methods and integration patterns, such as *one-way, two-way, direct* and *indirect, asynchronous,*

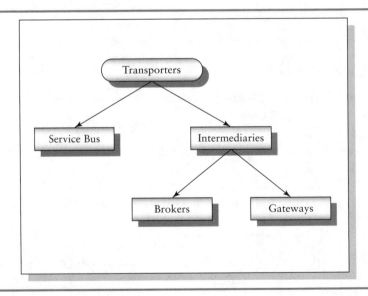

EXHIBIT 5.25 Transporters

and *synchronous*. Service bus frameworks can provide management and work flow tools to administer message routing, transmission flows, and business processes.

In environments where availability and scalability of service producers are a concern, service bus platforms can assist with interoperability, increase reusability, and reduce implementation complexities. Furthermore, service transportation enablers can be scaled, by clustering for example, to satisfy increased demand for service communication bandwidth and large transaction volumes between participating parties. Exhibit 5.26 depicts an interoperability solution that enables a mainframe system to utilize .NET and J2EE services by leveraging a centralized service bus that provides seamless and reliable communications.

Intermediaries are message interceptors that provide a wide array of message transmission, routing, and data manipulation functions. Intermediaries are known by different names, such as interceptors, brokers, hubs, and gateways. Their duties can overlap with service bus and services management implementations, but intermediaries tend to provide more granular services and largely do not support elaborate queuing systems that service buses are designed for.

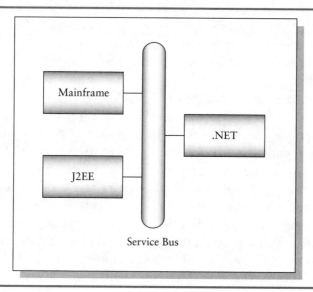

EXHIBIT 5.26   Interoperability by Service Bus

Intermediaries, while usually deployed as an integral component of services management and SOA run-time stacks, are often leveraged by policy engines and SOA governance solutions, whereby they employ rules engines and policy evaluation algorithms to enforce standards and services policies. They also act as services performance "sensors" and message delivery mechanisms by supporting load balancing and failover, service monitoring and management, and workload management features to manage traffic and efficient message delivery.

Intermediaries support decoupled security and policy enforcement models in SOA networks. For example, intermediaries can provide security enforcement functionality, which is vital to service operations. They can contribute to credential verification, enable digital signatures and certificates by employing industry-standard enabling technologies such as X. 509 and SAML assertions, and facilitate consumer authentication and authorization activities. Furthermore, intermediaries can provide SOA governance and policy enforcement, including service-level agreement monitoring, service performance, and consumption monitoring as well as alerts and alarm facilities, audit trail mechanisms, and management reporting.

Data transformation is an essential process that is performed on incoming and outgoing messages. Format reliability, schema validation, and data integrity are fundamental to service consumers and producers. These transformation processes ensure the fluency of consumer-provider conversations. Intermediaries provide protocol conversions to increase interoperability and enhance communication across heterogeneous environments. An example of this is a SOAP conversion to RMI/IIP and JMS, or SNA to HTTP.

Some vendors provide gateways that offer customization and adaptor capabilities in the form of application programming interfaces (APIs), and also provide management tools that can fill security gaps, and enable dynamic service binding and searching capabilities. Gateways mainly enable legacy consumers and producers that operate on proprietary platforms to communicate with external service consumers and producers that do not share their technology.

Intermediaries can be chained for the purpose of process and function decoupling. They can reside between service consumers and producers, or be deployed on service end points and act as agents. Exhibit 5.27 depicts a typical intermediary-based deployment. A banking portal that operates on a .NET platform provides branch-searching

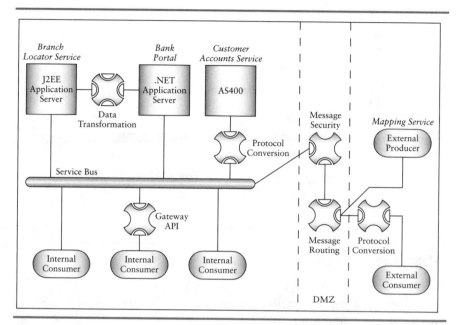

EXHIBIT 5.27 Intermediaries and Service Bus Integration Scenario

services to its base consumers. The actual searching is performed on the JAVA J2EE application server. The *mapping* service provider is an external entity. Intermediaries in this example provide data transformation, protocol conversion, message security, and message routing functionality.

Governors Governing messages and transaction flows are types of responsibilities that should be offloaded from service functionality. By most standards, services should focus on processing business logic and related operations while leveraging standalone rules engines, orchestration, and work flow platforms to perform those activities. Services in general should not implement complex inference algorithms, orchestration, or work flow logic within the service. Rules engines and work flow management tools are governing products that can control message routing and influence transaction work flows. They can assist services by operating externally or internally. Externally, they are centrally positioned and accessible by entire service communities. Internally, they are dedicated, conform to service policies, and take part in internal governance activities. Exhibit 5.28

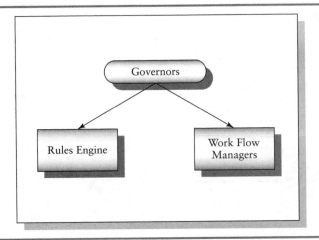

Exhibit 5.28   Governors

illustrates service integration governing mechanisms—rules engines and work flow managers.

Two service integration governor mechanisms should be considered when modeling SOA integrated environments:

1. *Rules engines.* Rules engines are decision support solutions that can provide binary and context outputs based on sets of business rules stored in their repositories and owned by line of business (LOB) personnel who are responsible for rule definition, modification, enhancements, and maintenance utilizing out-of-the-box rule orchestration and management capabilities. Rules engines that take part in service integration initiatives should be configured to provide context-based routing services.

2. *Work flow engines.* Work flow engines manage the integration and orchestration between services, and control routing and flow of messages and transactions in service communities. Work flow engines provide state, context, and support for long-running transactions involving atomic or composite services. Work flow engines include orchestration solutions based on BPEL and support choreographed transactions between organizations. They are activated by process rules that provide event schedules and logic routing. Work flow engines manage steps, streams, and sequences of occurrences, and incorporate message delivery mechanisms.

Some work flow management products offer data and protocol transformation functionality much like intermediaries do.

Dispatchers   Dispatchers are largely concerned with software delivery processes and software message routing mechanisms as depicted in Exhibit 5.29. They can be embedded in rules engines, work flow managers, service bus middleware, or intermediaries. Dispatchers are tuned to service consumption rates and can be configured to handle different styles of message delivery behaviors. Delivery of messages should be controlled and managed by resource capacity and allocation governing policies that apply to service community requirements.

Services can utilize two major types of dispatchers:

1. *Load balancers.* These are dispatching mechanisms that control flow of messages based on preconfigured parameters, taking into account SLAs, service consumption capacity rates, and operating environment constraints and influences such as network bandwidth and hardware configurations. They are tuned to real-time occurrences and events, enabling message rerouting to alternate services and devices.

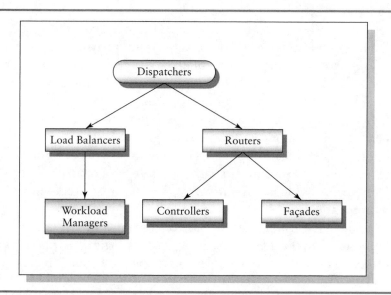

EXHIBIT 5.29   Dispatchers

Workload management facilities are a type of load balancer, capable of managing and routing flow of traffic to services to avoid service delinquencies and time-out conditions. They are embedded in intermediaries and service bus middleware, and can be part of service hosting frameworks and containers such as application servers, Web servers, and proxies. They have failover capabilities, and their dispatching behavior can be configured and set to a variety of delivery modes such as *round robin, random,* and *weighted.* Horizontally and vertically scaled services can benefit from this diversity of delivery approaches and provide service coverage to high-volume transaction consumers. One of the most effective delivery modes is the *weighted* approach, which monitors message volumes to comply with service capacity consumption rates. For example, the delivery weight of messages can be set to a high value for services that are installed on powerful servers, or conversely, low-consumption-rate environments can be treated in the opposite fashion.

2. *Service routers.* Service routers are responsible for delivering messages to participating parties based on built-in logic that controls the process flow. Controllers and service facades perform the matching between incoming requests and their end points. They invoke *service locators,* which have the knowledge to identify required services.

   Controllers are state machines. They are central dispatching facilities that invoke a set of actions to provide efficient disbursement of requests. *Controllers* are preprogrammed and preconfigured to facilitate rapid deployment and maintenance.

   Facades are business routers that direct messages to business logic. They hide complex service implementations and interdependencies, minimize their exposure, and simplify access to underlying service components by enabling usage of public interfaces. Standardization of central remote procedure calls to services can provide easier software customization, versioning, and maintenance.

   Dependencies imposed by service consumers on producers can be reduced by *facade* layers, which act as logical partitions positioned between business implementations (embedded in services), and *facade* elements, which manage message distributions. Both are depicted in Exhibit 5.30. Establishing standard interfaces

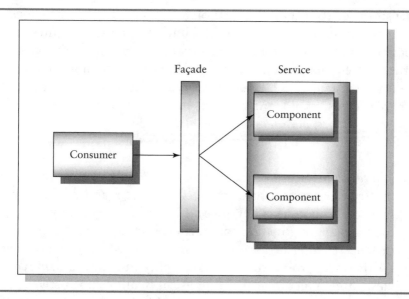

EXHIBIT 5.30 Facade Implementation

between service consumers and producers eliminates the need for direct interactions between these message exchange parties by establishing coarse-grained service access and, as a result, reduces network traffic by restricting calls to finer-grained service functions.

Service Integration Facilitators

Service integration facilitators rely on and are supported by existing integration backbone elements such as *transporters, governors,* and *dispatchers.* They enable connectivity between participating parities, assist with data and protocol transformation, provide service consumers with searching and discovery capabilities, and enable publishing and registration of services.

Connectors   *Connectors* enable parties to exchange messages with service communities and facilitate communications with partners that may not share common technologies, platforms, or protocols. They provide logical and physical connectivity and simplify message exchange between service consumers and producers. *Connectors* can be customized to specific application needs and are often provided as modular entities that can be plugged into existing service integration facilitator platforms. Intelligent *connectors* rely on industry standards and enable customization and tailoring to support popular applications such as SAP, Seibel, Oracle, and other enterprise software platforms. Exhibit 5.31 depicts three major types of connectors: *route connectors*, *adapters*, and *agents*.

Services can utilize three types of connectors:

1. *Route connectors*. These are simple connectivity mechanisms that enable services to distribute, exchange, and facilitate message transmissions. They present routing relationships between the participating integration parties, such as service consumers, producers, intermediaries, and related messaging middleware. Furthermore, *route connectors* simplify integration deployment views and depict logical and physical relationships between service community entities. *Connectors* identify three major association types between integration parties: service producer and consumer links, conversation partners, and message delivery participants.

   Route connectors can express direct and indirect affiliations and provide visual representation of deployment blueprints. Exhibit 5.32 depicts a *connector* that links a service consumer to its two service producers through intermediaries and a message bus middleware implementation.

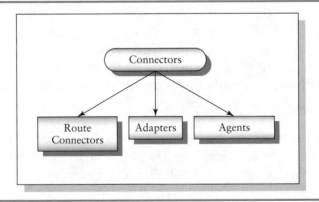

EXHIBIT 5.31   Connectors

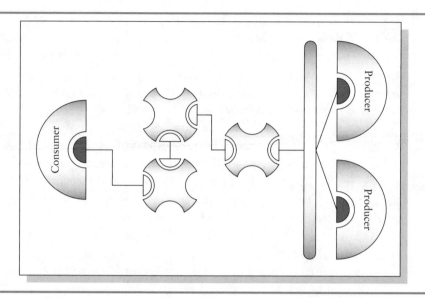

EXHIBIT 5.32   Route Connectors

2. *Adapters.* *Adapters* are *connectors* that serve as interfaces and facilitate seamless service consumer and producer communications in heterogeneous computing environments. They fill integration and interactions gaps and translate conversation dialects, such as protocols, into both unique and universal formats. They are pluggable entities that can be installed on service consumer and producer premises to enable transformation of data, validate schemas, marshal and unmarshal transmitted messages, and create a holistic view of exchanged information.

Services and third-party products that do not comply with an organization's technology-specific standards can leverage *connector* solutions by providing bridging adapters that can mitigate compatibility and interoperability concerns. *Adapters* can be supplied in different configurations, such as off-the-shelf products, vendor black-box *adapter* libraries, or *adapter* frameworks that enable customization to particular service consumers' and producers' needs.

For example, SUN offers a J2EE connector architecture (JCA) standard, which enables service consumers to communicate with various types of enterprise systems such as mainframe transaction-oriented applications and enterprise resource planning (ERP) services. Vendors can increase their product compatibility and adaptability to various environments by conforming to *connector* standards. To do so, vendors provide J2EE *connectors* that can be plugged into various application servers to enable communications with external products.

The IBM's CICS Transaction Gateway provides J2EE Connector CICS resource adapters that can access mainframes services.[6] These adapters enable real-time access to services that reside in CICS regions by invoking external call interfaces (ECI) and external presentation interfaces (EPI)—a set of APIs that enable the invocation of 3270-based transactions.

Exhibit 5.33 illustrates adapter technology that enables connectivity to a SAP R/3 system and to mainframe services. *Connector* frameworks and adapters are utilized to access these service providers.

3. *Agents. Agents* are another type of connector. They are designed to facilitate interoperability challenges in heterogeneous environments. Agents are mobile, independent, adaptable, and reactive to environment events and occurrences. They are distributed

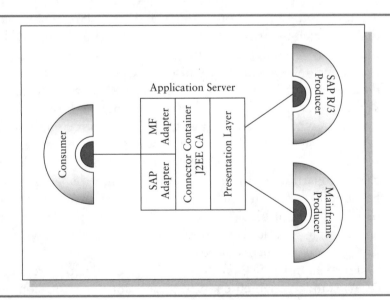

EXHIBIT 5.33   Service Adapter Technology

elements that can be installed on a variety of platforms and in different styles, such as standalone or chained (to increase peer-to-peer agent communications). *Agents* are utilized for services profiling, resource management, network management, monitoring and provisioning, tracking quality of services and consumption rates, and enforcement of SLAs.

Transformers Transformation is a vital function in a service community. Messaging platforms such as service buses and related messaging middleware, intermediaries, and *adapters* can facilitate conversions of protocols and data (as illustrated in Exhibit 5.34), enforce data integrity and schema validations, and enable flawless service producer and consumer conversations.

Transformers facilitate data conversion needs by intercepting exchanged messages, extracting their content, and transforming them to match the receiving parties' data formats. Service bus middleware, *adapters*, and intermediaries utilize contextual *metadata* and *rule-based* transformation frameworks to enable configuration and administration of their data conversion functionality and facilitate the automation of data and protocol translation, both of which are based on predefined rule sets.

Preserving the characteristics and identity of data types during transformations would require utilization of intermediaries or hubs that contain sophisticated *transformers*, which provide *customized data type treatment* methods to avoid generic treatment of data types. *Transformer* facilities should utilize *template-driven data*

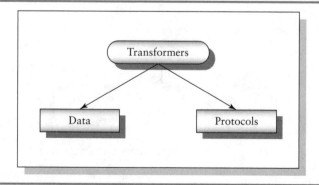

EXHIBIT 5.34   Transformers

models to control integration of data by leveraging predefined data models and schemas (see the earlier discussion of data integration principles).

The underlying transformation of data can be accomplished by a wide array of technologies, frameworks, and libraries. For example, conversion and extraction of XML content can be achieved by using eXtensible Stylesheet Language Transformations (XSLT), which is a part of the eXtensible Stylesheet Language (XSL) defined by the World Wide Web Consortium (W3C). Another example, XQuery, which is written in the XQuery language, provides query and retrieval of XML data services.

Service Facilitators *Service facilitators* constitute an integration layer that specifically addresses service environments, exposure, and access requirements. These elements provide rudimentary support that facilitates seamless business and technological activities provided by services in service communities. Thus, *discoverers, publishers, binders,* and *invokers* enable service searchability, assist with service identification, expose service interfaces, and allow service providers to publish, bind, and invoke services. As a result, service reusability can be enhanced, service consumption can accelerate, and the service consumer base can be increased. Exhibit 5.35 illustrates these three major service facilitators: *discoverers, publishers,* and *binders/invokers.*

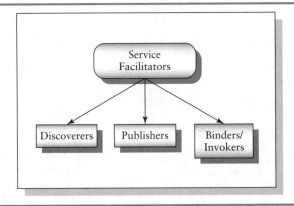

EXHIBIT 5.35 Service Facilitators

Services can make use of the three major service integration facilitators:

1. *Publishers.* Service providers publish their services to service registries that enable the discovery of published services, permit service consumers to query their repository structures, and allow retrieval of business- and service-related information by organization-specific metadata taxonomies. For example, the industry standard registry specification, universal description discovery and integration (UDDI), provides publishing, service query, and discovery tools, along with repositories and registry structures. UDDI registry vendors have recently added repositories to their solutions to enhance their functionality. Furthermore, SOA governance is also being added to UDDI solutions by managing enterprise policies and supporting distributed enforcement through the services lifecycle. In addition, service registries and metadata repositories support service version management by notifying service consumers of changes to the services they utilize. These common structures consist of service providers, and business and service technical and nontechnical information. The common elements in these structures are:

   - *BusinessEntity.* Provides description of service providers from a business perspective
   - *BusinessService.* Contains nontechnical description of services
   - *BindingTemplate.* Contains pointers to service description ports
   - *tModel.* Provides pointers to service description files

   The Java API for XML Registries (JAXR) enables service providers to utilize a registry's *lifecycle manager* to perform a variety of registry-related functions, such as publish business providers and references to their services (i.e., *saveServices* and *saveOrganizations*).[7]

   An SOA integration and deployment paradigm should grant registry accessibility, and service searching and discovery capabilities to service consumer communities. In heterogeneous environments, where compatibility of platforms, protocols, and operating systems poses integration difficulties, strategies should support federated publishing approaches, where interconnected chained registries reside on numbers of platforms and enable seamless publishing and service discovery operations.

2. *Discoverers.* *Discoverers* provide query capabilities to enable registry information searching on service providers, service descriptions, and binding information. Queries on their structures can return a rich set of data that is affiliated with business entities, their offerings, and type of services they provide. Furthermore, services can be listed based on various selected categories. For example, consumers can query a variety of XML registries, by utilizing JAXR libraries that provide searching capabilities via a rich set of interfaces that facilitate discovery of service providers and their respective services. *findOrganizations, findServices,* and *findServiceBindings* are examples of such JAXR API calls, which are typically embedded into consumer products.

3. *Service binders and invokers.* Binding and invoking services are the sole responsibility of consumers. Once a service query or service discovery request returns a satisfactory result, binding and invocation of services are the next logical step. Binders can operate both statically and dynamically. In static scenarios, usually at design time, service consumers locally retain service interface stubs and implementation descriptions. Dynamic binders acquire this information by querying registries. *Binders* and *invokers* are not deployable assets, as they are embedded in service consumer operations. Exhibit 5.36 depicts the collaboration between various *service facilitator* components. The service registry is the focal management point for service publishing, querying, and discovery. First, a service provider publishes services. Once consumers receive service information, they bind and invoke their target service producers.

Building SOA Integration Models

Modeling service integration is the art of mapping logical elements to physical entities. A top-down approach is required when building integrated service producer and consumer communities in an SOA. Thus, the environments in which services operate are fundamental to integration initiatives.

Modeling integration entails a profound understanding of the surrounding technology landscape, examining middleware capabilities,

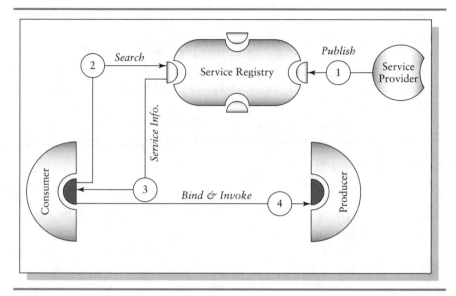

EXHIBIT 5.36   Service Facilitation

studying the characteristics of services and their clients, and complying with SLAs between the participating parties. Organizational service integration policies and standards should be followed. Capacity, consumption, and resource plans should provide guidance for the construction and integration of collaborative service environments.

Bottom-up integration approaches, such as addressing service-publishing issues or incorporating *adapters* and *connectors*, can succeed to a certain extent. Nevertheless, these methods overlook the big picture. They are tactical in nature and largely do not furnish strategic solutions to SOA and service integration challenges.

Service Integration   The SOA ecosystem in which all parties engage and collaborate is layered and hierarchical. Integration modeling efforts should be conceived as pyramids of construction initiatives. The base layers are integration foundation environments, and include elements such as networks, subnetworks, middleware, and tiers. Reusable organizational assets such as services, consumers and producers, intermediaries, and enabling integration platforms reside on the very top of the pyramid. (Consumers and producers in this sense refer to nonhuman consumers such as systems, applications, and other services.) Once positioned, these layers become an integral part of the service integration landscape and, to a large extent, depend on their surroundings.

This aggregation and containment method of integration generates an internal dependency between child and parent layers and provides a solid foundation for hosting, managing, and administering SOA interactions. Viewing these ecosystems as hierarchical and supporting building blocks can greatly simplify service-integrated environments and provide a different perspective for the achievement of integration milestones and targets.

The ultimate goal of integration work is to position an organization's reusable services on the top of the pyramid and to validate the assumptions that were made during the integration design phase. Thus, integration modeling is about proving concepts and eliminating the need for costly and time-consuming experiments. Modeling initiatives should be guided by the *service integration modeling component* design blueprints and follow the *service integration strategy component* principles and patterns.

SOA Integration Pyramid   In the integration pyramid model, *my world* is the foundation of all integration initiatives, since it identifies a specific environment for which the integration work is being done. This world is the base layer of the pyramid. All other layers are aggregated and contained, should be a part of this environment, and share its characteristics. Thus, integration is subjective to specific enterprise environments. The pyramid is a customizable model that allows the visualization of deployment and integration in a more personal and individual manner. Organizations can create their own layers and construct their distinct integration pyramids. Exhibit 5.37 depicts this idea. It illustrates a layered deployment environment that hosts a service producer on top of its integration pyramid.

Formal Service Integration Presentation   Three-dimensional displays of integrated environments are visual and easy to understand. Unfortunately, when constructing large and complex environments, they can consume space and require more work, and in some ways are counterproductive. A formal presentation of integrated environments can simplify these constructs and still express the SOA ecosystem in which services operate. A more compact, compressed, and flattened

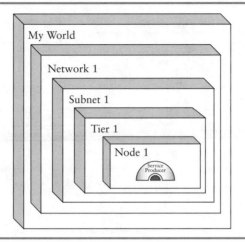

EXHIBIT 5.37   SOA Integration Pyramid

view would eliminate the three-dimensional effect and provide a simpler view in which all levels can be observed, their behaviors captured, and their characteristics identified. Such a blueprint model can express larger SOA scenarios, formalize service integration model views, and better depict logical-to-physical mapping aspects. Exhibit 5.38 depicts this concept. It is the formalized representation of Exhibit 5.37.

Service Integration Modeling Process   The service integration modeling process is comprised of five rudimentary steps. These modeling activities map reusable assets to their environments to ensure proper communications and interactions between service producers and consumers, intermediaries, middleware products, networks and hardware assets. This SOA network architecture building exercise yields a formal deployment blueprint that can be employed to construct efficient and reusable service environments. These five steps outline the service integration process:

Step 1. Define integration environment. Define base operating environments for services and their supporting entities.

Step 2. Position reusable assets. Position services in integrated environments.

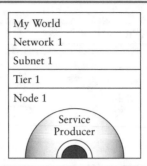

EXHIBIT 5.38   Formal Service Integration Model Diagram

Step 3. Define asset touch points. Identify *adapters* and *agents* that are employed by services.

Step 4. Incorporate delivery methods. Identify routing, dispatching, and message distribution mechanisms.

Step 5. Add transportation paths. Discover routing paths in designated service environments.

Exhibit 5.39 depicts this five-step process.

The following sections elaborate on the service integration modeling process and introduce a step-by-step modeling methodology that captures the essence of service architecture activities.

Step 1: Define Service Integration Environments   A logical approach to model service integration would be to position reusable organizational assets on the top of the pyramid and start connecting the dots. However, first the supporting environment must exist. Service consumers, producers, and services infrastructure cannot operate in a vacuum. A construction foundation should support further building activities and reflect organization environment characteristics.

My world is the fundamental concept of this activity. It provides a starting point and defines the service integration boundary for this initiative. It is possible to create multiple worlds, if these environments extend beyond the initial one. *Their world* can define other deployment regions and other worlds that collaborate with *my world*.

Construction of layered environments demands the assembly of strong foundations first. Thus, supporting entities should be positioned

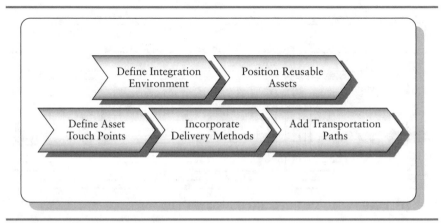

EXHIBIT 5.39 Service Integration Modeling Process

initially. For example, in many installations, enterprise networks can be conceived as the preliminary building blocks and pillars of integration and deployment. Subsequently, aggregated entities, such as subnetworks, tiers, clusters, service, and middleware, should be defined and layered just as real pyramids are constructed.

Step 2: Position Reusable Assets   Enterprise services should be positioned on the top layer of the integration pyramid and be recognized as the integration driving forces. They are provided with easier access, are exposed to participating parties, and are reusable across enterprise organizations. Service consumers and producers and service bus middleware and intermediaries are major contenders for placement in the top layer. They are business and technology solution providers that must receive the most attention from an organization. Exhibit 5.40 depicts a combined network environment, subnetworks, and four nodes that support the deployment of a service producer, an intermediary, a message bus, and a service consumer.

Exhibit 5.41 represents the same configuration in a formal deployment blueprint.

Step 3: Define Asset Touch Points   Collaborating services should be interconnected. They depend on their peers and in some cases *are not* self-sufficient and independent. A service integration model diagram should illustrate and elaborate on how assets are associated and

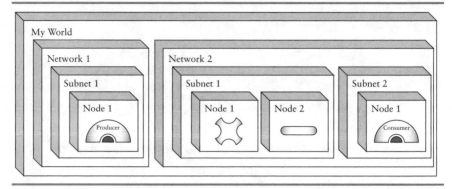

EXHIBIT 5.40   Service Integration Model Diagram

My World			
Network 1	Network 2		
Subnet 1	Subnet 1		Subnet 2
Node 1	Node 1	Node 2	Node 1
Producer			Consumer

EXHIBIT 5.41   Formal Service Integration Model Diagram

depict touch-point mechanisms that are employed to facilitate their dependencies.

Integration practices can offer a wide array of connection facilitators. Touch points are intersections or adjacent points between organizational assets and their connectors. The *touch-point methods layer* is a region where service integration *connectors* can be utilized. *Adapters* and *agents* are the main players in this section. They should facilitate integration of assets on a more granular level and follow vendor-specific installation and configuration best practices. Exhibit 5.42 illustrates three major integration layers:

1. *Environment layer.* Foundation entities, such as networks, subnets, and nodes

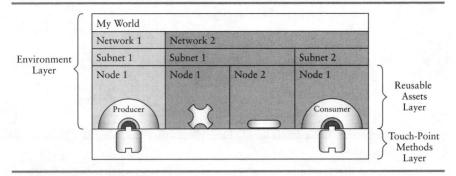

EXHIBIT 5.42   Touch-Points Method Layer

2. *Reusable asset layer.* Service producers and consumers, intermediaries, and service bus middleware
3. *Touch-point methods layer.* Adapters section

Step 4: Incorporate Delivery Methods   Delivery methods are important for
controlling the scalability and the availability of deployed services.
These delivery methods identify dispatching mechanisms in integration model diagrams. Dispatchers reside in the *delivery methods
layer.* They are comprised of software *routers* and *load balancers* that
control the manner in which messages are dispatched to various services. *Load balancers,* such as *workload managers,* and routers—
controllers and *facades*—can be built-in capabilities of commercial
products, applications, or even services. Nevertheless, in the *delivery
methods layer,* these mechanisms should be identified and described
separately since they are a crucial part of a well-functioning SOA
integrated environment. Exhibit 5.43 depicts a *delivery method layer*
that is comprised of a load balancer.

Step 5: Add Transportation Path   And finally, the path to the participating
organizational assets should be identified in the *transportation path
layer* region of the integration blueprint. This layer is comprised of
route connectors that specify the process flow and the direction of
messages and transaction transmissions in an SOA ecosystem utilizing network connectivity, and environment transportation enablers
and delivery methods.

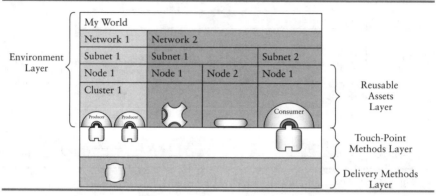

EXHIBIT 5.43   Delivery Methods Layer

Exhibit 5.44 presents a *two-way* conversation pattern. A consumer (on network 2/subnet 2/node 1) posts a request on a service bus (on *network 2/subnet 1/node 2*), which then is routed to an intermediary that performs data transformation (on *network 2/subnet 1/node 1*), and then activates a load balancer (located in the delivery method layer), which delivers messages to a vertically scaled service producer cluster (deployed on *network 1/subnet 1/node 1/vertical cluster 1*). The response is sent back to the same service bus (on *node 2*), and waits until the service consumer (on *network 2/subnet 2/node 1*) retrieves it.

SERVICE PRODUCT MAPPING COMPONENT: INTEGRATION PRODUCT MAPPING STRATEGY

Integration Product Mapping Strategies

SOA integration and enablement products should be assessed against a set of organization product evaluation and adaptation standards. The product mapping process should be guided by business and technological requirements as well as by the formal organizational integration model. This top-down approach to integration should be driven by mapping integration requirements to product offerings. In subsequent steps, product manufacturers should provide agility certificates to prove the quality, compatibility, and stability of their products.

Products should not be the driving forces behind integration projects. This is a bottom-up approach that results in very narrow views

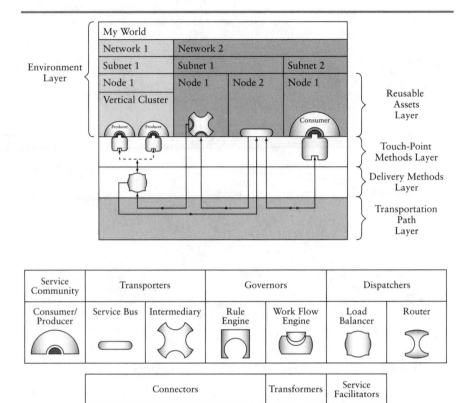

EXHIBIT 5.44   Transportation Path Layer

of product evaluation and selection initiatives, and may ultimately only provide short-term tactical solutions.

Integration products should be selected based on organizational integration strategies as reflected in Exhibit 5.45.

A product features and concepts checklist should be used to verify and confirm products against your organization's SOA product requirements. A checklist example follows.

✔ *Accommodation of business requirements.* Provide mechanisms to implement and maintain business requirements and rules.

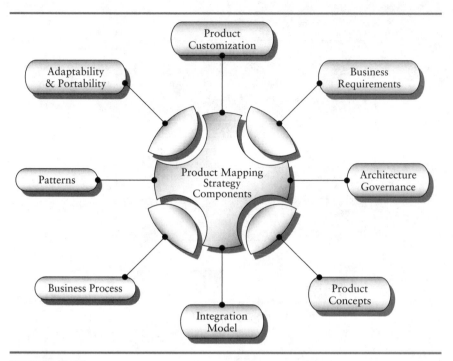

EXHIBIT 5.45   Product Mapping Strategy Components

✔ *Compliance with architecture governance.* Comply with architecture governance policies, best practices, and standards of organizations.

✔ *Facilitation of integration model.* Adhere to organization service integration model requirements.

✔ *Facilitate business processes.* Provide support for business rules, orchestration, choreography, and work flow and business process management functionality to service consumers and producers.

✔ *Adhere to integration patterns.* Enable service consumer and producer interaction and collaborations based on integration model patterns.

✔ *Adaptability and portability.* Fit in the integrated environments and support service community activities and interactions.

✔ *Furnish customized mapping.* Provide product mapping and adaptation capabilities to organization integration requirements model.

What Certification Should Vendors Provide?

Product mapping can be an arduous process that may not facilitate rapid product evaluation and their compatibility with your current IT environments and service integration requirements. In most cases, vendors provide high-level architecture blueprints and operating guides. The underlying problems arise down the road, when vendor products do not communicate with others and their reusability decreases with time. In some cases, products fail to provide customization capabilities, and therefore the return on these investments diminishes.

In a rapidly evolving SOA and services industry, vendors should provide agility certificates that prove their product's ability to adapt and be portable across a range of current, anticipated, and even unanticipated organizational needs. Providing these certificates is the sole responsibility of product manufacturers, and should be verified during organization product evaluation, selection, implementation, and adaptation processes.

Use this product agility certificate checklist in the product evaluation, selection, and negotiation phases, and even during request for information before formally engaging with short-listed vendors.

✔ Product service-level agreement offerings

✔ Product capability certificate, such as capacity and consumption rates

✔ Reusability factor of involved products

✔ Integration touch points, such as inventory of adapters, connectors, and their architecture capabilities

✔ Delivery methods of the products, such as routing and workload management

✔ Product quality certificate, which demonstrates its stability, reliability, and availability

✔ Management run-book and operational procedures

✔ Benchmarks and market feature comparisons

✔ Interoperability certificate, such as protocols, operating systems, and platforms compatibility

✔ Enabling expandability APIs and data transformation format capabilities

✔ Product security certificate

SUMMARY

This chapter provides an in-depth service integration methodology, and depicts crucial elements of service integration enablers. The path to success is emphasized by various integration principles, patterns, and best practices that can simplify and abstract complexities of today's integrated computing environments. Furthermore, the proposed service integration processes can facilitate establishing new organizational integration strategies, and provide a solid foundation for the formation of service communities that provide seamless execution of business transactions.

This integration model introduces a modeling approach that treats services environments and their surroundings as dynamic ecosystems that are reusable and can span heterogeneous platforms and operating systems boundaries. This methodological approach to modeling service integration can facilitate a self-consuming service community that adheres to SOA interoperability principles and complies with reusability fundamentals.

NOTES

1. Stephen T. Albin, *The Art of Software Architecture* (Hoboken, NJ: John Wiley & Sons, Inc., 2003), p. 117.
2. Eric Newcomer and Greg Lomow, *Understanding SOA with Web Services* (Addison-Wesley, 2005), p. 166.
3. "Patterns: Service-Oriented Architecture and Web Services," IBM RedBook SG24- 6303-00, April 2004, pp. 46–69.
4. Sudhir Jah, "Customer Data Integration: Why Application Vendors Are Inadequate. A New Approach to Building Open Customer Hubs" (Siperian Corporation, 2005).
5. Martin Keen et al., "Patterns: Implementing an SOA Using an Enterprise Service Bus," IBM RedBook SG24-6346-00, July 2004, pp. 26–29.
6. Mark Endrei et al., "Patterns: Direct Connections for Intra- and Inter-Enterprise," IBM RedBook SG24-6933-00, February 2004, p. 94.
7. Sun Microsystems, Inc., "JavaTM API for XML Registries (JAXR) Specification ('Specification')," April 10, 2002, pp. 14–111.

CHAPTER 6

Fundamentals of SOA Asset Reuse: Service Reusability Model

Information technology (IT) asset reuse is an important topic given the post–Internet bubble focus on the bottom line and IT spending. IT asset reuse is currently being approached from a number of dimensions. Hardware asset reuse falls under a number of labels, such as utility computing, on-demand computing, grid computing, and other approaches to achieving greater utilization of hardware resources by pooling capacity and focusing computational resources on areas of need within an enterprise. Other approaches enable or disable capacity at the server level to accomplish similar objectives. These hardware reuse or optimization approaches are all similar in their goal to convert what were once fixed costs—capital assets such as IT hardware and infrastructure—into variable costs that can fluctuate according to actual utilization. These models are gaining in popularity and can be expected to continue to make inroads into corporate and IT strategies.

Software reuse is not a new concept either. Software reuse strategies have always been contemplated regardless of the generation of programming technology—mainframe paradigms, client-server paradigms, object-oriented programming models, and more recently with services in the emergent service-oriented architecture (SOA) approach to software. Software reuse efforts, however, did not enjoy great success in IT organizations. The failure of software reuse initiatives boils down to technical and behavioral/cultural issues: the very same factors that can either facilitate or inhibit success of SOA initiatives.

Software reuse challenges on the technical dimension involve issues related to finding and consuming software assets that are available to reuse. In other words, developers must know where to look for reusable software as well as what to look for, which can make reusing software more challenging than writing it from scratch. Any incremental effort for developers makes reuse a burden, not an opportunity. This reuse challenge has been addressed largely by metadata catalogs that facilitate the process of identifying, cataloging, and searching for software assets that are available for reuse.

In addition to the searching aspects of software reuse, developers often had to leave their native programming environment in order to locate potential software assets that could be reused. The recent solution is to integrate software reuse metadata repositories with the programming tools, or integrated development environments (IDE), which eliminates any lost productivity attributed to switching environments to achieve reuse.

Finally, there is the creative aspect of writing software. Developers are creative problem solvers; most often they prefer to write code rather than to reuse someone else's code. This goes to the heart of the cultural and behavioral issues of reuse. Reuse initiatives fail because there are no behavioral reinforcement mechanisms to encourage and enforce software reuse. Achieving software reuse requires individual and organizational incentives, rewards for good reuse behavior and penalties for failing to reuse assets, and metrics and employee reviews to continually reinforce the desired behavior.

These cultural and behavioral challenges are addressed further under the topic of SOA governance. Realize, however, that the very same organizational, cultural, and behavioral issues of software reuse will either support or inhibit SOA and services reuse.

SOA requires that services be created or exposed as reusable capabilities within domains, across domains, and organization-wide for various classes of services. Achieving the business value of SOA, as we discuss in the return on investment (ROI) model in Chapter 9, requires that organizations at least reach the reuse threshold of SOA value in order to enable the other more advanced benefits of SOA, such as service and process orchestration, integration cost avoidances, information latency benefits, and the accumulated overall value of SOA. The first stage of SOA value, however, is the creation of a portfolio of reusable services that can be leveraged for current and future processes, orchestration and choreography benefits, and more.

This chapter offers an approach for realizing services reuse in an SOA. This reuse model describes the strategy, disciplines, and best practices for achieving maximum reuse of services in an SOA.

MAJOR INFLUENCES ON SERVICE REUSABILITY

A number of factors influence the reuse of services, including business and technology strategies, technical enablement of reuse, the business environment, and the consumers of services:

- *Business and technological strategies.* Business and technology strategies can affect reusability of organizational assets immensely. These forces include business standards and best practices as well as service lifecycle activities such as service analysis, design, construction, and management. Business strategies that favor particular business units or lines of business over others can increase reusability of their supporting services by providing adequate service development and maintenance funding, enhancing their service infrastructure and operating environments, and allocating budget to expanding their service portfolio. Furthermore, technological strategies can increase service reuse by encouraging architectural solutions and enabling technology for reuse, such as asset decoupling mechanisms, asset cataloging and distribution tools, and services design and architectural layering approaches.
- *Technical enablement of reuse.* Service consumption capacity, performance, scalability, and service availability can be enabled through various technology solutions that support asset reusability. Furthermore, optimization of network environments, removal of security barriers, and integrating heterogeneous environments can increase potential service reuse and consumption in support

of transition to a service consumer-provider model that facilitates reuse.

- *Business environment.* Market events can influence demand for products and services, and thereby influence the creation and reuse of supporting information assets and services. Often reuse of assets in response to market conditions derives from compelling business events, such as increased competition, lost market share, and other negative conditions that force cost reductions and the demand for productivity and greater asset leverage. However, positive factors, such as a surge in customer orders or reduced demand for certain products, can affect supporting business initiatives and service reuse requirements as well.
- *Consumers.* Increased consumer demand can influence reusability of services. This increased demand might trigger demand for new versions of services, customizations and enhancements of existing services, and new product and process configurations based on services. Moreover, increased network traffic volumes and transaction rates between service consumers and producers can affect service reuse as well.

SERVICE REUSE MODEL

The *reusability model* is comprised of reusability strategies, disciplines, and directions. The model permits adjustments to organizational reusability standards and strategies that will help an organization face new business and technological challenges. Thus reuse strategies are dynamic and must be adjusted and tuned as needed.

Exhibit 6.1 depicts the reusability model that is comprised of three components: a *strategy component,* which facilitates reuse strategy and requirements; a *construction component,* which offers service development best practices; an *integration component,* which facilitates reuse of assets in integration initiatives; and a *management component,* which provides reuse policies via asset monitoring, SLAs, provisioning and lifecycle management.

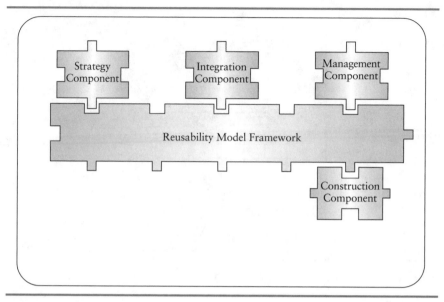

EXHIBIT 6.1   Redefining Reusability Strategy—Component View

SERVICE REUSABILITY STRATEGY

A *service reusability strategy* facilitates creation of an organization's service reuse strategy, standards, and technical requirements. Service reuse is an enterprise requirement and outcome of an organization's technology strategy and environment. Hence, reuse requirements should be based on asset reuse characteristics of individual environments and lead to specific reuse disciplines appropriate for a given organization.

For example, *accessibility* of services is an essential requirement for reuse and can be addressed differently in various information technology environments. A commodity trading development facility, based on J2EE and stateless Java beans operating in EJB containers, enables consumption of a *commodity information service* through the RMI/IIOP transportation protocol. Thus, this accessibility standard proposes a specific message delivery protocol and identifies a distinct platform for the *commodity information service*.

Exhibit 6.2 depicts *service reusability strategy component* factors, which are essentially a set of service organizational reuse requirements.

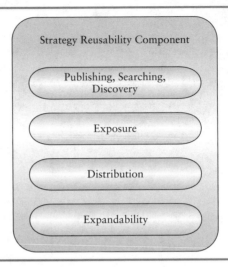

EXHIBIT 6.2   Strategy Component Factors and Reusability Requirements

Maximization of Service Reusability

The *service reuse strategy* should encompass baseline requirements that can be adapted, modified, and customized to the particular needs of an organization. They should enable maximum service reuse and be applied during various service lifecycle stages. Baseline reuse enabling requirements include:

- Service publishing, searching, and discovery
- Service exposure
- Service distribution
- Service extensibility

Service Publishing, Searching, and Discovery   This requirement is related to publishability, searchability, and discoverability factors of asset reuse. Service reuse can be increased if services are published and advertised to potential consumers. The publishing process should announce service availability, functionality, and other relevant consumer information. A published service should identify its location, specify how to obtain its service description, and be searchable. A service can operate and provide value to consumers without being published to a service registry. However, services that are published and advertised will achieve higher use and reuse rates. Achieving service reuse depends on identifying targeted reuse for services at the business, process, and technical level initially. In other words, before a service is published, the reuse potential for the service and consumption patterns for that service must be defined. This is "planned reuse." However, there is the real possibility of "emergent reuse," where services are reused by consumers who, by virtue of the services being published within the enterprise, can locate and consume services that they find useful even though they may not have been the target consumers for the service. This pattern of emergent reuse is a tremendous value proposition and enabler of service reuse. It encourages new consumption patterns that may not have been the originally intended use of the service, and yet they offer value to the businesses by obviating the need to develop a new service. Hence, service reuse depends on the amount of requesting consumers, how frequently they utilize services, transaction volumes, and consumption rates. All can be greatly influenced by publishing a service.

Service publishing and discovery are supported by service registries and metadata repositories. Establishing centralized or federated registries in organizations, such as Universal Description, Discovery, and Integration (UDDI), Discovery of Web Services (DISCO), and Advertisement and Discovery of Services (ADS), can facilitate service publishing, discovery, and search capabilities. Publishing and subsequent discovery of services and related assets can occur across the services lifecycle, from design and development to discovery within registries to dynamic discovery and invocation during run-time execution of services.

Service Exposure Service accessibility and exposure are important aspects of service reuse. Service accessibility should be carefully planned when distributing, deploying, and configuring services in production environments. Blocking routes to services can reduce their usefulness and reuse. Frequent reconfigurations of operating environments and modifications of deployment parameters can impair services and block transmission of messages and transactions. Thus, service accessibility should be based on static environment parameter sets that seldom change and are based on governance policies and defined deployment strategies.

Designing alternate network paths to service operations and eliminating unnecessary security barriers, such as firewalls, proxies, and gateways, can maximize accessibility to services. Environments with strict security policies should consider relaxing these configurations to promote accessibility without exposing networks to external and internal attacks or increasing the risk of security threats.

Intermediaries such as hubs and gateways hide service end points from consumers yet in some cases limit alternate routes to services. They also play a major role in policy enforcement, asset security, service distribution, enhancement of workload management, improvement of service scalability, and interoperability. Adding more functionality or complexity to these intervening layers may reduce response time to requests and decrease service use and reuse. There should be a balance between the value and potential downside of using intermediaries based on their potential impact on service consumption and reuse.

Service exposure should be considered during service design, architecture deployment, and implementation. Offering multiple service protocols, such as SNA, HTTP, RMI/IIOP, and TCP/IP, can increase reuse of services and provide flexible connectivity in heterogeneous computing environments. Conversely, this approach may increase service maintenance, version management complexities, and customization efforts.

Adding design patterns to facilitate access to services can protect assets, increase service security, and standardize and simplify service exposure mechanisms. However, these pattern layers potentially can reduce service reuse by limiting accessibility and privatizing their interfaces. For example, excessive usage of *facade, service locator,* and *router* patterns that are built into unnecessary layers can reduce service accessibility.

Service Distribution   Service distribution is the ability to migrate services to heterogeneous environments and platforms without altering functionality. Service distribution can be planned, designed, and architected to increase service reuse in an SOA.

If service operations are highly dependent on local resources such as networks, operating systems, middleware, and peer services, they can be confined to their local environments. In this scenario, though, their interaction and interfaces with external services, consumers, and producers can be significantly reduced. For example, a *customer* service, which provides name and address information, depends on a *customer account balances* service. They both operate in the same network and communicate via a local message bus. Migrating and distributing the *customer* service to a different network and operating system could be a challenge unless the service is highly interoperable. This localized resource dependency can reduce distributability and reuse of assets in organizations.

Decoupling of service abstractions, such as processes and logic, can increase service dependencies on external resources, since each decomposed element would depend on its newly formed peers. Unfortunately, decoupling is not the ultimate solution for increasing service reuse. Furthermore, this practice can reduce distributability and interoperability services. Thus, proper architecture and service design can strike the balance between software decoupling and aggregation of abstractions, which can enhance distributability, interoperability, and reusability of services. Exhibit 6.3 depicts tight-coupling versus loose-coupling distribution scenarios and illustrates resulting influences of such operations.

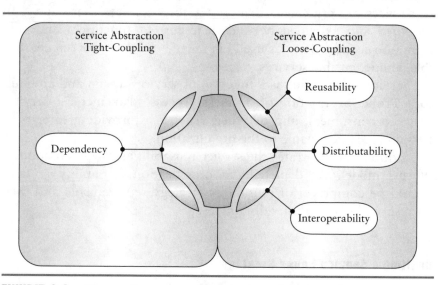

EXHIBIT 6.3 Decoupling versus Aggregation of Service Abstractions

Interfaceability enables consumers to communicate with services directly or indirectly via intermediaries, proxies, and gateways. Exposing service interfaces and enabling easy access to services can facilitate standardized access methods by consumers. Many types of adapters are available to facilitate exposure and integration of services across heterogeneous technology platforms while supporting greater reuse.

Service interfaces should be versioned and cataloged when they are customized or updated. Employing service version management techniques and supporting technologies will help eliminate the need to modify deprecated service versions, which may still be used by consumers. Maintaining multiple versions of service interfaces can increase reuse and broaden planned and emergent consumption patterns.

Service Extensibility   Service extensibility and customizability provide business and technological agility, facilitate managing change, and enable rapid response to market events and competitive business challenges. Service extensibility supports rapid time-to-market by accommodating new business requirements into services. The inability to provide time-to-market business value can decrease services life span and reduce their utility. Thus, extensibility and customizability of services are critical to their reusability. Services that cannot be modified and extended beyond their current functional and consumption scope are not as useful in an agile SOA as more agile, flexible, and extensible services.

Service extensibility is a function of services design and architecture. Proper abstraction of business processes can increase services value to consumers, improve their reuse, and provide greater business and technical value to the organization.

Exhibit 6.4 illustrates the service reusability strategy component of this model. As depicted, an organization reusability strategy should be comprised of reusability strategy requirements and their corresponding reusability disciplines.

Crafting a Service Reuse Strategy

The *service reuse strategy* captures reusability requirements, which are used to derive corresponding technical specifications and ultimately

Reusability Strategy Requirement	Reusability Discipline
Publishing, Searching, & Discovery	Publishability
	Searchability
	Discoverability
Exposure	Accessibility
	Exposability
Distribution	Distributability
	Interfaceability
	Interoperability
Expansion	Estensibility
	Customizability

EXHIBIT 6.4   Strategy Component Requirements and Disciplines

build the foundation for service reusability. This process involves three steps:

1. List the organization's reusability requirements, such as exposure and distribution. Provide organization-specific reusability requirements that apply to particular lines of business, process or functional domains, environments, and business processes.
2. List the corresponding reuse disciplines. For each listed requirement, indicate one or more reusability disciplines.
3. Provide corresponding technical specifications for each reuse discipline.

Exhibit 6.5 illustrates an organizational reusability strategy based on service reusability requirements.

SERVICE CONSTRUCTION

Service reusability construction component requirements are concerned with fundamental analysis, design, architecture, and software development practices, which facilitate asset reuse as well as governance of reuse disciplines across the services lifecycle. Design-time governance process and enforcement of design-time policies drive service reuse by encouraging and enforcing appropriate industry and organizational standards that will increase reuse of services. In fact,

Revise Requirement	Discipline	Service	Technical Specification
Publishing, Searching, & Discovery	Publishability	Customer Profile Service	• Use standard UDDI registry to publish the Customer Profile service • Store service description file (WSDL) on Customer Web Container
	Discoverability		Utilize UDDI registry to provide consumers service discovery capabilities
Distribution	Interoperability	Loan Origination Service (a J2EE service)	Install and configure a SOA intermidiary, such as a hub or gateway, that can enable the Loan Origination service to communicate and exchange trasactions with Mainframe and .NET consumers
	Interfaceability		Build 2 main interfaces to Loan Origination service: *Get Customer Credit*, and Get *Loan Exposure*
	Distributability		Provide appropriate design and architecture to reduce Loan Origination dependencies on its immediate surroundings

EXHIBIT 6.5   Organizational Reusability Strategy Example

most aspects of service reuse are influenced during service identification, analysis, and design. Furthermore, reuse itself is a policy that must be enforced to help achieve reuse. This influence places great importance on the process of services modeling, design-time SOA governance processes, and supporting tools, such as process modeling utilities and advanced IDEs. Thus, the service reuse construction component is a critical advisory element that provides development standards, service construction best practices, and oversight and governance from an organizational reuse requirements perspective.

Exhibit 6.6 depicts reusability construction component best practices that should be followed during service development phases.

Service Reusability Best Practices

The reusability best practices that are discussed next are concerned with abstraction reuse, generalization of concepts,[1] decoupling and granularity of services, componentization of software, and layering.[2]

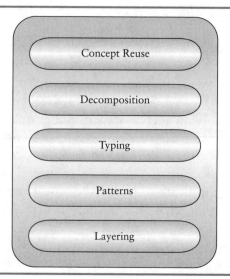

EXHIBIT 6.6   Service Reusability Construction Component Requirements

These concepts provide compelling reasons to logically and physically separate service operations.

Concept Reuse   Abstraction[3] and generalization of concepts are fundamental and critical disciplines of service reuse. Abstraction is the process of formulating high-level concepts that express commonality of concrete instances and specific examples. Abstraction is an approach for dealing with complexities. The abstraction process helps establish solutions that address larger business problems and provide direction for designing and architecting software solutions for these business problems. Service abstractions comprise ideas, concepts, and processes that are implemented by their underlying constituents, such as concrete elements and components. These contained entities are responsible for executing abstraction goals and providing tangible service solutions to problems.

Abstractions represent horizontal views of concerns in an organization. Services are grounded in abstraction concepts and thus can benefit from a higher degree of reusability because they address a wider spectrum of enterprise problems. For example, a fine-grained *account ID service* provides account identification to consumers, while a *customer service*, which is a more abstracted entity, can provide customer account information, customer balances, and even include the account identification information.

A rule of thumb suggests that services should be based on abstraction levels that are above and beyond the initial problem scope that they are focused on. Hence, abstractions should aggregate common problems to increase service reusability. For example, a defined business problem such as *duplicated customer accounts limits management capabilities of customer records in the firm* can be abstracted and elevated to an organizational concern level that can lead to the origination of the *customer service.* This approach not only addresses the duplicate records issue, but it can provide a better way to manage other customer requirements, such as *customer accounts lookup* and *customer account balances.*

Generalization is a process of simplifying complexities by generalizing concepts and creating hierarchies of entities that are *type-of* elements of their parents.[4] Service abstractions are not only horizontal layers; they express vertical generalizations of the problem as well. For instance, *brokerage account, mutual funds account,* and *checking account* are types of financial accounts. Thus, *financial account* is the generalized parent in this hierarchy. The next step up would be *product,* because *financial account* is a *type-of* product offering of that firm. Exhibit 6.7 depicts these generalization ideas.

Generalization is one of the most important aspects of service reuse because it utilizes hierarchal structures to develop generalized concepts that can be applied later to the creation of service abstractions.

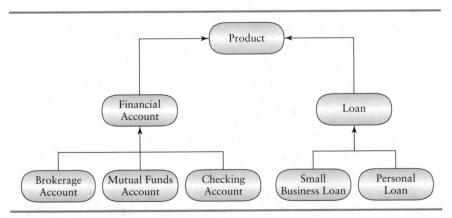

EXHIBIT 6.7   Generalization of Concepts

Consequently, reuse of parent concepts can increase service reusability greatly and eliminate redundancy of processes in underlying service implementations. Proceeding to lower levels of this generalization hierarchy, from the parents down to the children, facilitates requirements definition and development of finer-grained and more concrete components.

Decomposition   Granularity, modularity, decoupling, and componentization are service reusability disciplines that identify size, spectrum, and extent of software decomposition. Service reuse depends on decomposition activities of software components during architecture and design and through deployment into production.

Modularity of software depends on how source code is organized, managed, and packaged during development. Software modules can be grouped into logical units based on their context—mainly physical grouping versus conceptual collections. Utilizing these modules can reduce design, architecture, and implementation redundancy and encourage reuse. Hence, more modular software can better influence development for reuse and lead to the deployment of more reusable services as compared to less modular software.

Components are a part of a software assembly—a system, a subsystem, or a service.[5] They are combined to form self-contained executables. Componentization of abstractions and logical grouping of business context, business processes, and operations can increase reusability of software by enabling its future expansion, customization, and portability. Furthermore, a service is assembled from interrelated components and other elements that provide its core functionality. Service frameworks manage components and their ability to interact. Thus, service constituents do not need to be published, registered, or searchable because they operate from within a service context. Components offer internal reusability regardless of their physical deployment location. They should not be accessed by external services or systems directly. Exhibit 6.8 depicts this idea. Here componentization of services is expressed by internal and external components.

Service design and architecture practices should employ subdivision and demarcation techniques and encourage concepts of loose-coupling and logical segmentation of processes to enhance service reusability. Loosely coupled architecture facilitates reduction of

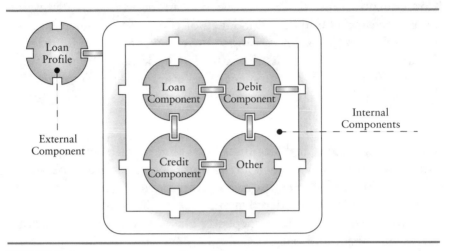

EXHIBIT 6.8 Componentization of Services

consumer-producer and environmental dependencies. Thus, malfunctioning services should not affect the operation of related peer services or negatively influence consumers. As mentioned previously, tightly coupled assets can influence service reusability and affect their distributability.

Granularity of services is related to identification, analysis, design, and architecture disciplines. Fine-grained services are smaller in size, provide less functionality, and are simpler to manage. In the grand scheme of service reuse, fine-grained services may not have a large consumer base to justify their distribution. Thus, their reduced reusability confines them to local implementations. Coarse-grained services are larger in size and provide larger segments of functionality and information. *Customer profile service* and *trading history service*, for example, can be viewed as coarse-grained services that provide greater business value, and hence they will experience greater consumption and reuse.

Typing Polymorphism, typing, and aggregation are related disciplines that impact development for service reuse utilizing language-specific capabilities.

Object-oriented software development practices encourage the utilization of polymorphism, because methods can appear in different forms and demonstrate different types of behaviors. A single operation may be defined in different classes, in which methods can have different implementations. This type of approach can be carried out through structural reuse of classes and their definitions. There are language- and platform-specific characteristics and capabilities. For example, definitions of printing operations can be expressed throughout class hierarchies in many forms and appearances. Printing functionalities can yield various outputs, such as images, that are rendered to monitors or serialized to files. Hence, this type of functional reuse can influence underlying service implementations and provide standardized and reusable interfaces to be exposed and utilized by various consumers.

Languages that support weak typing enable reusability of their methods because of their implicit run-time data-type conversion capabilities. Type checking during compilation time, or explicit checking (strong typing), limits the generalization of data types and further affects abstraction of concepts in the design model. When using weak typing implementations, the receiving end may have to cast these generic data types to specific ones unless these types are utilized as abstract interfaces to be used for generic purposes. Once again, this underlying implementation of services can influence generalization of functionalities that are critical to targeted services.

Language aggregation capabilities are a special form of association. It is a relationship between data types that includes other data types, for example, a *has-a* correlation. Data types as part of such aggregations can be shared and reused. This type of affiliation is not enabled by inheritance or generalization, but rather is a horizontal type of data utilization that increases reusability and eliminates the need for creating new types.

Design Patterns Patterns are solution knowledge bases that provide templates or models that express customary ways of implementing functionality or process behavior. They facilitate the development of rapid and high-quality solutions, which are based on expertise and experience gained in specific practices. Furthermore, patterns introduce development implementation standards and systematize the expertise they provide. They enable reusability of solutions and reduce the need for analysis, research, and in some cases proof of concepts and testing. Hence, patterns provide guidance for addressing recurring problems by generalizing source code algorithms and increasing code reusability.

Patterns can provide insightful system technical knowledge, reveal architecture and design approaches, and offer technology reference guides that can be used to communicate internal compositions of applications, services, and other products. For example, a *customer information center* application based its design on the *model-view-controller*[6] (MVC) paradigm—a common application design pattern. The MVC pattern can uncover design and architecture approaches and expose aspects of underlying implementations such as code structure and style. The *customer information center* application architecture employs the MVC pattern to facilitate the decoupling of its major layers: the presentation layer (*view*), dispatcher layer (*controller*), and a business logic layer (*model*).

Patterns in general can be applied to various service lifecycle stages. They provide solutions to business architecture, software analysis, development, design, and the formation of architecture concepts and strategies. More granular patterns usually are applied to underlying solutions of design and construction. They provide tactical solutions. Coarse-grained patterns largely apply to strategic decisions, concepts, ideas, and approaches.

Services can benefit from patterns by exploiting SOA patterns. Yet the underlying implementation of services should follow basic best practices utilizing software development patterns. As the SOA industry evolves, more patterns are being discovered, developed, and offered along with emerging products, methodologies, and strategies. Services can greatly benefit from patterns that offer reusability of producer and consumer implementations. Currently, known SOA industry patterns can assist in the following domains: business, design and architecture, construction, integration, deployment, and management.

For example, *service locator* is a popular and widely used pattern that enables service presentation layers or facades to locate proper business layers and implementations that are isolated or hidden. This pattern has the ability to map consumers' requests to service interfaces and to locate appropriate business logic that is executed by specialized services.

Other examples of SOA patterns are *service bus* and *broker inter-ception* patterns (see the service integration model in Chapter 5). They are types of integration reuse templates that facilitate distribution of services and assist with the creation of loosely coupled environments.

Layering   Layers provide architecture decoupling mechanisms to facilitate the distribution, disbursement, and deployment of processes and data. Layering is a logical segmentation approach that enhances service reuse and enables access to various implementations and information. Exhibit 6.9 depicts the reusability aspect of layers in a distributed environment. Consumers can access individual layers rather than using the presentation layer as an access mechanism.

Layering paradigms can provide logical segmentation of concepts such as *presentation layer, data access layer,* and *business layer.* They tend to bundle and bind architecture entities and reusable assets, and facilitate the formation of architectural partitioning standards. Layers provide context and support the deployment and accommodation of services in their domains. Services best operate in distributed and loosely coupled environments, based on layering concepts, that enable portability and facilitate their management. Layers are not affiliated with, and do not depend on, physical environments.

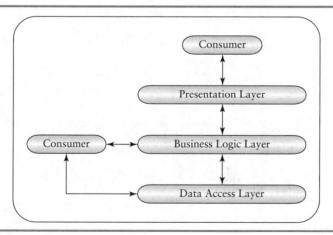

EXHIBIT 6.9   Reusability of Layers

They can be deployed and distributed on separate physical nodes or work from within one physical machine. Exhibit 6.10 illustrates a business logic layer that is comprised of *employee* and *customer* types of services. Such layers can be distributed and migrated easily to different platforms along with their constituent services.

Exhibit 6.11 depicts service construction component requirements and their corresponding reusability disciplines that should be adopted and followed during service construction.

SERVICE INTEGRATION

Integration management of assets in complex and dynamic environments should embrace integration policies and disciplines for the purpose of maximizing service reusability. The *service reusability integration component* captures organizational dependency, interoperability, adaptability, and service positioning requirements that are critical for enabling service reusability during integration (Exhibit 6.12).

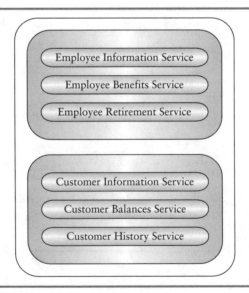

EXHIBIT 6.10 Containment of Services in a Business Logic Layer

Service Reusability Construction Component Reusability Best Practices and Disciplines	
Reusability Construction Requirement	
	Reusability Discipline
Concept Reuse	Abstraction
	Generalization
	Aggregation
Decomposition	Granularity
	Modularity
	Decoupling/Loose Coupling
	Componentization
Typing	Data and Parameter Typing
	Polymorphism
	Aggregation
Patterns	Template Formation
	Model Formation
Layering	Segmentation
	Loose Coupling
	Partitioning

EXHIBIT 6.11 Construction Component Requirements and Disciplines

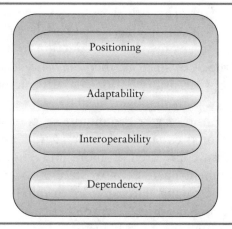

EXHIBIT 6.12 Integration Reusability Model Component

Reusability Aspects of Integration Positioning

A reusability integration component offers process as for evaluating criticality and strategic value of services and determining which services should be granted special attention and integration privileges to maximize reusability.

Service integration environments, such as networks, deployment facilities, middleware, and hardware, should follow a tiered business structure. Revenue generating services—mainly strategic assets or service-supporting technologies—should be positioned in top tiers; this is called horizontal positioning. Tactical services that return lower income should be positioned in lower tiers; this is vertical positioning. Services that are not affiliated with revenue, such as technical services and supporting utilities, should be evaluated by their criticality to the service-integrated environments and should be positioned accordingly. This type of classification should facilitate integration service positioning process and help to prioritize integration resources, fund allocations, and technological availabilities. For example, a personal business banking division offers products such as *loan, credit, ATM, monthly statements,* and *daily business news* to its base customers. *Loan, credit,* and *ATM* were ranked as its business tier one because they are revenue-generating services and are thus considered strategic assets of that organization. *Statements* and *daily business news* are free services; thus, they are tier-three rated. Organizations must prioritize their services based on their business and IT imperatives. If top-line revenue growth is the primary SOA goal, it should be in tier one. If cost reduction or asset leverage are the objectives of the SOA strategy, then they should be in tier one.

The outcome of such prioritization analysis can influence physical positioning of services in deployment and affect their accommodations and integration in service communities. As a result, horizontal services can be granted enhanced network access and can be better scaled, installed, and configured on more powerful hardware. Their integrated environments can employ state-of-the-art technologies, middleware, and messaging. Furthermore, technological superiority, such as advanced collaborative environments and improved asset management and monitoring mechanisms, can potentially increase a service's consumer base and maximize reuse.

Service Adaptability

The following principles of service adaptability and portability are disciplines of the integration component adaptability requirement:

- *Service portability principle.* Services should have the ability to interoperate in heterogeneous environments without reconstruction and customization.
- *Service adaptability principle.* Services should dynamically adapt to fluid environments. They should provide business and technological continuity, demonstrate solid performance and behavior, and preserve their quality of service. Services should maintain consumption volumes, support increased reuse, and continue to obey service-level agreements (SLAs).

Service reusability, adaptability, and portability can be affected by technological challenges, such as migration to different platforms, enhancements or deployment of new middleware products, changes in operating environment and security policies, installation and configuration of networks, and amendments to deployment strategies or architecture.

Reusability Interoperability Discipline

Consumers should have the ability to communicate and interface meaningfully with desired services with no special or incremental effort and regardless of technological barriers, such as operating system incompatibilities, variety of protocols, different supporting vendors and proprietary products, diverse networks, and middleware.

Service interoperability requires good service design practices and appropriate enabling technology such as gateways, hubs, and proxies that can remediate incompatibilities and address reusability concerns arising from heterogeneous computing environments. Two major interoperability challenges impact service reuse:

1. *Standardization of protocols.* Reusability of services can be affected by incompatibility of communication protocols that are

utilized by service consumers and producers. These protocols are responsible for transmission of data between message- and transaction-exchanging entities.

2. *Data transformation.* Data transformation between service producers and consumers should be seamless. The transmitted information must comply with data formats and semantics of the conversing parties.

   Third-party intermediary products offer message interception and translation mechanisms to facilitate data transformation between consumers and producers. Some solutions include APIs and conversion tools to accomplish these tasks. For example, XSLT is a language for transforming XML documents to other XML documents.[7] (It is part of XSL,[8] a stylesheet language.) It can facilitate XML transformations between partners that have different formatting structures and canonical forms.

These interoperability challenges can be resolved by taking proper technological measures.

Exhibit 6.13 depicts the reusability aspects of interoperability. Mainframe and .NET consumers that operate on different platforms

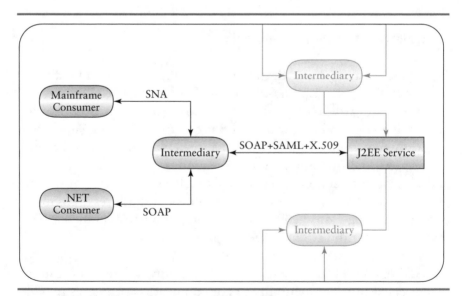

EXHIBIT 6.13   Reusability Aspect of Interoperability

can communicate with a J2EE service by utilizing intermediaries (hubs or gateways), which perform protocol and data transformations.

Furthermore, services may depend on distributed components that do not physically reside in the same operating environments, yet they are integral to the services' operations. To enhance service reusability, communication between these elements should comply with service interoperability disciplines and transmission and transformation standards defined by architecture organizations.

Dependency

Distributed services may depend on their peers, supporting applications and components, their operating environment, and related service infrastructure. Realistically, complex service topologies do not permit asset self-sufficiency and independence. A loosely coupled architecture supports distributing services and their components on the network to increase reuse and reduce logical complexities. Nevertheless, this distribution scheme increases the dependency of services on their peers and supporting service infrastructure. Thus, increasing services dependencies can diminish the reuse gained by decoupling them. There must be a fine balance between asset decoupling and dependence on internal or external resources. Exhibit 6.14 depicts these ideas.

Consider the following integration discipline guidelines and best practices when implementing integration for service communities:

- Decoupling activities can increase dependency of services on their environment, peer services, and components.
- Tight coupling may reduce service reusability. Exhibit 6.15 illustrates the relationship between reusability factors and tightly coupled design and architecture activities. The service reusability factor decreases if it is tightly coupled to its peers and supporting environment.
- Dependency of services may reduce service reusability. Exhibit 6.16 depicts the relationship between service reusability factors and service dependency on its environment and peer services. In this case, while the dependency factor increases, the service reusability aspect decreases.

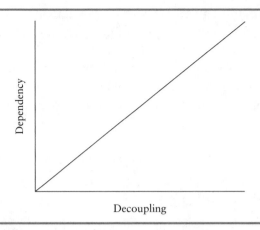

EXHIBIT 6.14   Dependency and Decoupling Factors

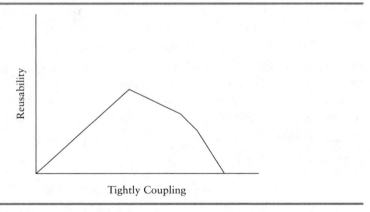

EXHIBIT 6.15   Tight Coupling and Reusability Factors

Modifying service functionality with high dependence on peer services may trigger a wide array of environmental reconfigurations and service customizations. For example, changes to a service interface may cause changes to consumers' requests, to service description files such as Web Services Description Languages (WSDLs), and to intermediaries that may handle data conversion and transformations. This domino effect may impose development challenges and impact production environments. Some organizations prefer to avoid this scenario and instead create new services by duplicating their existing functionality rather than reusing existing services. This solution to remediate service dependencies is not recommended. Good architecture strategies and resource planning can facilitate reusability solutions in high-service dependency scenarios.

Exhibit 6.17 depicts the reusability integration component requirements and their corresponding reusability disciplines that should be adopted and followed during service integration initiatives. These requirements and disciplines facilitate establishing reusability standards and strategies in the organization.

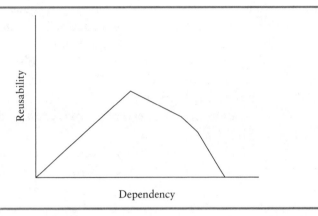

EXHIBIT 6.16   Dependency and Reusability Factors

Reusability Integration Requirements	Reusability Discipline
Positioning	Evaluating Strategic Values
	Asset Prioritization Analysis
	Resource Prioritization
	Horizontal and Vertical Positioning
Adaptability	Adjustability
	Dynamic Adaptability
	Portability
Interoperability	Interfaceability
	Remediation by Intermediaries
	Standardization of Protocols
	Foundation of Data Transformation Mechanisms
Dependency	Loose Coupling

EXHIBIT 6.17   Integration Component Requirements and Disciplines

SERVICE MANAGEMENT

Dynamic and complex deployment environments, asset interoperability requirements, and service topology dependencies demand organizational reusability management processes and methodologies to ensure quality control, consolidation of deployment initiatives, reduction of configuration and installation efforts, and proper utilization of enterprise assets. Consumption of services can be measured and controlled by employing monitoring and traceability tools, visual dashboards, and alerting systems to quantify, evaluate, maintain, and maximize asset reusability in organizations.

A key ingredient of service reuse is an SLA, which can be negotiated by service consumers and producers. The goals and targets of service reusability management rules and disciplines should reflect reusability expectations; the goals are provided by the *service reusability management component.*

Exhibit 6.18 depicts reusability management component requirements that are critical for increasing asset reusability in organizations.

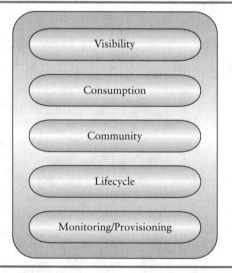

EXHIBIT 6.18   Management Component Requirements

Service Visibility

Services should be monitored and managed to ensure run-time conformance to policies and performance requirements. Load balancing, failover, throttling of performance, and performance tuning are important to maintaining services reliability. Tools and utilities should be employed to track services state and real-time execution. Service reusability should be analyzed and evaluated against SLAs, which are stipulated prior to their deployment.

Service Consumption

Controlling and managing service consumption is critical for service reusability. Service consumption can be measured by monitoring access, exposure, and usage of services, by observing service quality, and by assessing service performance. Service reuse should be governed by predefined rules and agreements, many of which are organizational policies and portfolio management and technology management issues. Thus, service consumers and producers should abide by SLAs and comply with committed consumption rates. Various compliance measures can be taken when consumers exceed permitted utilization capacity. These measures include alerts, denial of access, or temporary blockage of access to services. Services that do not deliver business value should be examined, analyzed, enhanced, or, if deemed appropriate, decommissioned or replaced.

Systematic tracking of consumers and producers, and the ability to control their interactions, enables management to quickly assess real-time performance for the SOA and make decisions to enforce reuse in production environments. Analyzing historical reuse and service consumption data can facilitate resource allocation and optimal consumption of services within a given reuse strategy.

Service Community Management

Management of network grids populated with communities of services can challenge operations management practices, demand rigorous monitoring efforts, and involve multiple disciplines in IT organizations. The three vital aspects of service community management are:

1. *Service integration.* Maintain overall service reusability in communities based on SLAs.
2. *Service dependencies.* Manage and monitor service community dependencies to ensure the maximization of service reusability.
3. *Interoperability.* Guarantee proper communications in heterogeneous environments to increase service reusability.

Managing the SOA big picture and error-free operations will require engagement rules and solid SOA strategies. Such tasks involve environmental issues, such as network management, security management, deployment and configuration of intermediaries (hubs, gateways, and proxies), and end-point administration. Promotion and demotion rules can be applied to services for the purpose of controlling reuse. Statistical usage and strategic value of services should determine their relative ranking in their communities. A service that is subject to promotion should be horizontally positioned in its surroundings and should enjoy the privileges of its class. Demotion of services usually occurs when services are about to be decommissioned or their business value is decreased.

Reusability Lifecycle Management

Reusability lifecycle management is discussed in detail in Chapter 2. Lifecycle management is concerned with service reuse through all phases of a service, from identification through analysis, design, production, and management. There are four levels of reuse for a service: business/process reuse, functional reuse, technical reuse, and consumption reuse (intended and emergent reuse).

Service reuse can be determined from a business and process perspective early in the service's lifecycle. At this point, service reuse focuses on the ability of business units and related organizations to reuse a given service. This is the first point of reuse analysis, and speeds the other aspects of services design and implementation. It is also at this point where the funding and ownership of services can come into play.

Functional reuse of a service is when decisions are made during services modeling around the functionality of a service, and the utilization of business processes, relative to its desired reuse model. To achieve reuse, more functional scope may have to be incorporated into the service. Functional reuse has a direct impact on the granularity and overall solution coverage for a service. Once functional reuse has been established, technical reuse must be determined.

Technical reuse is concerned with the ability to abstract from specific technology platforms the business logic and transactions that will be encapsulated within the services. Technical reuse is where the business/process reuse and functional reuse are realized through a physical solution service.

Consumption reuse is where reuse of services is the desired and intended outcome—where consumers are discovering and using services within the SOA. Remember, there are two forms of consumption for services: the targeted consumption for services that was planned during the requirements definition and implementation activities, and the unplanned, emergent consumption of services by other business units, processes, or consumers within the organization. This emergent reuse of services is a delightful outcome for an SOA and helps increase the overall value of the portfolio of services.

Service management initiatives should provide reusability policies and controls to monitoring activities, business modeling and alignment, portfolio and asset inventory management, asset administration, and quality of services (QoS). Service reuse should be managed through all service lifecycle stages:

- Motivation stage
- Conceptualization stage
- Modeling stage
- Realization stage
- Management stage

Reusability Provisioning, Service-Level Agreements, and Service Monitoring

Managing transaction expectations, granting access, agreeing on reusability enablement mechanisms, and tracking and monitoring consumption of services are the essence of SLAs and enforcement methods. Service producers, consumers, and governing management rules are the three major participants in this endeavor.

Service Producers   Service producers that expose and publish their services to the public should document their capabilities and transaction capacities within their interface descriptions, such as WSDLs and supporting metadata and documentation. Such documentation can include service consumption limits, volume limitations, availability, and response time. Subscription to these offerings should be governed by binding contracts with involved consumers. Consumption and reusability planning enable producers to share capacity with their requesting partners. Services should be responsible and accountable for their delivery as defined in the service contract, regardless of their dependence on other resources or environments they may operate in. For example, services may depend on their peers to satisfy a single consumer request. This type of service aggregation should require the responsible parties to participate in these agreements as well.

Producers of services should include these elements in their service contracts and SLAs:

- *Consumption limits and ranges.* Minimum and maximum allowable transactions and utilization rates
- *Reusability and utilization parameters.* Reusability factors that are supported by service providers in the agreement, such as interoperability, exposure mechanisms, searchability, and so on
- *Guaranteed service performance.* Message response time and estimated performance benchmarks
- *State management methods.* Methods of message and transaction state management, such as stateless and stateful implementations
- *Quality assurance.* Quality guarantees (e.g., smooth transactions, free of defects, and delays)
- *Interface descriptions.* Description of exposed interfaces
- *Service availability.* Hours of operations, and restricted access time

Service Consumers   Consumers should be able to subscribe to service offerings and abide by the contract they agree on. They should be granted with access to service interfaces, be provided with authorization and authentication, and network security permissions to services they acquire, and be allowed to submit requests and execute transactions up to their approved consumption and service utilization limits. Consumers should be notified when contracts are breached and be provided with periodic reporting, activity summaries, consumption rates, and reusability measurements and assessments.

Consumers should include these reusability requirements in SLAs:

- *Service requirements.* Type of services needed, interface descriptions, and returned values
- *Access requirements.* Requests for accessibility, authorization, authentication descriptions
- *Response time requirements.* Maximum message response time tolerated by the consumer
- *Reusability requirements.* Reusability parameters required by producers, such as publishability, customizability, and interoperability
- *Reporting requirements.* Transaction and consumption reporting requirements

Governance and Provisioning   Service provisioning policies should ensure that service consumption is not excessive (relative to planned consumption and specified operating parameters of the infrastructure) and quality and reusability levels are maintained. Governance policies should ensure that consumers and producers honor SLAs. A notification system should provide warnings and alerts if SLAs are approaching violation limits. Notifications that can be sent to the consumers and providers during policy and SLA enforcement include:

- Services about to be interrupted
- Services halted
- Service reusability factors in decline
- Consumers experiencing service interruptions
- Consumers planning to stop utilizing services
- SLAs breached

Breach of contracts can prompt controlling actions, such as service interruptions, reduction of consumption to the agreed level, and delay of services. Consumers should have the ability to notify their producers concerning service satisfaction levels and provide detailed reusability and quality reporting.

Consumers can be charged for their consumption and utilization of services by provisioning mechanisms that enable asset utilization measurement capabilities. Chargeback schemes can be applied based on usage time, transaction rate, or type of service. SLAs should contain governance sections that bind consumers and providers to general SLA policies.

These governance requirements should be included in service contracts:

- *Reusability strategies.* Reusability strategies employed in agreements
- *Capacity strategy.* Services capacity planning and the allowable consumption rates by particular consumers
- *Cost and charges.* Service price structures
- *Alerts and notifications.* Alerts levels and severity of notifications
- *Monitoring scope.* Specified parts of agreements that should be monitored
- *Access terms.* Authorization and authentication specifications

Development of organization provisioning models should facilitate quality assurance of services, proper distribution of resources and capacity, maximization of service reusability, and the enforcement of governance policies. As depicted in Exhibit 6.19, these models should

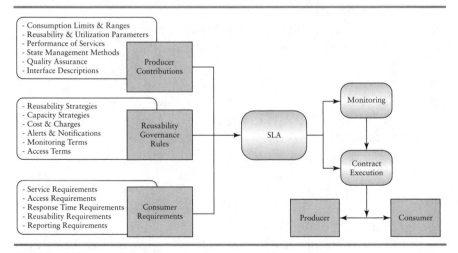

EXHIBIT 6.19   Reusability Provisioning Mode

aggregate producer offerings, consumer requirements, and governance policies into service contracts and SLAs. These SLAs should be monitored, supervised, and controlled by specialized service and reusability tracking software products. These monitoring tools should track producers and their subscribing consumers' activities.

Exhibit 6.20 depicts the requirements and disciplines of the service reusability model management component.

Reusability Management Requirements	Reusability Discipline
Visibility	Service Exposure
	Employment of Tools and Utilities
Consumption	Resource Planning
	SLAs
	Capacity Planning
	Tracking and Monitoring
Community	Service Topology Management
	Monitoring Service Community
	Standardization of Protocols
	Service Dependency Management
	Interoperability Management
	Integration Management
Lifecycle	Lifecycle Monitoring
	Business Modeling and Alignment Management
	Asset Portfolio and Inventory Management
	Asset Administration
	Quality of Services
Monitoring/Provisioning	Provisioning Model
	SLAs
	Consumption Planning
	Resource Planning

EXHIBIT 6.20 Management Component Requirements and Disciplines

SUMMARY

Service reuse is one of the most important criteria for identifying potential services to build or expose in an SOA. This chapter provides a model to help treat service reuse as a primary consideration in the services lifecycle, from identification to implementation, as well as in the selection and implementation of enabling technology. Implementing reusable and interoperable services is critical for establishing critical mass for an SOA. Reuse is the first step in achieving the business value of SOA, but that is only the beginning. Service reuse is essential, but it is only the beginning of the SOA value proposition for an organization. Getting beyond reuse to orchestration and the other SOA benefits is a must. But first service reusability must be achieved.

NOTES

1. Grady Booch, James Rumbaugh, and Ivar Jacobson, *The Unified Modeling Language User Guide* (Addison-Wesley, 1999), p. 64.
2. Alan Brown, Simon Johnston, and Kevin Kelly, "Using Service-Oriented Architecture and Component-Based Development to Build Web Service Applications," Rational Software Corporation, 2002, p. 6.
3. Grady Booch, *Object-Oriented Analysis and Design with Applications*, 2nd ed. (Benjamin/Cummings Publishing Company, 1994), p. 20.
4. Ian Graham, *Object Oriented Methods*, 2nd ed. (Addison-Wesley, 1994), p. 19.
5. Graig Larman, *Applying UML and Patterns: An Introduction to Object-Oriented Analysis and Design and Iterative Development*, 3rd ed. (Prentice Hall PTR, 2005), p. 624.
6. Eric Gamma, Richard Helm, Ralph Johnson, and John Vlissides, *Design Patterns: Elements of Reusable Object-Oriented Software* (Addison-Wesley, 1995), pp. 4–5.
7. www.w3.org/TR/xslt, "XSL Transformation (XSLT)."
8. www.w3.org/Style/XSL/, "The Extensible Stylesheet Language Family (XSL)."

CHAPTER 7

SOA Governance, Organization, and Behavior

Service-oriented architecture (SOA) is a challenge for both business and information technology (IT) organizations in light of the organizational and behavioral issues that attend an SOA initiative. However, SOA has the potential to impact IT governance and enterprise architecture perhaps more than any other processes.

There are many symptoms of the need for change in an IT organization. Among them are stovepiped architectures, where various applications and computing platforms cannot share data or interoperate in support of common processes or business functions. They also include costly and brittle integration strategies implemented to alleviate the problem of stovepiped architectures. Such strategies may address some of the immediate integration challenges, but they only push the root cause further under the carpet, hidden from scrutiny. Imagine that you are an archaeologist. Your job is to analyze physical remains and artifacts in order to draw conclusions about the behaviors of the people who left the artifacts behind. Often these physical artifacts must be carefully excavated and documented to record the spatial context and position in the earthen matrix in which they have been found. These artifacts include flint tools, ceramics, animal bones, fire-cracked rocks from fire pits, decorative beads, and so forth.

Now, some of these artifacts will provide immediate clues as to the date of the site and the cultural affiliation of its prehistoric peoples. Arrowheads and ceramic styles often quite accurately point to the period in history when a particular group inhabited an area. However, other behavioral issues cannot as readily be ascertained. Why were these people at this specific location? Why were houses located as such? Around what organizational principles was the village structured? How was their society governed? What were the rules? Was there class differentiation or was this an egalitarian group?

Examination of physical remains can answer some, but not all, of these behavioral questions. No matter how skilled you are as an archaeologist, you will have a difficult time drawing conclusions about behavior from the assemblage of artifacts. The behavioral granularity is very coarse and cannot eludicate the thought processes of individuals or the collective civilization.

Now, imagine you're an IT archaeologist (of course, there are no such titles, at least not yet...). Your job is to reconstruct the behavior patterns that resulted in the assemblage of technology artifacts in an organization. What were the collective and individual decisions that led to the purchase of a particular mainframe system? What behaviors led to a decision to install client-server platforms for enterprise applications? What caused the organization to pick a particular vendor platform over another? Why are organizations so interested in Open Source software now? What behavior patterns does that choice imply?

An organization's current IT architecture is a collection of artifacts, an assemblage of physical (and even mental) artifacts in the form of employees with specific knowledge of these "heritage" systems that accumulated through years of organizational and individual behaviors and choices. Behaviors caused your current IT architecture to be in its present state.

However, behaviors not only resulted in your current assemblage of IT artifacts; they also attempted to resolve challenges by implementing processes and chartering organizational functions whose sole purpose was to make sure IT systems worked and supported business needs. Central architecture organizations were formed, sometimes as federated teams from various business units and sometimes as central organizations chartered to oversee IT architecture and govern the technology and standards allowed in the architecture.

The organizational recognition of the increased complexity of IT systems required dedicated oversight and architectural attention. This role befell the chief technology officer (CTO) and chief architect. In the past, generally it was the CTO who had oversight for the organization's architecture and technology. Now, however, the SOA movement is presenting new challenges to enterprise architecture organizations. The architectural goal of "build things and make them work" is no longer good enough.

ARCHITECTURE'S ROLE IN AN SOA

The definition of "architect" is: *one who designs and supervises the construction of buildings or other large structures.* The appropriateness of the building construction metaphor has been discussed at length by others. Here we only say that the notion of building IT architectures that emulate rigid fixed structures has clearly been realized, much to the chagrin of business leaders who need a better way to respond dynamically to changing business conditions without being hindered by the digital concrete of current IT architectures and enterprise applications. Perhaps the very title "architect" has resulted in artifacts that are like buildings—fixed, rigid, sturdy, unchanging— as opposed to fluid, agile, flexible, nimble, or malleable. The "building" metaphor of architecture is too static to suit the requirements of IT based on SOA. "Architecture" must become an adaptive process that mediates business and technical changes and ensures that IT solutions can adapt and change in conjunction with business changes.

The current role and process of architecture must be reexamined in light of the demand for SOA and reusable services. The past role of enterprise architecture must be attuned to the nuances of SOA in today's business enterprise. Again, recall the IT artifacts we are left with. The behavior that caused these artifacts indicates processes and capabilities that did not emphasize interoperability and shared reusable services. These IT artifacts consist of rigid IT architectures characterized by legacy systems, inflexible "digital concrete" of enterprise applications, and a portfolio of applications cemented with integration software to make them interoperate.

The process and role of enterprise architecture must be reengineered to provide the vision, leadership, and active participation in the implementation of SOAs based on services. Architects must adapt to the new realities of IT and enterprise architecture—from getting systems to work to making services work together.

SOA will fail unless the process of architecture is radically changed from one of static advice and creation of color PowerPoint slides, application blueprints, and architecture roadmaps to one of actively shaping and implementing flexible and reusable IT assets that support business processes. In other words, SOA.

DYNAMIC ARCHITECTURE VERSUS STATIC ARCHITECTURE

Agile SOA is the key concept. What is agile SOA? Agile SOA is based on services that can be enhanced and extended without negatively impacting current consumers. Agile SOA is predicated on an agile services lifecycle process of identifying, modeling, and implementing services quickly in response to business and IT requirements. Agile SOA is predicated on flexible enabling technology solutions that can facilitate and accommodate the inevitable environmental, business, and technology changes. Service-oriented agility is the concept most organizations seek, yet they have not determined how "agility" translates into an operational concept of SOA, services, the enabling infrastructure and management processes SOA requires.

Once SOA is under way in organizations, they must adjust their enterprise architecture process from a static offline advisory function to an active shaping of IT flexibility and asset reusability. Exhibit 7.1 depicts the potential impact of an SOA on existing IT organizational structures—IT governance and IT architecture. The drivers of an SOA initiative, which are the motivating forces for SOA change in an organization, will superimpose an SOA governance model onto the existing structural makeup of an IT organization. The SOA governance process will impact IT governance, enterprise architecture, and other governance processes within the organization. The impact on each of these IT institutions may be minimal, but chances are the impact will be somewhat profound. Either way, an organization should be prepared to tune and adjust the IT governance and enterprise architecture models as the requirements of SOA become more mission critical.

Before taking this task on, we first have to devise a general model of IT architecture. Once this model is established and understood, we will adapt this to an SOA initiative. Chapter 8 addresses the new

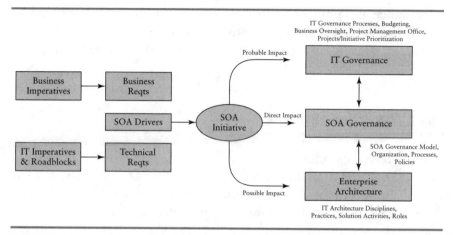

EXHIBIT 7.1   SOA Governance vis-à-vis an IT Organization

requirements of enterprise architecture to meet the demands of SOA. Here we shift our attention to the bigger picture of SOA: SOA governance and behavior.

SOA: SPATIAL AND TEMPORAL CHALLENGES

SOA is not a big bang implementation model based on a single momentous event. SOA is a conceptual IT architecture, based on reusable services, that is achieved over multiple implementations of "services" projects across an organization through time. The "services" are not implemented centrally. They are implemented through many projects over time, potentially across multiple departments, business processes, and business units, eventually to reach some critical mass of SOA benefits. SOA is accomplished through continuous iterations.

However, SOA is a spatially and temporally distributed process, and these features of SOA are very challenging for many organizations. How do you enforce a consistent set of design, reuse, and interoperability standards across a spatially diverse organization so that the ultimate benefits of SOA can be realized? How do you manage the temporal challenges of SOA, where services developed using one generation of Web services standards have the potential for incompatibility with a later generation of Web services standards? SOA governance and policies address these issues. Policies are enforced by a combination of decree, education, employee management, incentives, and overall enforcement during service design, publishing/discovery, and at run-time.

SOA GOVERNANCE OVERVIEW

SOA governance refers to the organization, processes, policies, and metrics required to manage an SOA successfully. A successful SOA is one that meets defined business objectives over time. In addition, an SOA governance model establishes the behavioral rules and guidelines of the organization and participants in the SOA, from architects and developers to service consumers, service providers, and even applications and the services themselves. These behavioral rules and guidelines are established via a body of defined SOA policies. SOA policies are specific and cover business, organizational, compliance, security, and technology facets of services operating within an SOA.

SOA governance consists of the organization and processes required to guide the business success of an SOA. SOA governance defines and enforces the policies that are needed to manage an SOA for business success.

SOA governance is crucial to transitioning from point-to-point Web services to reusable business services. SOA governance involves defining the organizational issues, the governance processes and procedures, and the necessary SOA policies required to manage services and the SOA infrastructure throughout the SOA lifecycle. While governance addresses the organization, processes, and required policies for managing an SOA, the SOA policies are the essential ingredient that must be enforced at service design, publishing, discovery, invocation, and management. Policies can be business policies, security policies, standards compliance policies such as WS-I, or internal standards and other technical policies.

For an SOA, SOA governance:

- Provides overall SOA oversight and management
- Defines architectural standards, developer guidelines, and specific policies that are enforceable across the services lifecycle—from design, development/enablement, publishing, discovery,

and run-time and across all architecture and development processes

- Clarifies services ownership and stewardship across the organization, including budgeting processes, maintenance responsibilities, infrastructure management, and so forth
- Defines services development and lifecycle management issues (e.g., service design, development/enablement, publishing to a services registry, discovery, invocation/run-time, management, maintenance, quality assurance, versioning and reuse)

SOA governance is a master thread running through the organization, processes, and roles in an SOA. It holds everything together and guides the activities of an SOA toward achieving its stated business and technical goals. An SOA governance model includes these elements:

- *Organization.* Defines the organizational structure and management processes for SOA oversight and management control.
- *Processes.* Defines the roles, responsibilities, and procedures for managing SOA processes and activities, including design, development, publishing, maintenance, and so forth.
- *Policies.* Consists of the body of SOA policies that will be enforced at design and run-time, including business policies, industry and organizational standards, security standards and policies, release procedures, publishing, reuse.
- *Metrics.* Must include business metrics, process metrics, performance metrics, service-level agreements (SLAs), and SOA governance metrics, such as SOA conformance and developer exception reporting.
- *Behavior.* Creates a behavioral model through its body of defined policies, which instills and enforces the behaviors necessary for the business success of an SOA. Behavior includes human behavior, such as management, architects, developers, consumers, and providers of services, but it also includes behavior of services as they interact and interoperate with the context of orchestrated business processes enabled by services. Behavior, culture, and both organizational and individual incentives are critical to instilling a reuse and SOA culture. Change management practices will help organizations drive the necessary changes in order to shift behavior to support SOA initiatives.

Each of these dimensions of SOA governance is explored in subsequent sections.

ORGANIZATION OF GOVERNANCE

If you are assigning an SOA core team, an architecture oversight board, an XML core team, or the like, you are creating an organizational model for SOA governance. Marks and others have captured the impact of organizational structure on the performance of a given process.[1] SOA governance is no different. How the governance organization is established will determine how it functions in a specific enterprise context. Therefore, attention should be paid to the structure, participants, and roles of the SOA governance organization as well as how it impacts existing IT and business governance functions.

SOA initiatives can impact IT organizations in a number of ways, as shown in Exhibit 7.2. An SOA initiative, along with an appropriate SOA governance model, will impact existing IT governance processes and the existing enterprise architecture model. SOA places new decision emphasis on projects where in some cases reuse and interoperability take precedence over the needs of individual projects within business units. In other words, the SOA greater good will overrule specific requirements of a business unit if there is reuse and leverage to be obtained from such an initiative.

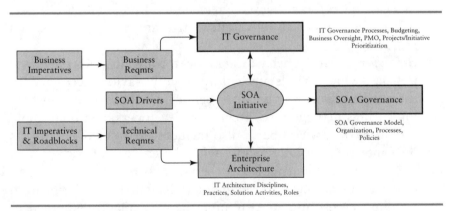

EXHIBIT 7.2   Relationship of SOA Governance to Overall IT Organization

Consider the case where a project budget may increase to obtain reuse of services. If reuse can be clearly demonstrated, then the increased budget can be justified. However, any incremental budget may have to be provided by a central SOA organization that is responsible for overall SOA projects, shared infrastructure, and special investments that are SOA-specific. Furthermore, reuse metrics suggest a 50% incremental cost to develop software for reuse. Although these numbers may or may not be appropriate for services, especially when the development process is different in many ways, the incremental cost and potential elapsed time to ensure reuse must be factored into budgeting and governance decision criteria.

SOA governance will force certain decisions to be resolved above the individual business unit and project level. The governance organization and processes must accommodate these scenarios.

SOA governance impacts existing enterprise architecture as well. (This topic is covered in Chapter 8.) Note, however, that the SOA governance model must incorporate decisions about the current architecture model, organization, process, and skills. We have documented the fact that current architecture practices are not tuned to the nuances of SOA. Enterprise architecture, application architecture, data architecture, and related architectural disciplines will have to be upgraded and tuned to a services model based on an SOA.

Exhibit 7.3 depicts how an SOA initiative may impact existing IT architecture within an IT organization.

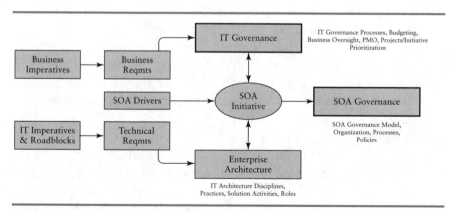

EXHIBIT 7.3   Enterprise Architecture May Be Affected by an SOA Initiative

Based on the specific SOA strategy, enterprise architecture, and IT governance model, an SOA governance model and its associated body of policies will be developed to implement and enforce those SOA and enterprise architectural goals.

WHAT DOES SOA GOVERNANCE DO?

What specifically are the activities that SOA governance provides oversight for? How is SOA governance accomplished? And who does it? SOA governance encompasses high-level activities and processes. SOA governance:

- *Determines SOA architecture oversight.* Who is responsible for the SOA technical architecture? Who owns the standards and monitoring of conformance to the SOA policies? How does the role and process of enterprise architecture change in an SOA context? Who determines appropriate levels of business service granularity and generality?
- *Establishes SOA policies.* Defines and enforces policies that will ensure conformance to the SOA goals, standards, and overall objectives across all process of SOA, including design, publishing, discovery, and run-time. Who will have access to the service? How will credentials be managed? What are the security policies for the SOA?
- *Establishes funding models.* Budgeting practices and funding models are challenges that must be addressed early in the SOA process. Who will pay for building and maintaining services? Who will pay for new shared SOA enabling technology when it is required by a specific project yet will be shared across business units? How will the *SOA greater good* be funded for shared services and infrastructure? Many organizations budget at the project level, where the project and its funding are subsidized by one business unit. This model creates conflict when SOA seeks the development of shared reusable services across business domains. A funding model that creates organizational incentives to develop reusable services for the greater good of the organization is essential. Creating this will require some creativity, new incentive models, and authority to implement these kinds of changes.

- *Implements the SOA governance process.* How will the interdependencies of shared services be managed within the SOA? What organizational and process challenges will be faced? Who will mediate conflicts between organizations?
- *Governs services definition, creation, and publishing.* How will services be defined, developed, and later modified? Who will have design authority? Upon whose requirements? Who owns the services? Who governs publishing and discovery? What technology platforms are necessary to implement SOA governance?
- *Establishes policies and processes for quality of service/SLA management.* What quality of service will be provided? Is high availability required by some but not others? Who will enforce the SLAs? What enabling technology will enforce policies and implement management for services?

SOA governance affects more areas, but this list sets the stage for its complexity and criticality.

SOA GOVERNANCE ORGANIZATIONAL MODEL

The SOA governance model below, based on typical preexisting structures within most organizations, may prove useful. The categorization of services follows a tiered model based on whether the services are business process services, infrastructure services, or hybrids.

Exhibit 7.4 illustrates this tiered model for SOA governance based on a tiered approach.

Supporting this generic tiered model, the following SOA governance organizational model may make sense. Depending on the organization, its IT organization and its enterprise architecture model, newly formed teams may be required to implement SOA governance. An SOA core team can assume multiple responsibilities until a formalized SOA governance and organizational model is established.

As you determine the organization, structure, and roles of your SOA governance model, you must consider the existing structures and processes you have as well as possibly adding overlay organizations onto them. This is a challenging exercise, as the process of SOA governance must not be additive to already-burdened job tasks. SOA governance must become the "company way" in all behaviors

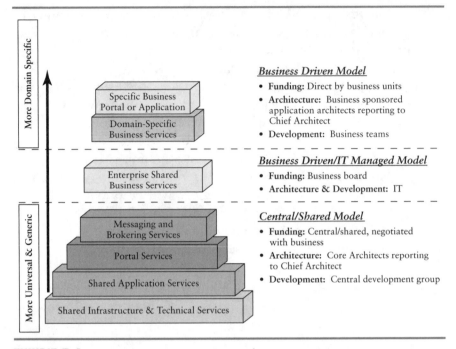

EXHIBIT 7.4   Tiered Governance Example
Source: Graphic Courtesy of BEA

and decision-making processes. The list below describes common SOA governance organizations and structures that may apply to your organization:

- *SOA leadership team (steering committee).* Executive team comprised of business and IT leadership.
  - *Goal.* Ensure SOA efforts align to business and IT strategic goals. Ensure budgets and funding are in place for SOA infrastructure and initial services rollouts. Review and approve SOA roadmap and business initiative roadmaps, project plans, budgets, and so on.
  - *Duration.* Ongoing, quarterly meetings or on-demand as projects dictate.
- *SOA core team.* Senior team composed of senior business and IT leadership.
  - *Goal.* Develop the initial SOA strategy, vision, policy, and governance model, standards and infrastructure, and spearhead

the initial services rollouts. Serve as a catalyst for ongoing SOA efforts. Evangelize the SOA benefits to the IT and business organizations. Be SOA coaches for the enterprise.

- *Duration.* May disband once formal SOA governance structure and processes are in place and these functions are absorbed by other processes and structures to be described.

■ *Process services team.* Senior business team composed of business leadership, process owners, and IT support personnel.

- *Goal.* Identify and prioritize business initiatives for SOA inclusion. Identify opportunities for services within and across business units. Determine ownership for business services, common process services, and budgeting for these initiatives. Develop business initiative roadmap with SOA core team. Review business initiatives with SOA core team/SOA leadership team, architecture services team (via SOA review board).
- *Duration.* Ongoing. Chairs Process Services Review Board for inclusion into business initiative roadmap.

■ *Architecture services team.* CTO, chief architect, and IT services leads (enterprise services, information service, process services).

- *Goal.* Create SOA policy and governance model. Identify and enforce architecture compliance to standards, development goals and guidelines, security policies, and business policies. Chair the SOA Architecture Review Board for infrastructure and process services proposals. Ensure all initiatives conform to the SOA governance model.
- *Duration.* Ongoing.

■ *Enterprise services team.* IT infrastructure services team members.

- *Goal.* Implement and manage the enabling infrastructure for the SOA. Includes baseline horizontal services for SOA enablement as well as security, messaging, audit, and related functions. Member of the SOA core team and Architecture Review Board.
- *Duration.* Ongoing.

■ *Information/data services team.* Data warehousing, analytics, data modules and information delivery team members.

- *Goal.* Implement and manage the enabling capabilities for information harvesting and delivery to consuming business units, processes, and users. Includes identifying and selecting infrastructure unique to delivering information services, such

as metadata management. Also includes development and ongoing stewardship of the canonical data model.
- *Duration.* Ongoing.

Specific SOA governance roles and responsibilities must be defined for each organization based on its SOA strategy, governance model, and specific business services. This SOA governance organizational reference model may prove useful in establishing an organizational model suited to your particular needs.

SOA GOVERNANCE PROCESSES

The SOA governance process is more than establishing the governance model and the policies that will be enforced. It actually is the process of governing the SOA. The governance process can be challenging because it may be partially manual. SOA governance can include design-time activities, such as design reviews, code reviews, testing and quality assurance processes, and the like. However, SOA run-time processes may require automated management platforms to ensure quality of service, reliability, load balancing, and failover, among many other requirements. Clearly these processes must be automated, using automated policy-enforcement. In the big picture, SOA requires policy enforcement across all SOA lifecycle processes. We call this closed loop SOA governance.

CLOSED LOOP SOA GOVERNANCE

SOA governance must also be enforced in various SOA and IT processes, such as services lifecycle processes (e.g., design, development, and deployment), as well as during SOA and services management, monitoring, analysis, and optimization. We advocate a closed loop SOA governance model. By "closed loop governance," we mean the ability to centrally define governance and SOA policies as well as enforce them across all SOA lifecycle processes—from service design and development to publishing and discovery, and ultimately through services operations and run-time. Policy and run-time feedback should be captured and fed back into the service design process to provide important feedback on services performance, SLA effectiveness, and overall consumer experience with services. Doing this ultimately provides the closed loop SOA governance model.

Implementation of closed loop SOA governance must include the key lifecycle processes of an SOA, including design, publishing/discovery, and run-time operations. The SOA governance aspects of these major lifecycle processes follow.

Design-Time Governance

Design-time SOA governance is accomplished by discovering, identifying, and inventorying business and technology assets using metadata catalogs. Metadata catalogs are repositories for various IT assets, including executables, design patterns and related knowledge assets, object libraries, software modules, and even services and related artifacts. Metadata catalogs provide support for developers who are implementing reuse policies and best practices. These design-time metadata catalogs integrate with developer tools and integrated development environments (IDE) for all major application development platforms to enable developers to use their normal development tools and processes when they reuse services and other software development assets.

Increasingly, these design-time metadata catalogs provide tools that support SOA governance where the specific policies intersect with the software or services development process. The increased convergence of offline design-time metadata repositories with run-time metadata solutions, such as service registries, will be interesting to watch as SOA implementation efforts mature.

At the completion of service design, the service will be prepared for publishing to a service registry.

Design-time governance requirements include:

- Application of SOA policies to services development processes
- Process policies, such as reuse, design reviews, code reviews, release procedures

- Technical policies, such as schema usage, WS-I conformance, security policies, compliance policies
- Automation through service validation processes
- Access to operational and run-time metadata

Publishing and Discovery Governance

When publishing services to a service registry, there are clear governance processes and policies to be enforced. For example, the publishing process may require eight predecessor steps to be completed satisfactorily first:

1. Complete exposing or development of service.
2. Unit test service.
3. Check SOA conformance of the service to governance model and policies of your SOA.
4. Receive "certification" that the service complies with your policies sufficient to be published.
5. Store the certification into a metadata registry with an association to that service.
6. Begin publishing process; verify that user has authorization to publish services to the registry.
7. If user does not have publishing authorization, he or she must submit the service and conformance certification to the registry owner or librarian who has authorization to publish to the registry.
8. Upon review of the service, test data, conformance certification, it will be published to the registry.

With respect to discovery governance, when locating services available in an SOA, whether by role, function, authorization, or what have you, policies are ultimately what determine a system or individual's access to services.

Publishing and discovery governance issues include:

- Application of policies controlling the service publishing process
- Roles, security, authorization, validation of services and metadata

- Conformance validation prior to publishing
- Application of policies affecting the discovery of services (design-time and run-time discovery)

Run-Time Governance

When consuming or invoking services, policies are enforced by inspecting the SOAP message headers for WS-Policy metadata in the form of assertions about policies asserted by the service providers. Run-time governance and policy enforcement will be essential sooner than most people expect, as major software vendors are planning to offer their software products as bundles of services contained in a services registry that will ship with their software. The real issue here is the potential proliferation of registries in the enterprise with no clear path toward federating them into a single view of the enterprise. A single federated view of all the metadata in an SOA or in an enterprise is essential to optimize reuse of these assets and to manage them all under a given set of governance policies. When there is no federated view of assets, services, and the associated metadata in an SOA, chaos is likely to ensue. Multiple fiefdoms of metadata and services will arise with no possibility of reuse, central management, or overall SOA policy enforcement. Failure to enforce SOA policies means that services may not interoperate because there is no consistent implementation of interoperability conventions and standards or implementation of specific standards and policies specific to that particular organization.

Run-time governance requirements include:

- Enforce policies during service consumption.
- For internal services, enforce internal policies, monitor services, feedback.
- For external services, enforce policies using acceptance criteria to allow consumption of external services.
- Close the loop to design governance by pushing metadata back to the design process.

WHAT IS THE SOA GOVERNANCE PROCESS?

Defining and implementing SOA governance is a series of steps that begin with SOA strategy and planning, business and IT objectives, and the standards and guidelines that are targeted for the SOA. SOA governance is a process that occurs through three high-level steps:

1. Define overall SOA governance model, organization, and process.
2. Define SOA policies to be enforced:
3. Implement SOA governance policy and enforcement

Define the Overall SOA Governance Model, Organization, and Process

The first task is to define the overarching governance model, which determines high-level organization, governance processes, services ownership, budgeting, and funding issues for an SOA. This step establishes ownership and funding models for various classes of services that will be defined and implemented in your enterprise. This overall SOA governance model establishes the operating model and rules for the SOA.

- Define SOA goals and objectives. (This step should have been completed already during the SOA strategy and planning process.)
- Define the SOA metrics, such as business, process, return on investment (ROI), performance and SLA metrics, as well as SOA conformance metrics.
- Define the SOA governance organizational model and governance processes required.
- Define services ownership across the organization and process model. Note that a service taxonomy may be required first to determine who owns what kinds of services. We suggest a simple service taxonomy initially: process services, enterprise services, technical services, and infrastructure services.

Define SOA Policies to Be Enforced

Next we turn to the policies, or the specific "rules of engagement," for designing, building/exposing, and operating services within an SOA. SOA governance is an exercise in futility without enforceable policies that will drive conformance to the SOA vision, goals, and standards. The policies that will be enforced include specific design-time and run-time policies. These policies must support and enable the higher-level SOA governance model. Four steps are necessary for defining policies to be enforced during SOA governance:

1. Define SOA policies needed based on business and technical requirements.
2. Define conformance processes across the services lifecycle (e.g., design, development/enablement, deployment, publishing, discovering, operation/run-time, management, and maintenance activities).
3. Govern the SOA and associated services using the defined policies.
4. Measure conformance to the SOA governance model by examining multiple areas of conformance.[2]

   Policies. What are our policies? Where are they implemented? How are they enforced during design, development, and run-time? Where are the gaps?

   Enterprise services. What enterprise services are being developed or exposed? How are policies being enforced during development? Is policy enforcement automated during the services lifecycle?

   Conformance status. Do our services (and others we consume) conform to our policies? What is the impact of nonconformance on service operations or business processes (e.g., security intrusions, SLA degradation, inoperable services)?

   Impact analysis. What happens to the SOA and associated business processes and business services if a policy is changed (e.g., SOAP policy, adding new metadata to SOAP message headers, message encoding policies, etc.)?

Interdependencies. How will business processes and operations be impacted by changes to services? What mission-critical processes will be impacted or fail due to a service change or enhancement? What regression testing processes must be followed when a service changes and other processes or business units rely on that service?

Exception management. How will policy exceptions be granted for services used by a specific project? What is the impact of policy exceptions? What minimal tier of policies must always be enforced in order for a service to be consumed? Should there be tiers of policies to handle the exception process?

The concept of SOA policies is explained in detail next.

SOA POLICIES: WHERE SOA GOVERNANCE GETS REAL

SOA governance is the body of policies that drives the overall behavioral model of the participants of the SOA and ensures the interoperability of the services operating in the SOA. Behavior of services and behavior of the participants on the SOA are the real challenges of an SOA. Policies define the parameters for the acceptable behaviors of both.

SOA governance is accomplished by policies. Policies are the specific rules that services adhere to at design time and run-time as well as the behavioral policies that developers and architects adhere to. There are thus enterprise policies that all SOA parties must adhere to (e.g., "Reuse services before developing/exposing new services") as well as granular technical policies that ensure architectural compliance, such as "avoid RPC Encoded Web services operations," or "use document-centric messaging wherever possible." The nature of the policies is driven by business and technology requirements, which feed into the overall goals of the SOA.

SOA governance is achieved through the definition of policies. However, it is critical to understand that defining clear enforceable policies as part of the SOA governance model is not enough. Policies must be enforced, at design time, at publishing and discovery time, and at run-time. Enforcement of policies in these offline and online capacities brings into play the technical implementation of policies that comprise the SOA governance model. But what do we mean by offline enforcement versus active online enforcement of SOA policies?

Offline policy enforcement occurs in meetings according to the governance model, organization, and overall governance process. It can involve design reviews, code walk-throughs, and other checks and balances during the development lifecycle that help architects understand how well SOA policies are being incorporated into various IT projects and adhered to. This is not far from the normal architectural enforcement model of the pre-SOA enterprise. Policies are reduced to documentation, which must be distributed to architects and developers and reinforced to them with active mentoring and ongoing education and training.

However, policies should not be institutionalized as documentation only. Somehow policies must be integrated into the services design, development, and deployment processes and the services publishing, discovery, and operational processes, or at run-time. Policies must be enforced at run-time by consumers and providers as well. Remember, behaviors are conditioned and shaped for all participants and roles in an SOA—human participants, services, applications, and enabling infrastructure.

Enforcing policies in an automated fashion using various technology solutions is essential for run-time SOA policy enforcement. SOA policy enforcement requires the appropriate enabling technology, including tools such as Web services management (WSM) platforms, policy validation engines, service registries, and metadata management solutions (for both run-time policy enforcement and offline enforcement during development). For example, consuming a service from an outside provider requires that the service contract, or WSDL document, be validated for compliance to the consuming organization's SOA and policies, such as the security assertions contained in the SOAP message headers, and the message encoding specified in the WSDL (e.g., RPC encoded versus Document-Literal, etc.).

Even when consuming an internal service, the policies supported by that service should be validated against the SOA policies to verify conformance. This step is important; in some cases, there may not be a solid process for enforcing policies during the development/enablement process and subsequent publishing of the service to a registry. In fact, a service registry may not even be implemented as part of the SOA enabling technology. Although service registries can help with the enforcement of policies prior to publishing, there is often debate as to when a service registry is needed to manage a particular volume of services. How many services dictate the need for a service registry? Gartner Group, for example, has arbitrarily settled 50 as the number of services at which registries and other SOA infrastructure will be necessary. These are all decisions that must be made case by case, as there are not enough empirical data to suggest a general pattern.

Who Defines Policies?

Policies are defined by multiple members of the IT organization who play a role in the definition of the SOA governance model and overall SOA vision and strategy. IT managers, chief technology officers, chief architects, architects, development managers, team and/or project leaders all can play a role in defining the policies that will comprise the SOA governance model.

Policies ultimately are derived from the business and technical requirements of the SOA initiative and the portfolio of services that will operate in the SOA over time. Therefore, it is likely that an initial body of policies will be defined by an SOA core team to spearhead the implementation of services and SOA in a given organization. In fact, many organizations define their initial policies without calling them policies at all.

Many organizations begin their SOA effort by defining their services design guidelines and best practices within various business process domains. These initial service design guidelines will become the basis for identifying and enforcing specific policies through code reviews and manual SOA governance processes under the oversight of the architects and IT management. Eventually these policies can be implemented as enforceable policies using automation and tools that provide centralized policy definition, management, and policy enforcement across the organization and SOA lifecycle processes.

What Policies Are Required?

Many types of policies must be defined, including:

- *Enterprise policies.* Policies that affect all business units, processes, and roles, such as reuse, security policies, design best practices and standards.
- *Business policies.* Address business issues, including process policies, SLAs and performance criteria, approval levels, spending limits for external services, and more.
- *Process policies.* Who is allowed to publish a service? What minimal standards must be adhered to for a service to be published to a registry? How will versioning of services be managed? How many versions will be allowed? How will new versions of services be advertised to consumers? How will deprecation of older versions be handled?
- *Compliance policies.* Policies that implement regulatory compliance standards and other industry-specific standards, such as HIPAA for healthcare, FIXX and IFX for banking and financial services, and ACORD for Insurance.
- *Technology standards compliance.* Web services standards also apply here, such as compliance to WS-I, appropriate versions of SOAP, WSDL, and UDDI, as well as other related standards including XML Schema, Xpath, and Xquery.
- *Security policies.* Policies that implement the organization's security model and technical standards, such as authorization and authentication policies as well as the standards that will be used to implement security policy. WS-Security standards, SAML, XML Signature, and XML Encryption may be specified for specific use cases of services or the messages sent or received by services.

The body of specific policies will be determined by the overall SOA governance model, defined standards, goals of the SOA, and, of course, the nature of the services that will be exposed or developed internally as well as services consumed from external service providers.

SOA GOVERNANCE IMPLEMENTATION AND INTEGRATION

Implementing SOA governance occurs through a combination of tactics. For organizational aspects of SOA governance, such as services ownership, budgeting issues, and mediating conflicts between organizations and functions, a series of SOA governance forums will suffice. However, some thought must be given to the organizational model for SOA governance. In addition, once an organization model is determined, the processes that implement SOA governance must be considered, such as how SOA governance will be implemented during the service design process, during the architecture process, and during key design reviews and development lifecycle checkpoints. Finally, the nuts and bolts of SOA governance revolve around enforceable policies. Who defines policies, and how will these policies be enforced and results reported on such that the SOA vision and goals can be achieved? Regularly scheduled SOA governance reviews should be planned, along with design reviews, architecture compliance reviews, conformance reviews, and the like.

Eventually, when the SOA enabling technology is fully deployed, an organization may be able to automate enforcement of policies across the full SOA lifecycle, from centralized policy definition and management to the automated enforcement from design to publishing and discovery to run-time operations. At a minimum, organizations should consider automation options when defining their SOA governance processes. The more automation that is put into place, the less intrusive governance becomes to the organization and the more likely that governance processes will be executed consistently.

SOA Governance: Three Basic Steps

SOA governance is a three-step process.

1. The overarching governance model determines high-level organization, governance processes, services ownership, budgeting, and funding issues for an SOA.
2. Policies, or specific "rules of engagement," are created for designing, building/exposing, and operating services within an SOA.

3. SOA governance is implemented and integrated. Often this requires multiple solutions working together to enforce policies across the many processes of an SOA. The integration of services management, messaging platforms, service registries, metadata repositories, development tools, and security solutions must be considered to achieve SOA governance across the SOA lifecycle.

Exhibit 7.5 depicts a generic SOA governance model in two ways: organizationally and functionally. Governance often begins with addressing the organizational aspects of SOA, such as ownership of broad categories of services, budgeting and cost allocation for services and shared enabling infrastructure, and aspects of the development lifecycle that may be impacted by SOA. Exposing and/or developing services is different in some respects from traditional software development, for example, in that additional steps are necessary before services may be consumed. The transition from the requirements-driven waterfall process of software development to a producer-distributor-consumer model requires new processes for asset management, application and enforcement of design-time and run-time standards and policies, and management processes. These may include publishing to a service registry, which would require services to be discovered prior to being invoked.

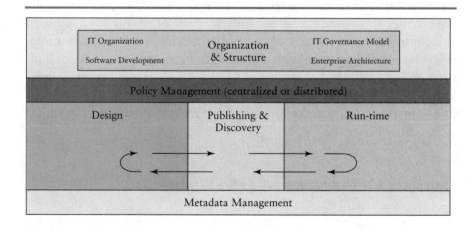

EXHIBIT 7.5   SOA Governance Model: Organizational and Functional View

In addition to organizational and procedural aspects of SOA governance, there are other lifecycle issues to be considered once an overall governance model has been devised. In order for governance to be effective, it must be built on a foundation of specific enforceable policies that will be used to encourage conformance to the goals, standards, and specifications of an organization's SOA governance model. This body of policies will be enforced at multiple points of the services lifecycle, including design time, during the publishing and release process, during the discovery process, and ultimately at run-time.

ENABLING TECHNOLOGY OF SOA GOVERNANCE

SOA governance, like SOA in general, is more than technology. Implementing SOA governance as a body of enforceable policies, or what is known as policy-driven governance, requires automation of policy enforcement as well as an integration and interoperability model across multiple platforms for governance, design, publishing/discovery, and run-time. For example, policy engines would define and manage enterprise governance and policies across the services lifecycle. Design-time governance would enforce design policies during the design, construction, and unit testing of services, as well as determining when they are allowed to be published to a registry. Design-time governance requires processes and policies, and can leverage metadata repositories to provide enforcement. Run-time governance, however, requires a different set of enabling technology in conjunction with a centralized policy engine, such as an intermediary-based architecture with agents and interceptors to enforce run-time policies as services are invoked and routed between consumers and producers. If the vision of a closed loop SOA governance model is to be realized, the governance integration and interoperability issues must be solved.

Centralized SOA Governance and Policy Engines

A new class of SOA enabling technology provides a centralized metadata catalog of enterprise policies as well as the ability to import and export policies from various run-time and design-time platforms. A centralized policy engine allows the decoupling of policies from service design and implementation, which is critical for services version management and maintenance of services. Commercial solutions specialize in providing enterprise SOA governance and automated enforcement across the diverse portfolio of SOA enabling technology that supports design and run-time lifecycle processes. In addition, service registry vendors are extending their UDDI-based (Universal Description, Discovery, and Integration) solutions to include SOA governance and policy management capabilities, as well as adding repositories to their registry solutions.

Policy Enforcement Models

The enforcement of policies within an SOA governance architecture can be accomplished in a variety of ways. One common scenario is to use an SOA intermediary model, where an agent or Web services intermediary actively intercepts SOAP messages and then references a central policy engine to apply the appropriate policies for that service before allowing the message to be routed to its next destination. The SOA intermediary model or agent model is implemented most often in Web services management frameworks and similar run-time fabric implementations where a distributed active intermediary model is used.

In an enterprise service bus (ESB) solution, where end points are integrated by virtue of a highly distributed run-time container, the policy information is provided through configuration of the ESB through centralized administration of the solution. In this policy enforcement approach, care must be taken that policies are clearly abstracted or decoupled from the services that run over the bus. In this model, the ESB acts as a distributed run-time container. Therefore, the policies are applied by "rules" that are defined and managed centrally for the container, or ESB. However, each end point will have its own policies for services, and the ESB must be able to aggregate or know the policies for all participating end points and represent them as enforceable and decoupled policies.

In an application server model, central administration and enforcement of policies will follow a similar set of rules. In this model, policies will be centrally defined, but ensuring that they are decoupled may be a challenge because the rules and administration of SOA policies in an application server architecture are closely related to the design process. Abstracting policies from the service design and development may pose a challenge for developers.

SOA Governance Architecture and Integration

The discussion of SOA governance always turns to the enabling technology and the mechanisms that will be used to enforce policies. Of course, SOA policies may be enforced through manual oversight processes, which were always the purview of design reviews, architecture compliance reviews, and traditional IT governance. However, given the nature of an SOA and the spatial and temporal distribution of services projects in a large enterprise, automating aspects of policy enforcement will help facilitate conformance to the SOA standards and goals that the policies represent.

Therefore, the concept of an SOA governance architecture is important. In addition to the enabling technology required to develop and operate services, which absorbs much of the attention of SOA practitioners in the early adoption phase of SOA, there is a need to ensure that the tools and technology solutions will support an SOA governance model with automated policy enforcement. For example, many organizations are exploring various SOA run-time and integration technology solutions, including ESBs, Web services management (WSM) solutions, application server suites, business process management (BPM) tools, service orchestration solutions, as well as enterprise application integration (EAI) solutions. In addition, supporting these core run-time stacks with service registries, metadata management platforms, and supplemental development tools such as XML modeling and diagnostics solutions adds to the mix. Organizations should also consider expanding services policy enforcement back into the services development lifecycle to minimize the cost of design errors by identifying them early in the development process.

The challenge, given this enabling technology confusion, is to define the SOA governance model and enforceable policies, as well as how those policies will be enforced, *prior* to selecting the enabling technology solutions. We believe that the SOA governance model and policies should be defined in parallel with identification and appropriate modeling of an organization's services before beginning to select technology platforms. This "services-driven architecture model" helps ensure that the technology solutions will support the technical requirements of the targeted business services, which is not always the case when a technology platform is selected and then identification of appropriate services begins.

SOA governance must also be considered in a similar fashion. Identify the SOA governance model and policies that must be enforced for the targeted services, then ensure that the chosen SOA enabling technology will be able to implement automated policy enforcement, either immediately or at least in some future versions of the particular class of technology.

In all cases, seek to decouple your SOA policies from your service.

Technology and Standards of SOA Governance and Policies

SOA governance as a discipline requires technology to implement. The technology and standards of SOA governance, and in particular policy enforcement, are relatively immature. Implementing policy-driven SOA governance relies on a body of extended Web services specifications that includes:

- WS-Policy
- Web Services Policy Language
- WS-MetadataExchange
- WS-Addressing
- WS-MessageDelivery

These emerging specifications fundamentally build on the established standards for Web services such as SOAP, WSDL, UDDI, XML, and XML Schema. However, the standards for policy management and SOA governance will continue to evolve in parallel with standards and approaches to managing metadata within an SOA. Here we focus briefly on the standards relating to policies at a high level.[3]

The primary standard for defining policies is WS-Policy. WS-Policy is actually comprised of three specifications: WS-PolicyFramework, WS-PolicyAssertions, and WS-PolicyAttachment. WS-PolicyFramework is the "container" specification that includes WS-PolicyAssertions and WS-PolicyAttachment and is referred to as WS-Policy.

Policies are simply assertions about a service that allow the consumer to find, evaluate, and invoke the services according to an agreed-upon SLA. Policy assertions "inform the requester about any additional information beyond 'plain' WSDL that may be needed to successfully invoke the provider's service."[4] The provider's service publishes its policy information so that potential consumers can access it, consume and process it, and successfully invoke the service. WS-Policy is an XML grammar for expressing policies such that they can be consumed and evaluated using rules or algorithms to determine whether the SLA can be met and thus the service can be consumed. Some policy assertions will be mandatory, while others may be optional. Some policy assertions will offer choices such as "exactly one," "all," or "one or more." For example, enclosing policy assertions in these various operators will tell a consumer what policies are mandatory, whether there are choices as to one or the other policy (e.g., security options or alternate transports), or whether a group of policies must all be applied (e.g., the "All" operator).

Without digging into deep technical details, the challenge of policy-driven SOA governance is to define the specific policies that will be enforced during services consumption. The body of policies will be codified in XML using the WS-Policy specification. A potential consumer of a service requests the policy information as an XML document conforming to the WS-Policy specification, so the consumer can format the request for the WSDL that will be used to invoke the service. There are a few issues and challenges related to SOA governance.

First, there is no consensus about how to codify and enforce policy in an SOA. As mentioned, three standards specifications cover SOA policy:

1. *WS-PolicyFramework.* Developed by BEA, IBM, Microsoft, and SAP
2. *Web Services Policy Language (WSPL).* Created by a subgroup of the OASIS XACML Technical Committee

3. *WSDL 2.0.* Includes the features and properties portion of WSDL devised by the WSDL Work Group at W3C to accommodate policy

The disputes range from which standard should prevail to questions around the inclusion of policy assertions within the WSDL documents. Policy management is a relatively immature domain, and the number of standards combined with the widespread industry buzz about SOA governance will ensure some volatility around policy for some time to come.

Another area of discussion involves whether policy assertions should be contained in the WSDL document. There has been recent discussion of the need to decouple policies from service descriptions because it is likely that an organization may apply different policies to the same service depending on who is consuming it (internal or external consumer), how it is being consumed, and by what process. Given this reality, decoupling policies from the service contract makes sense so an organization can centrally manage, modify, and update policies in an abstract fashion separate from the WSDL descriptions.

Finally, the process of evaluating policy assertions and determining which ones are mandatory versus optional is in flux. WS-Policy relies on a process whereby policies are expressed as a checklist that is matched between the provider and consumer, and numerical scores determine the relative preference for policies. If the checklist matches well enough, according to the mathematical criteria, then the service can be invoked successfully. However, WSDL relies on a scheme where policies are expressed as rules that are evaluated prior to invoking the service. The rules are evaluated as a tree structure, where the priority of the rules is established by the sequence in which they are specified.

As with the other standards of SOA and Web services, eventually the policy management standards will be resolved. In the meantime, workarounds for SOA governance are quite straightforward: Use manual policy enforcement for design-time governance, and automate policy enforcement of basic mandatory policies within the WSDL document. When the standards mature and the clear winner emerges, then the notion of decoupling policies from WSDL will most likely be realized. Decoupling policies from services will allow the central definition, management, and enforcement of policies in a holistic SOA governance and policy enforcement model.

To summarize, metadata management requirements for SOA governance:

- Provide a management framework across the entire SOA governance process.
- Must integrate software asset metadata (design time) as well as operational metadata (run-time).
- Must incorporate a federated view of metadata, including registries and repositories.
- Must support the processes and roles across the SOA lifecycle.

SOA Governance Integration and Interoperability

SOA governance requires the federation and integration of multiple solutions in an SOA depending on how various enabling technology solutions are implemented to support a given SOA strategy. The following SOA enabling technology solutions could be part of an SOA governance architecture:

- Policy enforcement engine
- Service registry
- Metadata repository (development and run-time, which may be provided by two separate solutions: one by software asset reuse repositories and one typically provided by WSM vendors)
- Web services management solution (to provide intermediary services)
- ESB (if no WSM is installed, this will provide the intermediary services)
- SOA run-time solutions

To implement an enforceable governance model, the various pieces of SOA enabling technology must be integrated in support of a coherent governance process.

Battle for Control of SOA Governance

In light of the amount of vendor activity focused on it, SOA governance is shaping up as a dynamic SOA subdiscipline. It seems as if all SOA software vendors are claiming to deliver or manage some aspect of SOA governance. The various SOA vendors may indeed have a role to play in the implementation of policy-driven SOA governance. However, the real question is one of control. Where should SOA governance be controlled, and by what solutions?

Recent entrants into the SOA software fray have created a new approach to SOA governance based on a policy-driven model. These solutions implement an approach to SOA governance that is based on two broad requirements.

1. SOA policies should be defined and managed centrally in a policy engine that manages and enforces all SOA policies across the entire SOA lifecycle.
2. Policies must be enforced across all SOA processes, from service design, to publishing and discovery, and at run-time.

This approach, which is fundamentally the right one, creates two further SOA governance requirements:

1. SOA policies must be decoupled from the services, not embedded in the implementation of the service.
2. SOA governance must be implemented across multiple technology solutions that maintain control of those SOA lifecycle processes (e.g., service design, publishing/discovery, and run-time). This creates a potential SOA governance integration issue.

Service registries, based on the UDDI standard, are trying to assert control of SOA governance by being the primary solution for defining and managing policies in addition to managing for publishing and discovery of services. This seems somewhat reactive since UDDI has not lived up to its originally envisioned role in an SOA. Furthermore, service registries do not maintain control of the design process or the run-time process. Thus a distributed model with a centrally defined and managed body of policies must be used to implement SOA governance.

SOA governance promises to be an interesting domain. Although there is much more to SOA governance than technology and integration, these challenges certainly will be very real over the next few years as automated enforcement of policies becomes mainstream for achieving the goals of SOA initiatives across widely distributed IT organizations and business enterprises.

Governance Summary

SOA governance is an essential ingredient for SOA success. We have shown what governance is comprised of, how policies implement an SOA governance model, and how these policies can be enforced using technology solutions. We also reviewed an approach to developing an SOA governance model and the required policies to achieve business and technology objectives. We also highlighted kinds of policies you will need in your SOA as you evolve it over time. SOA governance is critical to SOA success.

SOA BEHAVIORAL MODEL: BEYOND SOA GOVERNANCE

One area of possible change in many organizations to enable a more successful SOA initiative is the architecture process. However, the success of SOA also demands a new behavioral model for success. The behavioral model for an SOA is partially defined in the governance model, through the body of policies that will be enforced to drive conformance to the SOA standards, guidelines, and best practices. However, the behavior of an SOA also depends on structural and organizational factors, the roles and participants, and the processes that thread through the organization and roles and tie them together to achieve the stated mission and goals.

Many organizations now realize that the success of their SOA will demand the formulation of an SOA governance model and a body of enforceable SOA policies that will guide the desired management, architectural, and developer behavior within the context of the

SOA initiative. But attaining the desired SOA behavior from all its participants demands more than an SOA governance model.

SOA governance establishes the overall behavioral model of the SOA as it relates to the current IT organization, behaviors and skills, and culture of the organization. SOA governance is more than just the business and technical policies that define accepted development and run-time standards and procedures for services. It also guides the expected behavior of management, architects, developers, service consumers and providers, as well as IT management regarding the overall success of the SOA in achieving its defined objectives.

SOA governance specifies and enforces conformance to SOA policies, which define the overall behavior pattern of the participants of an SOA, such as architects, developers, services, service consumers, service providers, and others. As a recent WebLayers whitepaper notes, "Policies are the cornerstone of Governance. Policies set goals by which you direct and measure [SOA] success. Without policies there is no Governance."[5]

SOA governance is a major determinant of the organizational, technical, and behavioral success of an SOA. Governance is so essential that it must be built into the SOA planning and deployment from day one. In an SOA, the services are the lasting assets. Designing and implementing a portfolio of services in an SOA that are reusable, interoperable, and meet the needs of the business is fundamentally a behavioral problem. The necessary SOA behavior favors reuse over custom software development. The desired SOA behavior favors the SOA greater good over the needs of individuals, departments, and business units. The desired SOA behavior favors conformance to SOA policies such that interoperable reusable services can be achieved, which enables the additional SOA benefits of service and process orchestration, time to market, and increased business agility. SOA is a lifestyle change. It begins and ends with behavior and culture.

Role of Culture and Behavior in an SOA

How does behavior and culture affect the relative success of an SOA initiative? What are the moving parts of the behavioral and cultural machine that can be leveraged to positively influence behaviors toward a "services" behavior pattern? Behavior and cultural issues are major determinants of SOA success, because SOA is ultimately a composite behavior pattern that emphasizes multiple SOA themes, such as:

- Values reuse of services over developing new services
- Values reuse of components and other IT assets
- Requires conformance to SOA guidelines, principles and standards, and overall policies
- Achieving IT productivity through reuse
- Reusing fundamental services available within the SOA to develop business solutions faster, cheaper, and better
- Achieving faster time to market for IT services to the business

These behaviors all derive from the firm's organizational and cultural fabric. These behaviors have to be defined, agreed on, and enforced in order to achieve the benefits of SOA. The role of behavior in an SOA initiative is often overlooked because it is a very challenging aspect of SOA to solve. The organizational, process, and behavioral issues are among the most difficult to manage in an SOA.

Exhibit 7.6 depicts a high-level behavioral model that brings together the aspects of an SOA that relate to cultural and behavioral forces. Ultimately, the behaviors that will help make an SOA succeed derive from the current corporate culture and must be reinforced, modified, or completely reprogrammed. Changing organizational behavior is a challenging process.

It is important to recognize the impact of organizational factors on behavior and performance of an organization. Chapter 8 discusses the impact of SOA on enterprise architecture and suggests approaches to tuning the process of architecture to the needs of an SOA.

Many factors influence the behaviors related to SOA success. The major influences are:

- SOA vision, goals, and guidelines
- SOA governance model
- SOA metrics
- SOA organization and structure (vis-à-vis existing IT and business structures)

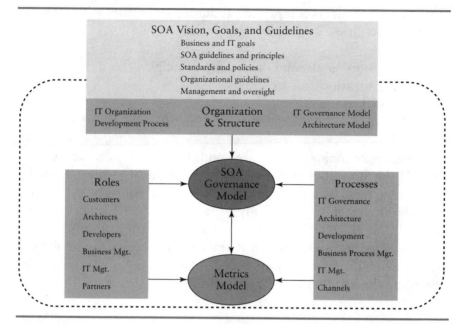

EXHIBIT 7.6 SOA Governance and Metrics Influence SOA Behavior

- SOA processes
- SOA roles and participants
- Input behaviors and the emergent behaviors
- Corporate culture and organizational behavior

SOA governance is a major contributor to the SOA behavioral model we seek. But SOA governance is not enough. Governance and its body of SOA policies require metrics and other social reinforcement mechanisms in order to drive the organizational behavior toward the norms and expectations of an SOA. Archieving the desired SOA behavior requires an understanding of the behavioral interactions in an SOA and how SOA governance, metrics, and other behavioral reinforcement mechanisms interoperate in their own right to achieve SOA success.

The behavioral interaction model of an SOA melds together the governance model, metrics, organization, processes, and roles of the SOA into a cohesive entity that can achieve the stated SOA goals. Let's explore the elements of an SOA behavioral interaction model further. This model is comprised of four major entities with two connecting subentities. The major entities are:

1. SOA vision, goals, and organizing principles
2. IT organization and structures
3. SOA/IT processes
4. SOA roles and participants

These four major entities are connected by two crucial subentities: (1) the SOA governance model and (2) the SOA metrics model. The SOA governance model and metrics model act to bind the other behavioral elements into a body of desired SOA behaviors, norms, and cultural expectations. The total model creates an SOA behavioral interaction model, which defines the expectations for the collective behavior of the SOA overall. These quotes are instructive regarding the importance of culture and behavior in an SOA:[6]

> *"Your current IT architecture is a behavioral artifact that resulted from patterns of organizational behavior over time, driven by corporate strategy and business goals."*
> *"The only way to achieve SOA is to address the cultural and behavioral issues first, then architect toward your SOA goals."*

Governance and Metrics Influence SOA Behaviors

You may be asking yourself what makes this behavioral model work. The answer is in the interaction of two mechanisms: the policies of an SOA, which are defined in the SOA governance model, and the SOA metrics, which provide the performance monitoring of elements of the SOA, including behavior of services, enabling technology, consumers and providers, and the human participants.

SOA metrics are critical. You need SOA metrics to know where you are and where you are going with your SOA initiatives. In other words, SOA metrics put a steering wheel on your SOA. Very often metrics are the afterthought of SOA initiatives because much of the early focus is on getting the technology implemented and working, then measuring the results later. We believe that metrics must be built into the SOA planning process, up front, and then assiduously monitored to help ensure goals are met.

The interplay of SOA governance and SOA metrics is how the total behavior of the SOA is determined and managed. For example, as discussed, SOA governance accommodates metrics for:

- SLAs
- Conformance reporting and policy breaches
- Enforcing reuse of existing services versus novel development of new services
- Enforcing "good reuse" versus "bad reuse," or reusing published proven services and not reusing rogue services
- Enforcement of service design best practices enterprise-wide as opposed to one-time design principles

The list could go on and on. The point is that from the body of policies in the SOA governance model, as well as the metrics defined during the SOA planning process, the overall target state behavior for SOA participants will be determined. These target behaviors must be supported by a combination of business metrics, process metrics, performance and SLA metrics, conformance metrics, and reuse metrics in order to really monitor and evolve the behaviors of an SOA.

Managing Individual SOA Behavior: Big Carrot, Big Stick

How are individual behaviors governed within the context of an SOA? Governing behavior requires a combination of clear metrics of the SOA, as discussed, and a means to relate overall SOA metrics to individual and group goals. All of these metrics and goals should be related and reinforce one another. For individual behavior, these approaches should be considered:

- Document SOA performance and behavioral expectations in annual plans for employees and contractors.
- Implement SOA performance and behavioral elements into employee review processes.

- Implement an SOA review process that helps reinforce the expectations and objectives of the SOA overall as well as the roles of various departments and individuals within the SOA context.
- Build SOA behavioral reinforcement into employee incentives and compensation plans. Consider a "profit" sharing approach for costs saved from SOA reuse and other hard-dollar and soft-dollar business benefits of SOA.

Influencing SOA behavior is going to require embedding enforcement of SOA policies and metrics within all employee annual plans and reviews as well as in compensation and reward systems.

Service-Oriented Culture and SOA

What is a service-oriented culture? In a service-oriented culture, SOA becomes the lifeblood of the IT organization. This is achieved after the organizational behavior model is implemented and there is a thorough understanding of the importance of SOA within the organization. A service-oriented culture is replicated by corporate tradition and reinforced behaviors through time. Like human culture, service-oriented culture is transmitted through learning and behavioral reinforcement.

Service-oriented culture binds the firm's vision, strategy, and objectives with its SOA strategy, vision, and governance model. We believe that our SOA behavior model describes the necessary interplay of SOA governance and SOA metrics to influence the overall behavior of the SOA, including all processes and participants. There must be ongoing training and reinforcement of the SOA goals, mission, metrics, and behavior in order to truly achieve a service-oriented culture. This is what leads to SOA results.

In order to help ensure SOA success, organizations must spend time understanding and planning for a behavioral model that will enable SOA success. Remember change management as a discipline that accompanied business process reengineering projects? At least change management was an explicit attempt to model behaviors that would help instill the process changes that attended BPR initiatives in the 1990s. What we need for SOA success is a new model, a behavioral model that begins with behavior and factors in the organizational, process, and behavioral elements that will result in a successful SOA. We have to begin with the behavior of SOA—the behaviors that lead to services reuse, SOA conformance, governance, and metrics—that will lead you to your SOA business goals.

SUMMARY

Governance is critical to the success of an SOA. We have discussed the overall requirements of SOA governance, including the elements of SOA governance, the organizational and process requirements, and the overall approach to SOA governance. Ultimately, SOA governance enforces an organizational behavior and cultural model. The interplay between SOA governance and a metrics model will determine the effectiveness of SOA governance and the overall culture and behavior that will determine SOA success. While we spend only a few pages on the cultural and behavioral challenges of SOA, in reality the effort will be the opposite. The organizational dynamics and behavioral aspects of SOA will require far more effort than the technology. The effort, however, will be worthwhile.

NOTES

1. Eric A. Marks, *Business Darwinism: Evolve or Dissolve* (Hoboken, NJ: John Wiley & Sons, 2003).
2. WebLayers, Inc., *SOA Governance Introduction* (Cambridge, MA: WebLayers, 2005), p. 11.
3. For a detailed discussion of the metadata management requirements for SOA, see Eric Newcomber and Greg Lomow, *Understanding SOA with Web Services* (New York: Addison-Wesley, 2005).
4. Ibid., p. 298[0].
5. WebLayers, *SOA Governance Introduction*, p. 9.
6. Eric A. Marks, *SOA Governance Overview* (AgilePath Corporation, 2005).

CHAPTER 8

Architecture Organization Model*

Enterprise architecture has become a critical organizational competency given the attention and market hype surrounding service-oriented architecture (SOA), software reuse, information technology (IT) integration imperatives, and related IT trends. We discussed in Chapter 1 some of the drivers for enhancing enterprise architecture capabilities, such as IT complexity and system integration challenges. Enterprises have recently embraced horizontal enterprise architecture management structures because they are better able to provide organizational strategy, establish planning and execution roadmaps, and manage standards, policies, and best practices for the entire organization. The need for an enterprise architecture organization is a sign of maturity and is a response to siloed technology and business organizations, lack of strategic IT direction, governance, and oversight, and to technology management inefficiencies.

The enterprise architecture model in this chapter examines the structure, disciplines, practices, and roles that will be required given the adoption of SOA and services in an organization. In light of emerging SOA methodologies, this model offers agile and adaptable disciplines that can be employed when organizations embrace SOA governance, best practices, and standards.

---

* This chapter is based on Michael Bell's "An Organization Model: The AOM-3 Architecture Organization Structure and Role Models; What Do Architects Do?" version 1.0.2, copyright (c)2005, Library of Congress, text and exhibits used with permission.

This model recognizes the significance of business and technology influences on the formation of an architecture organization. Business imperatives are motivating forces for establishing enterprise architecture organizations, while technological requirements impact the foundation of the organization charter, operations, and activities.

The response to the question "What do architects do?" unfolds through the introduction of the model components. These knowledge-driven management entities are depicted as the main pillars of an architecture organization. They influence management structures and help shape architecture roles, organizational occupations, individual activities, responsibilities, and accountabilities.

WHEN SHOULD ENTERPRISE ARCHITECTURE BE REVIEWED?

This enterprise architecture model should be used when a number of situations arise in an organization:

- *Establishment.* When no such organization exists in the enterprise.
- *Restructuring.* When the effectiveness of an architecture organization is questionable.
- *Alignment.* When business or technological requirements change, when new governance processes and policies are required (i.e., SOA governance), when there are changes to management structures, or when mergers and acquisitions are planned or in progress.
- *Major architecture shift.* SOA represents a major and fundamental shift from siloed IT architectures to horizontally structured services capabilities that represent shared IT assets across business units, process domains, and business functions. The adoption of SOA often mandates changes to the structure, disciplines, skills, and capabilities of most enterprise architecture organizations.

KEY QUESTIONS

What are the key questions that should be addressed?

- How should architecture organizations be established, reorganized, or aligned given the industry move to SOA and services?

- How should business and technology requirements be mapped to SOA enabling technology, reusable services, and related enterprise and solution architecture initiatives?
- What do architects do? How should enterprise architecture roles be defined? What are the required roles for an SOA initiative?
- How should architecture roles be established?

Constitution of Enterprise Architecture

An enterprise architecture organization is a reflection and artifact of the environment in which it operates. Enterprise architecture organizations should be established because of enterprise requirements to resolve and manage ongoing core business and technology challenges. The business and technology environment is responsible for shaping its four constituent dimensions (see Exhibit 8.1).

1. *Mission.* An enterprise architecture organization should proactively offer technical solutions to new business challenges. Enterprise architecture should discover, generalize, and abstract IT and business problems to help provide strategic[1] and tactical solutions via standardized, repeatable technology capabilities to business organizations, lines of business, and their constituents.

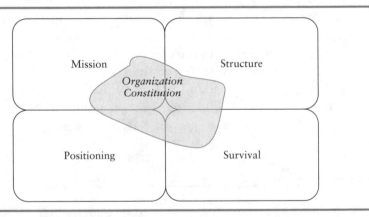

EXHIBIT 8.1 Architecture Supporting Constitutional Dimensions

2. *Structure.* An architecture organization structure should be aligned with enterprise business strategies, business initiatives, business concepts, and core business requirements. The vibrant nature of business, with the concomitant changes in business strategies, mandates dynamic architecture organizations to accommodate business and technology change. Furthermore, rapid technology cycles require the ability to accelerate architecture organizational changes to provide timely solutions and support.

3. *Positioning.* An architecture organization should be horizontally positioned in an enterprise. Enterprise architecture should not be another IT silo. Rather, it should operate across all business units, lines of business, and IT operations as well. It should assume center stage for technological solutions and be a proactive and driving force for strategic technological initiatives.

4. *Survival.* The existence of an architecture organization in an enterprise depends on the quality of its personnel, its human capital,[2] and the leadership they demonstrate in executing its mission. Ongoing architecture organizational viability then depends on quality operations, systems development, lifecycle effectiveness, and the methodologies it supports.

SOA-DRIVEN ENTERPRISE ARCHITECTURE MODEL

The SOA-driven architectural organization has two driving forces and three main components. The driving forces for the model are business and technology trends, which provide the business context and environmental inputs into the architecture organizational model. These are covered in Chapter 3 in the SOA Business Modeling section. In addition to the SOA business modeling inputs, the SOA governance model and organizational model is the other primary input. These two inputs provide the impetus for creating, restructuring, or realigning an enterprise architecture organization, process, and capabilities with the requirements of the business and SOA.

The three main components of an enterprise architecture organization are:

1. *Architecture practices.* These are the main operations of an architecture organization.
2. *Architecture disciplines.* There are subject areas or fields of expertise in an enterprise organization. We will highlight disciplines that are needed to support the transition to SOA.
3. *Architectural roles.* These are the roles and skills required to support the practices and disciplines of the enterprise architecture organization. These are derived using the architecture organizational model.

SOA initiatives have the potential to introduce new disciplines, practices, and architectural roles into an enterprise organization. These will be explored later in the chapter.

Exhibit 8.2 depicts the three critical aspects of an enterprise architecture organization, including practices, disciplines, and roles.

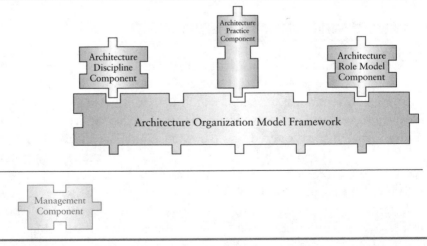

EXHIBIT 8.2 AOM—Architecture Organization Model: Component View

BUSINESS REQUIREMENTS

Business requirements describe the demand for solutions based on external or internal events that impact business health, such as profitability, competitive threats, or business weaknesses. Requirements help identify opportunities to address business challenges, increase business growth, achieve higher productivity, implement process improvements, and sustain business strength, reliability, and environment stability.

Reactive Approach of an Architecture Organization to Business Requirements Business events and environmental changes will require changes to business strategies, associated business models, business initiatives, and the creation or modification of business requirements.

Chapter 3 demonstrated a process of understanding business requirements, business context, and related environmental influences on enterprise architecture. SOA as an architectural paradigm offers the potential to address many business initiatives and requirements that organizations face today, such as faster mergers and acquisitions, business and process integration, regulatory compliance, and more. This reactive approach pressures the business organization to constantly track and pursue unforeseeable problems that cannot be controlled or resolved immediately. The architecture organization then is required to provide swift and timely solutions that depend on its readiness level, management capacity, and skill sets. Effective solutions can resolve or minimize the negative impact of business and regulatory problems. Exhibit 8.3 depicts an organization's reactive approach to occurring events, which may impact business activities if architecture solutions are not provided.

Proactive Approach of an Architecture Organization to Business Requirements SOA holds great promise to regain business agility and IT flexibility through reusable services and flexible architecture capabilities. Readiness initiatives and planning for uncertainty are investments in an organization's future.[3] These activities are designed to prevent business harm by utilizing existing and proven architecture solution models that have been developed over time. These experience-based architecture

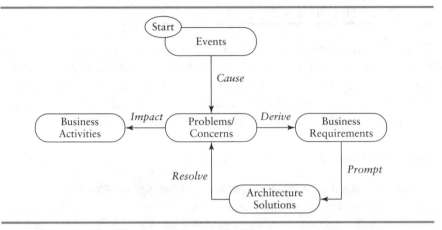

EXHIBIT 8.3 Reactive Approach to Business Requirements

solutions facilitate establishing or modifying proactive business requirements that can augment, enhance, or derive new solution models. The development of an architecture knowledge base, in the form of models, can shorten the architecture response time to business urgencies and provide proven, high-quality solutions used previously to address similar challenges. This proactive method helps position the business and technology organizations to anticipate change, thus eliminating uncertainty and risk of unforeseen challenges.

For example, a firm that is pursuing a merger and acquisition (M&A) strategy to spur business growth can expect data management challenges, such as customer names and addresses, with each acquisition and subsequent integration. The core of the problem may be the incompatibility of respective business models. The merging firms have different beliefs and strategies concerning data management and centralization. This clash of strategies can result in long-term disputes and confusion, business disruptions, and lost productivity, and even can impact M&A profitability until policies, standards, and best practices are established and implemented. Architecture solution models can alleviate the pain of data consolidation during M&A events since the requirements can be generalized and abstracted into a more generic form that provides a broad solution to data centralization versus data partitioning and segmentation. This proactive approach may not always provide ideal solutions to master data consolidation, but with each business event, a new set of proactive business requirements can improve existing architecture solution models. A progressive approach to solving problems, learning from past experiences, and adding to the architecture solution knowledge base can exponentially shorten the reaction time to business problems.

Impact of Business Requirements on Enterprise Architecture

Enterprise architecture greatly relies on business requirements because they provide motivation and justification for the organization's existence as well as substance for their operations. Requirements influence management structure and support the creation of architectural roles and responsibilities. Furthermore, enterprise architecture contributes to the creation of architecture disciplines and practices, which are main areas of operations and expertise.

Ranking Business Requirements

Business requirements tiers enable the ranking, evaluation, and positioning of business needs. They are arranged based on their potential impact on profitability, business opportunities, and revenue growth.

- Significant business requirements should be grouped into the upper tiers and classified as strategic targets and focal points for solution domains.
- Tactical business needs may not require immediate attention and thus should be positioned in the lower tiers or in separate lists. This arrangement provides solution roadmaps and helps prioritize activities. Exhibit 8.4 depicts these concepts. These three tiers comprise business requirements that are aligned with an organization's business values.

TECHNOLOGICAL REQUIREMENTS

Technological requirements are major contributors to the architecture organizational model since they provide different views and perspectives for enterprise architecture. SOA brings with it a variety of technology requirements, some of which are not new but are now

Tier	Name	Description
1	Time to Market	Shorten the length of time it takes to develop and enhance trading systems and trading tools, from product concept phase and submission of business requirements to initial deployment in production.
	Systems Performance & Response Time	Improve trending systems performance and user interface response time.
	Increase Storage Capacity	Increase storage capacity to accommodate 5-year history of trading data.
	Improve System Communications	Enable communications between applications to eliminate redundant customer records in Account Name & Address Lookup application, Customer Account Balances application, and Account Holdings application.
2	Improve User Interface	Provide customers with flexible trading system user interface, enable customization, personalization, and preferences system capabilities.
	Provide Important Trading Tools & Features	Provide customers with extended news on demand and financial market alert features and tools.
3	Improve System Administration Views	Enable systems administrator to view customer information from a single user interface.
	Look & Feel	Improve trading system look & feel.

EXHIBIT 8.4   Mappable Business Requirements

achievable given recent developments in standards, new middleware solutions, and related technologies. Four major technological requirement categories can contribute to the establishment, reorganization, and the realignment of an architecture organization: (1) fundamental technology requirements, (2) derived technology requirements from business requirements, (3) functional needs of IT organizations, and (4) innovation initiatives. Exhibit 8.5 depicts these four major technology requirements groups.

Fundamental Technology Requirements

Fundamental technology requirements are concerned with IT environmental and operational base practices and disciplines. The technology

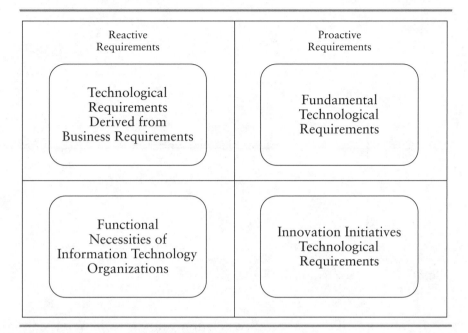

EXHIBIT 8.5 Types of Technological Requirements

"how to do" issues should be expressed in a collection of architectural solution models (reusable templates) with a core knowledge base comprised of methods, technological expertise, instructions, and routines that enable architecture organizations to provide rapid solutions to arising problems. For example, asset reuse is a leading concern in many organizations since it can impact IT expenditures, cost avoidances, and savings. Establishing an SOA reuse strategy and model can encourage utilization of organizational assets, result in consolidation of resources, and promote decoupling of intellectual assets to support reuse.

Requirements for technology solution models are the driving force behind an architecture organization since they provide motivation for the planning of architecture initiatives, creation of roadmaps, and definition of goals. These deliverables are critical for an architecture organization's existence. Technology models are grouped into four major areas of concern for technology solutions: (1) methodologies and processes, (2) discovery, design, and construction, (3) production, and (4) management, as shown in Exhibit 8.6.

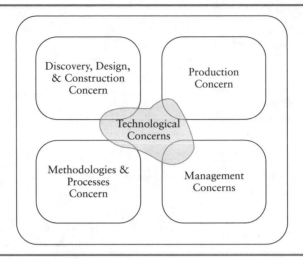

EXHIBIT 8.6   Information Technology Concerns

Exhibit 8.7 illustrates the correlation among technology concerns, requirements, and models.

Technology Requirements Derived from Business Requirements

Much as IT imperatives are derived from business imperatives, technology requirements should be derived from business necessities and placed in parallel tiers. This mappable format enables accurate alignment of essential needs on both sides of the problem and the solution domain. It facilitates the translation and the transformation of requirements from one context to another. A single business requirement can trigger multiple technical approaches, which should be expressed in technical terms. This type of mapping and alignment should be repeated each time business requirements are changed or redefined. New or modified strategic technology requirements should trigger an architecture organization realignment activity, which may impact architecture roles and management structure.

Technological Fundamental Requirements		
Concern	Requirement	Solution Model
Production	How should organizational assets be managed?	SOA Asset Management Model
	How should organizational assets be secured?	SOA Security Model
	How should organizational assets be configured?	SOA Configuration Model
	How should organizational assets guarantee its services?	SOA Provisioning Model
Management	How should an organization be established, restructured, or aligned? How should roles be established?	Organizational Model
	How should management provide strategies, direction, vision, and mission?	Strategy Model
	How should projects be managed?	Systems Development Life-cycle Model
Methodologies & Processes	How should organizational assets be reused?	SOA Reusability Model
	How should organizational assets be integrated?	SOA Integration Mode
	How should organizational models collaborate?	SOA Collaboration Model
Discovery, Design, & Construction	How should events be understood? How should the problem domain be understood? How should business requirements be understood?	Business Architecture Model
	How should organizational assets and services be designed?	SOA Design Model
	How should organizational assets and services be constructed?	SOA Construction Model

EXHIBIT 8.7   Fundamental Concerns, Requirements, and Models

Exhibit 8.8 illustrates these ideas in tier one. It includes transformed technology requirements next to their corresponding business requirements. The *time-to-market* business requirement relates to five technology requirements that can shorten the product delivery process by proposing various methods to accomplishing this goal, such as an efficient services development lifecycle and the adoption of *buy-versus-build* concepts.

Functional Requirements of IT Organizations

Technology needs of various IT organizations, such as assurance services, software development, and data services and infrastructure, can contribute to the establishment, reorganization, and alignment of

Business Requirements			Transformed Technological Requirements	
Tier	Name	Description	Name	Description
1	Time to Market	Shorten the length of time it takes to develop and enhance trading systems and trading tools, from the product concept phase and the submission of business requirements to initial production deployment	System Development Lifecycle	Adopt SOA development lifecycle process to expedite product construction and deployment to production
			Training Strategies	Develop training strategies to support advanced technologies and improve staff efficiency
			Asset Reusability	Adopt SOA reusability model to avoid product development redundancy
			Continuous Integration	Develop real-time product and application integration environment by establishing continuous integration processes and employing automated deployment mechanisms
			Buy vs. Build	Establish organizational policies, standards, and best practices to support buy vs. build strategies
	Improve trading systems performance and user interface response time	Improve trading systems performance and user interface response time	Middleware Support	Provide enhanced middleware to support high performance data transportation between services and applications
			Infrastructure	Improve infrastructure and hardware to support high trading volumes
			Scalability	Enhance vertical and horizontal systems scalability, provide efficient workload management, and enable distribution of services to maximize performance and response time

EXHIBIT 8.8   Mapping Business to Technology Requirements Example

an architecture organization. This is due to the close proximity in which these organizations operate and their mutual interest in resolving internal operational problems that ordinarily are not derived from business requirements.

A horizontally positioned and centralized architecture organization can add tremendous bridging value to siloed, semisiloed, or independent organizations by filling communication gaps, coordinating activities, observing and discovering commonalities, encouraging reusability of IT assets, and promoting integration of applications. Architecture should become the central hub of information by maintaining knowledge base repositories for technology studies, solution models, software development assets, and documentation. On the strategy level, an architecture organization should help define the IT organization's identity and assist with its mission, vision, and strategy.

An architecture organization should conduct three major functions:

1. *Base requirements.* These are fundamental requirements for establishing internal processes, methodologies, and environments that are affiliated with essential organizational operations.
2. *Consultation requirements.* These requirements are based on architecture consulting services provided to various business and technical groups based on short-term needs or on a project basis (e.g., software design and modeling, systems architecture, network architecture, data farm and data mining design, and architecture).
3. *Keep lights on (KLO) or keep the world going (KWG) requirements.* Ongoing support initiatives such as data recovery, configuration management, installation management, production support, production monitoring, and security services are a part of baseline IT organization activities. These initiatives are executed at all times regardless of any occurring business initiatives and events.

Technology Requirements of Innovation Initiatives

Technology trends and industry innovations influence the creation, reorganization, and alignment of an architecture organization because of their impact on readiness and adaptation activities, which should involve modernization of IT facilities, software platforms, systems, and infrastructure. Staying abreast of emerging and cutting-edge technologies can contribute immensely to the improvement of technical services. It can provide value to the business as well as impact productivity and profitability.

Requirements for IT innovation initiatives can include establishing a research and development (R&D) organization along with the foundation of R&D practices, standards, and policies. Other requirements can be affiliated with product evaluation and adaptation initiatives, which would require proof-of-concept and quality assurance efforts.

ARCHITECTURE DISCIPLINES

An *architecture discipline* is a solution domain framework with specialized knowledge, architectural assets, and intellectual property. The *disciplines* are managed by subject matter experts that enable an architecture organization to resolve problems by providing "what to do" guidelines in the form of detailed *technical requirements*. Architecture disciplines are responsible for assisting the architecture leadership in translating business requirements into *technical requirements* and solutions, as well as committing resources and support for their implementation. *Architecture disciplines* are derived from business requirements, technology requirements, or other inputs, such as governance and administration requirements. Exhibit 8.9 illustrates these relationships.

SOA will bring new requirements for architecture disciplines in an enterprise architecture organization. Expected disciplines will include SOA governance, middleware and integration, services modeling, and the like. For example, *deployment management, integration management, business architecture management,* and *security management* are architecture disciplines that can be conceived as execution frameworks, which provide *technical requirements*, plans of engagement, directions, and detailed roadmaps. Furthermore, administration requirements as well as SOA governance needs can derive various architecture management and administration management disciplines. These internal frameworks are important for the creation of management and administration roles in an architecture organization.

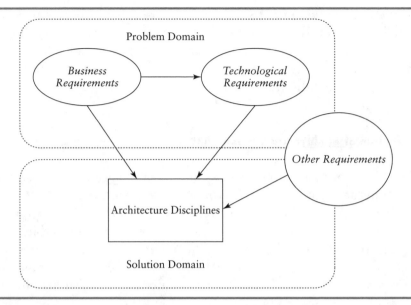

EXHIBIT 8.9   Contributors to Architecture Disciplines

Solution Activities: How-to-Do Aspects

A *solution activity* is a hands-on knowledge function that provides prescriptions, methodologies, and guidance for specific architectural requirements. It is managed by technical staff and chartered to provide the detailed technical solution guidelines in the form of *technical specifications*. An *architecture discipline* is comprised of one or more *solution activities*, which can address problems from multiple perspectives. These activities are the architecture organization's execution and implementation arms. They are where the rubber meets the road between enterprise architecture vision and solution implementation.

For example, a trading service consumer must communicate to a customer profile service by utilizing integration mechanisms. One of the selected solutions would be to utilize third-party SOA integration products. A *product integration support solution activity* can offer product selection and evaluation services, establish product adaptation processes, and provide integration best practices and policies. Furthermore, a *middleware strategies and architecture solution activity* can be commissioned to strengthen the solution by offering an *enterprise service bus* (ESB) architecture to provide messaging functionality between the customer profile service and trading consumer. The collaboration between *solution activities* to resolve problems often can result in the elimination of concerns and a collaborative, successful implementation.

Derivation of Architecture Disciplines

The ability to understand business and technology requirements and then translate them into *architecture disciplines* and *solution activities* can facilitate establishing an architecture organization as well as shape its management structure, roles, and responsibilities. In architecture organization restructuring or realignment initiatives, some existing disciplines may be decommissioned, which would then accommodate new architectural disciplines. The elimination or establishment of disciplines is a response to business and technology changes.

Disciplines and their affiliated *solution activities* should be derived from strategic requirements gathered from both the *problem* and the *solution domain*. We suggest basing the architecture management structure on long-lasting demands and requirements that are rooted in fundamental business and technology concerns. *Disciplines* can originate from business requirements alone, from technology requirements only, or from both. Requirements that are not derived from either are usually affiliated with management and administrative needs.

Exhibit 8.10 depicts how an *architecture discipline* can be derived from business and technological requirements. The discovery of duplicate customer records in various repositories and lack of a centralized administrative user interface application is a challenge to account management activities in this organization. Thus, the business organization demands a solution to better manage trading system complexities. It is interested in a technology proposal or plan that demonstrates a solution for centralizing of customer data. In this example, business and technology requirements derive two major architecture *disciplines*, which were selected to provide solutions:

1. The *SOA integration management discipline* is responsible for systems integration through the introduction of an ESB and

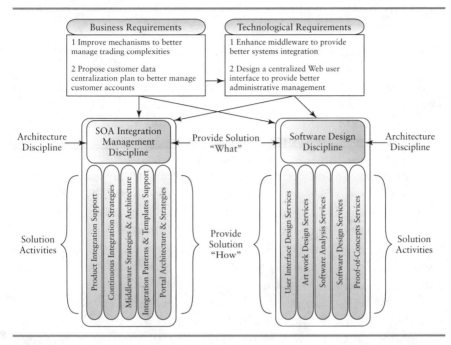

EXHIBIT 8.10   Derivation of Architecture Discipline and Solution Activities

incorporates other SOA integration products, such as service intermediaries.

2. The *software design discipline* provides design blueprints and artifacts to demonstrate a centralized customer user interface approach.

Contributions to Vision and Mission Statements

The categorization and prioritization of architecture solutions will potentially trigger or be inputs into the architecture vision and mission statements. *Architecture disciplines* and *solution activities* derived from top tiers of business and technology requirements should be recognized as strategic drivers of an architecture organization, and thus they form the basis for its strategy, vision, and mission. Tactical requirements should play a diminished role in shaping the direction and strategy of an organization but can provide short- and mid-term solutions to carry out architecture tasks.

ARCHITECTURE PRACTICES

Practices are the primary architectural operations. These are solution management functions comprised of *architecture disciplines* that provide core areas of expertise and problem-solving capabilities. These operations are managed by architecture teams that understand division of labor, staffing, and dispatching, and are capable of establishing communication with business leaders and implementing organizational reporting systems. This layer of leadership provides the high-level what-to-do direction while relying on *solution activities* to furnish the how-to-do aspects of architecture solutions.

For example, a *software architecture practice*, which is required to provide software-related architecture services, may contain disciplines that handle and support software solutions, such as *software analysis and design* disciplines, *application architecture* disciplines, and SOA modeling disciplines.

Exhibit 8.11 illustrates the relationship between *architecture practices* and *architecture disciplines*. The depicted organization contains two major practices, which are comprised of disciplines and their related solution activities. *Disciplines* can be shared among *architecture practices* because of their needed expertise and capabilities.

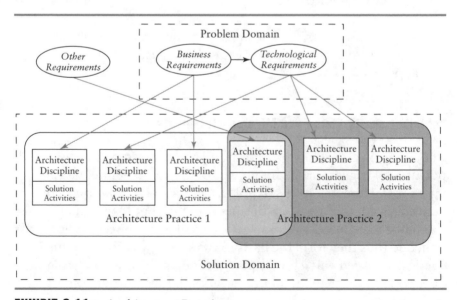

EXHIBIT 8.11   Architecture Practices

For example, an *architecture management discipline* can be shared by the *software architecture practice* and the *hardware architecture practice* because both have management capability needs.

Practices and Architecture Organization Management Structure

Disciplines provide solutions for enterprise challenges by utilizing their subordinate *solution activities* to address problems from multiple viewpoints and then developing *technical specifications* to accomplish those goals. Conversely, *practices* offer a baseline formulation of solutions. They serve as a valuable foundation for the architecture organization and are its fundamental management structure. Exhibit 8.12 depicts a *software architecture practice*, which is comprised of different *architecture disciplines* derived from business and technology requirements. The grouping of disciplines must be based on a common denominator (e.g., software-affiliated management tasks is the common attribute that makes this classification possible).

Practices Structure

Business, technology, and other requirements can affect the ratio of *practices* to *disciplines*. The specific ratio depends on organizational

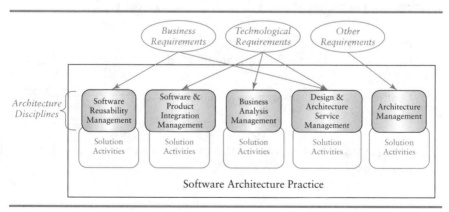

EXHIBIT 8.12   Categorization of Architecture Disciplines

requirements and the strategy, vision, and mission upon which the architecture organization was established. Since *practices* are a coarse form of management, they are established as high-level areas of expertise. Therefore, an architecture organization should be comprised of few *practices* regardless of its overall size. A large number of *practices* can increase the risk of redundancy and unnecessary operational overhead.

For example, an investment banking organization commissioned its technology advisory board to establish an architecture organization based on business and *technology requirements*. Their requirements focused on major areas of interest, such as repository strategies, storage integration facilities, development of new loan and credit applications, integration, consolidation of various client name and address services, and implementation of service registries. First the technology advisory board established a considerable number of *disciplines* and affiliated *solution activities*. Next, these *disciplines* were categorized into major areas of interest, which provided the motivation for establishing three major management practices: *software development practice*, *data and repositories strategies practice*, and *global architecture logistics practice*.

The suggested process for establishing practices in an organization is a bottom-up approach, working from the details to a more generalized construct, or the management structure. This method advocates first mapping of business and technology requirements to architecture disciplines, then developing solution activities, and finally grouping these disciplines into architecture practices. Exhibit 8.13 depicts the process of practice creation, as summarized in five steps:

1. Business requirements are determined.
2. Business requirements are transformed into technology requirements.
3. Business and technology requirements are used to derive disciplines.
4. Solution activities are created for each discipline.
5. Disciplines are grouped for the purpose of forming architecture practices.

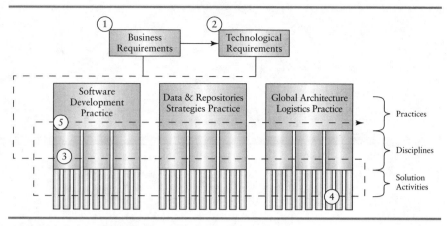

EXHIBIT 8.13   Formation of Architecture Practices

ARCHITECTURE ROLES

The answers to the question "What do architects do?" can be found in the solution domain. *Disciplines* and *solution activities* are the best place to start. Business and technology requirements must be developed first. Once *architecture disciplines* are defined and *solution activities* are finalized, architecture *roles* can be derived and then subsequently positioned in the organizational structure.

Composition of Architecture Roles

An *architecture role* should be defined based on *solution activities*. Activities can be selected from various *architecture disciplines* spread over an assortment of architecture practices. Exhibit 8.14 depicts the relationship among a role, *architecture disciplines*, *solution activities*, and *architecture practices*.

Realistically, a role that spans multiple *architecture practices* may be hard to fill since it would require a very broad and unique skill set. Moreover, from a management perspective, it would make sense to create roles that operate within one *architecture practice* because

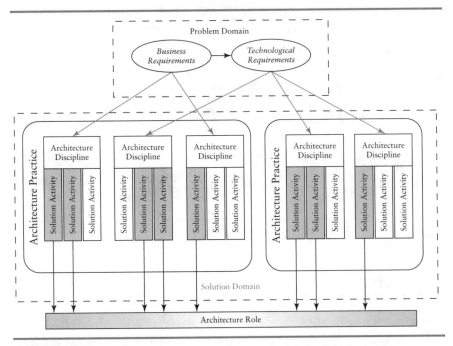

EXHIBIT 8.14 Architecture Role Comprised of Solution Activities

doing so can reduce accountability conflicts and can enable teams to focus and strengthen their skills in one knowledge domain.

Exhibit 8.15 illustrates the composition of an application architect role from various *solution activities*, which were selected from different *architecture disciplines* within one *architecture practice*. This role offers application architecture–level support that provides analysis, design, architecture, and programming services. The strategy and the methodology disciplines are not included because they are irrelevant to this position.

Grading Expertise

Grading solution activities expertise can further refine architecture roles. This skills scoring method can help better tune architectural roles to fit tasks within the scope of *architecture disciplines*.

Exhibit 8.16 depicts this idea. The *software design services solution activity* contained in the *design discipline* that is defined in the

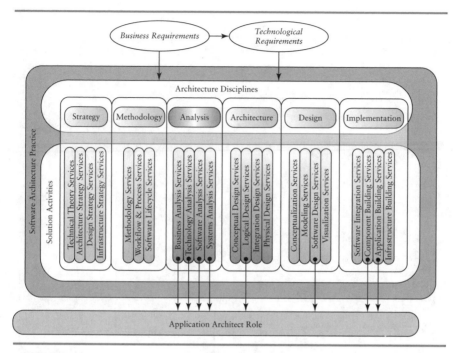

EXHIBIT 8.15 An Application Architect Role Defined by Solution Activities

software architecture practice. It has critical requirements for an application architect role, which would thus be valued at 100 on a 0 to 100 scale. Conversely, the required skill value of the *physical design services solution activity* contained in the *architecture discipline* is defined in the *software architecture practice* with a value of 40, since such a role does not require a high skill value in hardware design.

Methods of Deriving Architecture Roles

Architecture roles can be derived by employing two different methods:

1. *Using solution activities.* This method, which was described in the preceding paragraphs, can be applied successfully to small architecture organizations with fewer *disciplines, solution activities*, and roles to manage.
2. *Utilizing models.* This approach, explained next, supports construction of an architecture role model before deriving specific architecture roles.

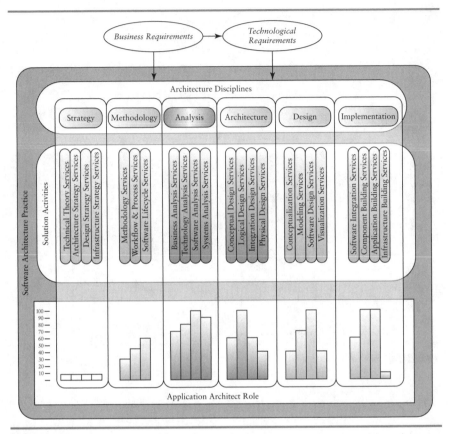

EXHIBIT 8.16 Tuning an Architecture Role

ARCHITECTURE ROLE MODELS

Roles are reusable skill templates that facilitate the creation and shaping of architecture roles by assisting acceptable value ranges to *solution activities* expertise, and then evaluating roles against those values. Role models provide supporting elements to the foundation of an organizational structure and set standards for various staffing initiatives in an architecture organization.

Creation of Architectural Role Models

The process of creating role models is similar to establishing architectural roles. Both are comprised of *solution activities*, selected from various *architecture disciplines* that are defined in one or more *architecture practices*. Models are different because they provide templates that define the required expertise value range for each *solution activity*. Selection of expertise values should fall within this spectrum when creating roles from role models.

Exhibit 8.17 depicts a *security architect role model* and the allowable range of expertise values for each *solution activity*. (Ranges are shown in dark gray on each *solution activity*.) The *security strategy services solution activity* in the *security management discipline*, defined in the *architecture logistics practice*, mandates a threshold expertise value of 85 (i.e., a low value) and a maximum value of 95. In the same fashion, the *deployment models development solution activity* defined in the *deployment management discipline* requires a

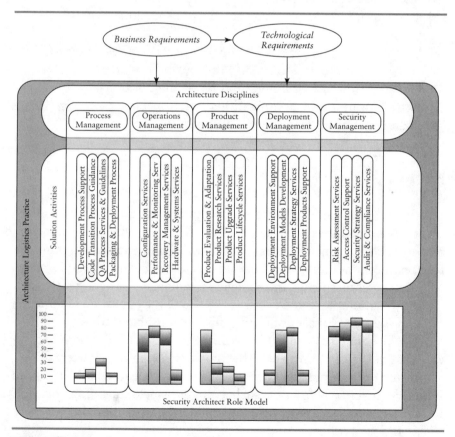

EXHIBIT 8.17 Architecture Role Model

minimum threshold of 45 and a maximum value of 85. This is a much wider range and thus a more lenient requirement.

POSITIONING OF ARCHITECTURE ORGANIZATIONS: AN SOA PERSPECTIVE

Determining the breadth of organizational influence and span of control is the act of *positioning*. Positioning establishes boundaries for the architecture organization's relative influence in an enterprise. Establishing organizational positioning dimensions, either vertically or horizontally, can set these limits. A horizontally positioned organization is better able to operate and execute across multiple domains and organizations. Vertical positioning limits organizational span of control and influence, which tends to focus an organization on a narrower scope of execution. Positioning organizations is fundamental for:

- Establishing management organizations, structures, and processes
- Assigning authority, roles, and responsibilities
- Construction of hierarchies and reporting relationships
- Foundation of interorganizational relationships
- Manifestation of enterprise cultures

Positioning

Positioning is required during establishment, restructuring, or alignment of an architecture organization. Dynamic and environmental aspects such as human factors, sociopolitical influences, corporate culture, market conditions, new business strategies, business requirements, technology requirements, or management changes may trigger this act.

For example, a surge in company growth may spur the facilitation of high-volume transactions by building reusable and scalable services, which may require extending the software development organization's role and influence beyond its original charter. Thus, positioning it as a partially dominant dimension can enable it to lead initiatives in a few IT groups, such as supervising data storage projects in the data services group or even mandating operational changes in the assurance services group.

Positioning Management and Strategies

Positioning management is about the formation of an enterprise positioning map, in which organizations recognize their site and operations boundaries in the enterprise. This type of influence can be expressed and graphically visualized by allocated space and orientation on that map. A few mechanisms can facilitate the creation of an enterprise positioning map:

- *Fully horizontal positioning.* This organization is empowered to oversee, lead, and direct all other vertically positioned organizations. In Exhibit 8.18, the enterprise is an "architecture-centric" type. It became architecture-centric because the architecture organization is *fully horizontally positioned.*
- *Semihorizontal positioning.* This scenario grants leadership over few organizations, yet others are allowed to operate under different management groups. Exhibit 8.19 depicts an architecture organization that provides leadership to the development group, training services group, and assurance services group, but the engineering group is not included under this supervision.

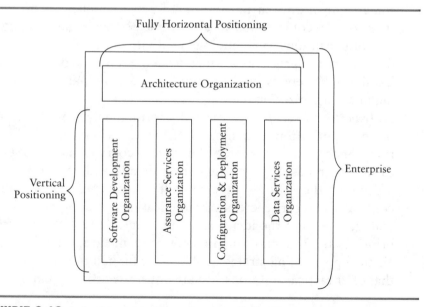

EXHIBIT 8.18   Architecture Organization: Fully Horizontal Positioning

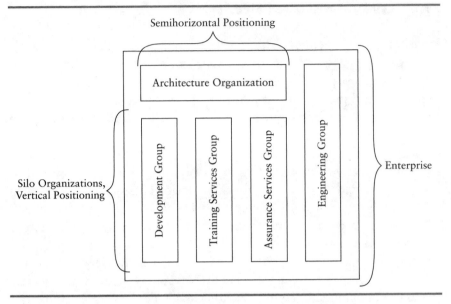

EXHIBIT 8.19   Architecture Organization: Semihorizontal Positioning

- *Partial domination positioning.* This positioning can guarantee partial involvement in other organizations' affairs, oversight for some groups, and partial or shared project management. This strategy is recommended in environments that regard architecture organizations as technology facilitation and training groups that are not engaged in leading strategic technology initiatives. Exhibit 8.20 depicts the concept of partial domination positioning in an organization.
- *Fully vertical positioning.* Vertical positioning narrows the scope of an organization to a siloed style of management and operations. Such a narrow span of horizontal control enables organizations to focus on implementation details and on the tactical aspects of the services they provide. This type of positioning constricts enterprise cross-communications and organizational dialog, may limit the identification of reusability for core enterprise assets, and may impair enterprise integration initiatives. Vertical positioning strategies should be limited to organizations that offer tactical solutions and are not strategic to the enterprise.

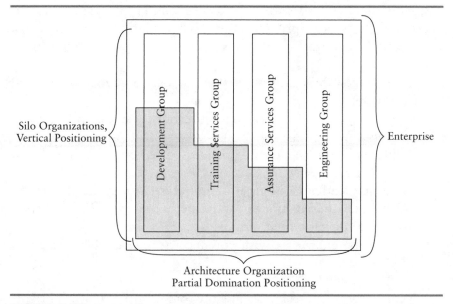

EXHIBIT 8.20 Partial Domination Positioning

Communications, Interaction Protocols, and Processes

Setting standards of communication between organizations, establishing interaction protocols, and defining interorganizational operating processes should accompany the act of positioning. Additionally, each organization located on the enterprise-positioning map should define its identity by providing its vision and mission, organizational structure, and governance rules conforming to the overall enterprise charter.

Positioning Architecture Organizations

An enterprise architecture organization should be completely horizontally positioned and empowered to set technology strategy and direction and to craft the vision and mission of technology initiatives for the enterprise. It should participate in and lead strategic and tactical initiatives across various business and IT groups, understand their challenges, and provide appropriate solutions. An enterprise architecture organization with this structure and positioning can:

- Increase communications between siloed organizations in the enterprise.
- Facilitate reuse of IT assets among vertical business and technical domains.
- Reduce redundant IT and business architecture initiatives in corporations.
- Assist and lead SOA integration initiatives across the enterprise.
- Aid various organizations in an IT institution to define their identity and to develop their strategies.
- Provide the enterprise with guidance, standards, best practices, and policies.

Exhibit 8.21 depicts an architecture organization that is horizontally positioned relative to enterprise silo organizations.

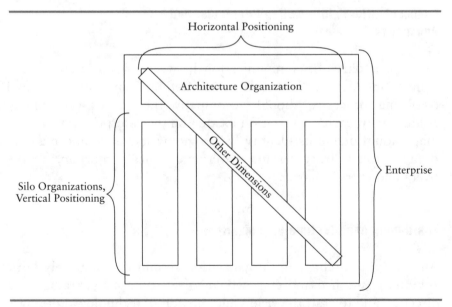

EXHIBIT 8.21 Positioning an Architecture Organization in the Enterprise

ARCHITECTURE ORGANIZATIONAL MANAGEMENT STRUCTURE

The structure of an architecture organization should correspond to *architecture practices*, *disciplines*, and *solution activities*. It should be dynamic and provide flexibility and agility for business and technology trends. Alignment with business and technology imperatives should be maintained through ongoing interaction, collaboration, and overall IT governance processes. Restructuring efforts should take place when the effectiveness of the organization is questionable.

Architecture Management Structure Model

There should be four layers to an architecture management structure. Management oversight is required for each of these layers.

1. Architecture leadership layer
2. Architecture practice management layer
3. Architecture discipline management layer
4. Architecture solution activities management layer

Exhibit 8.22 depicts this model.

Architecture management layers should synchronize[4] and orchestrate performance of their subordinates; be responsible for translating, transforming, and interpreting requirements into architecture initiatives; and provide subordinate management with more granular, detailed, and specific tasks and goals.

Architecture Leadership Layer   The leadership layer supervises the overall strategic direction of the organization by taking a proactive approach to resolving business and technology problems. It provides strategic and conceptual support, helps translate business and technology requirements into architecture tasks, and assigns them to *architecture practices*. The translation, interpretation, and transformation of business and technology requirements into architecture work are accomplished through analysis and discovery, which may

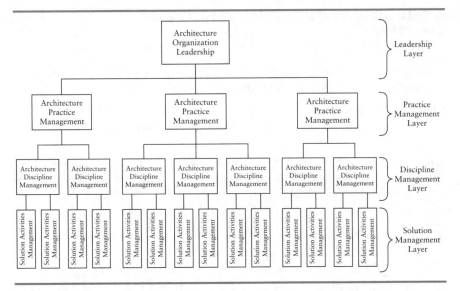

EXHIBIT 8.22 Architecture Management Structure Model

involve not only the leadership layer, but can include all four layers of the architecture organization, stakeholders in the business organization, and technology groups. Propagation of architecture tasks to the *architecture practice* management layer is the act of initiative coordination that is needed to control the flow and the division of work within the organization.

For example, the business requirement "provide customization, personalization, and preferences capabilities to enrich our customer experience on our Wall Street business newsmagazine site" would require building infrastructure, designing and architecting an enterprise portal, and utilizing advanced technologies to achieve such business imperatives. The architecture leadership layer divides this labor into architecture tasks and assigns them to various architecture practices.

Exhibit 8.23 depicts this idea:

- The *software architecture* practice is required to design and architect a portal.
- The *logistics architecture* practice is engaged to provide planning for supporting the portal infrastructure and evaluating various portal products.

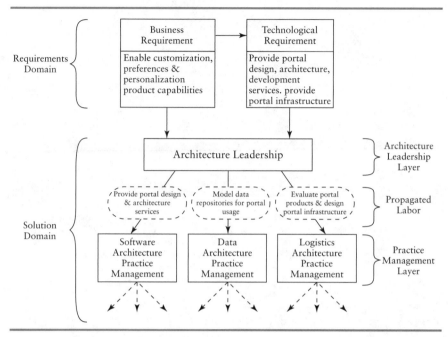

EXHIBIT 8.23   Propagation: Architecture Leadership to Practice Layer

■ The *data architecture* practice is commissioned to model the data and establish repositories.

Architecture Practice Management Layer   This layer is conceived as the foundation structure of an architecture organization, owned by architecture management and supervised by architecture leadership. It is a coarse form of solution management that is responsible for further refining and propagating the labor to its subordinating discipline management layer and is accountable for coordinating tasks among *architecture disciplines*. Practice management is occupied with providing the high-level what-do-to guidance of the solution, furnishing business architecture insights, assisting with processes and methodologies, and pointing to high-level technology remedies without providing the how-to-do detailed portion of the solution.

Exhibit 8.24 depicts delegation of responsibilities by the *software architecture practice* management layer. It involves and provides guidance to the *software and product integration discipline*

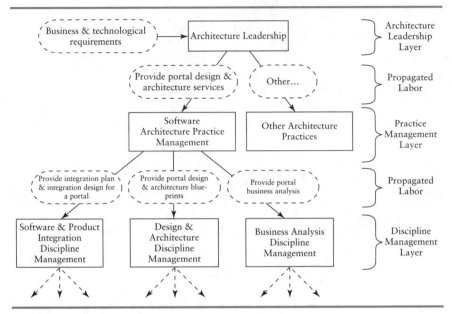

EXHIBIT 8.24   Propagation of Practice Layer to Architecture Discipline Layer

management, the *design and architecture discipline management*, and the *business analysis discipline management*. The practice management layer matches technical requirements to proper discipline management capabilities.

- The *software and product integration discipline management* is required to provide an integration plan, and a portal integration design blueprint.
- The *design and architecture discipline management* is commissioned to provide portal design and an overall architecture blueprint for this initiative.
- The *business analysis discipline management* is asked to furnish analysis of business requirements.

Discipline Management Layer   The discipline management layer is responsible for providing the *detailed implementation* of the what-do-to portion of the solution. This layer should be concerned with propagating the labor to its subordinating *solution activities* management layers by matching types of work to expertise capabilities of its various owners, providing methods of implementation, and coordinating *solution activities*. The what-to-do portion of its responsibilities should be translated into detailed *technical requirements*, tactical plans for each solution activity, roadmaps, and expected targets and goals.

Exhibit 8.25 depicts design architecture discipline propagation of work to its subordinating solution activities.

- *Conceptualization solution activity.* Develops software concepts from given portal requirements.
- *Visualization solution activity.* Designs a presentation layer, which accommodates customers with preferences, customization, and personalization.

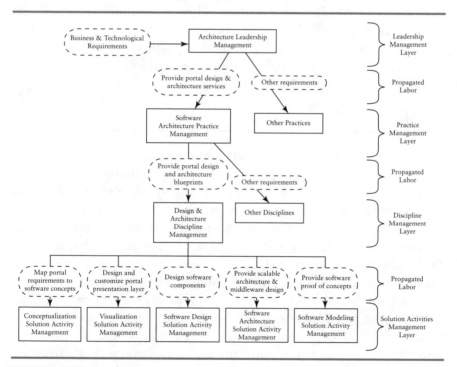

EXHIBIT 8.25 Propagation of Discipline Layer to Solution Activity Layer

- *Software design solution activity.* Provides design artifacts for handling the logic behind the portal presentation layer.
- *Software architecture solution activity.* Provides blueprints of components and services, and designs middleware solutions and an integration plan.
- *Software modeling solution activity.* Furnishes a working executable model to the suggested architecture.

Solution Activity Management Layer   This layer is a hands-on technical specification provider and tactical implementation entity. It is responsible for providing detailed implementation descriptions that elaborate on the how-to-do portion of the solution. Its main focus should be on achieving the goals and the targets assigned by the discipline management layer.

As seen in Exhibit 8.25, the *solution activity* layer should cover the solution spectrum by suggesting a range of combined activities that can resolve the problem. The conceptualization and the visualization groups should be concerned with providing detailed technical specifications, which should be used by the design, architecture, and software modeling solution activity manager.

SUMMARY

This chapter provides a model for establishing, redesigning, or restructuring an enterprise architecture organization in a business enterprise. This enterprise architecture organization model can stand alone, but in this case we have peppered it with SOA-relevant examples of disciplines, practices, roles, and skills that befit an organization exploring SOA and services. As we discussed in Chapter 7, an SOA initiative can have a dramatic impact on existing IT organizational structures and processes, including IT governance processes, development lifecycle processes, and enterprise architecture processes. This chapter provides a reusable model that helps delineate the SOA requirements of enterprise architecture organizations. Whether you must tune your current architecture organization, establish an enterprise architecture organization from scratch, or realign your existing enterprise architecture organization based on business, technology, or

SOA changes, this model should provide a lasting reusable framework for enterprise architecture.

NOTES

1. Henry Mintzberg, Bruce Ahlstrand, and Joseph Lampel, *Strategy Safari: A Guided Tour Through the Wilds of Strategic Management* (New York: The Free Press, 1998), p. 16.
2. Thomas A. Stewart, *Intellectual Capital: The New Wealth of Organizations* (New York: Doubleday, 1997, 1999), pp. 79–106.
3. Peter F. Drucker, *Managing in a Time of Great Change* (New York: Penguin Group, 1995), pp. 39–44.
4. Peter F. Drucker, *The Practice of Management* (New York: Harper & Row, 1986), pp. 341–342.

CHAPTER 9

SOA Business Case and Return on Investment Model

The return on investment (ROI) for a service-oriented architecture (SOA) initiative is a very interesting challenge for most organizations. As we know, SOA is not a new concept, yet very few organizations can point to their SOA and demonstrate crisply documented ROI proof points for their efforts. For example, XYZ Financial claims a 200 to 300% ROI from its SOA efforts, primarily driven from reuse. However, an ROI percentage or number requires one additional critical piece of data: the payback period. Stating or claiming an ROI without a payback period is like claiming $500 of savings by spending $3,000! "Look how much I saved you today, honey!" You get the picture. XYZ's ROI probably can be verified, but the example magnifies the stickiness of cost justifying new approaches to managing information technology (IT). Business case and ROI data for SOAs are starting to emerge, and more use cases of positive results from SOA initiatives are forthcoming every day. But this misses the point. SOA is about business value and strategic business enablement. ROI is a tool to justify and approve projects. It is not always the best tool to evaluate things like business value, business impact, and strategic business enablement.

There are documented ROI case studies for Web services, which are less about SOA than they are about simplifying development processes, lowering costs, and enabling future benefits through reusable services. Many initial Web services projects promoted with big ROIs were implemented before most organizations were truly thinking about SOA and the enterprise-wide benefits of reusable services. Depending on how these early projects where implemented, and in particular how the services were selected, designed, and implemented, their ability to interoperate in an SOA may be an issue. Many early services implementations were point-to-point services and were not designed for reuse and interoperability within the larger context of SOA.

The ROI for SOA has taken on new importance as more and more organizations are exploring SOA initiatives to see where they can positively impact their business. Organizations new to SOA place great importance on the business case and ROI analysis prior to launching these initiatives. Many times these organizations are early in their SOA implementation lifecycles, and so the business case becomes very important, along with selling SOA value to business unit executives.

ACHIEVING SOA VALUE

SOA offers many more strategic benefits for an organization, yet those strategic benefits can be difficult to tease into a hard dollar justifiable business case. How do you measure agility? How can you demonstrate the value of faster time to market? And even reuse metrics, which are very well documented for software and components, are not as accessible in the services case.

Recall the definition of an SOA: *An SOA is a computing architecture where application functionality is available as shared reusable services that are discoverable on the network.* A number of benefits arise from offering IT functionality as shared services in an SOA. There is a clear ROI associated with the reuse of services in an SOA. Once a portfolio of services is available to be leveraged in an SOA, these reuse benefits multiply in an "SOA network effect," where the value of an SOA increases with the number of available services and the number of consumers using and reusing those services. This benefit compounds over time as the SOA is leveraged internally by developers and business analysts and externally by customers and trading partners.

But how does an organization achieve the critical mass of services to begin to generate SOA network effects? How many services are needed to reach critical mass? How many consumers or unique clients are needed? And how much reuse of services constitutes critical mass? Extending conventional software reuse metrics to services is simple, yet there are clear differences in the type and volume of services consumption in an SOA context.

SOA VALUE CONSIDERATIONS

The ultimate business driver of SOA is the promise of business agility, as evidenced by faster time to market and lower costs for business initiatives. In addition, there are several IT benefits, including reduced IT costs, increased productivity, software and asset reuse, reduced integration and maintenance costs, faster development time, and overall increased IT flexibility and vendor independence.

Naturally, flexibility and agility are very challenging goals for an SOA initiative because of their slippery nature and the difficulty of putting a metric around them. Operationalizing the words "agility" and "flexibility" is the challenge. Explicitly linking an SOA initiative to tangible metrics is hard work, which is what drives many early SOA adopters to their reuse focus. Reuse, whether it is software or services, is tangible and easy to understand.

The reuse benefits of SOA alone are compelling enough. SOAs allow existing software systems and legacy assets to be exposed or rendered as reusable services, which can then be flexibly used and reused, combined into new services to solve other new business and IT challenges, and assembled into orchestrated business processes (comprised of reusable services), which can provide tremendous flexibility in supporting business process change over time. A business change in this case would involve reassembling services, which are already available and proven, into the new target business process as opposed to writing millions of lines of software code to address business changes.

SOA is compelling because changing business requirements can be addressed through reuse of proven, tested, and interoperable services in an SOA rather than following a traditional software development process. Cost savings of at least 80% over the traditional software development process are achievable in this new environment, not to mention the many cost avoidances such as fewer integration expenses, fewer integration software licenses and hardware requirements, and more optimal use of IT resources and assets.

SOA VALUE POINTS

The need for SOA is driven by two broad factors:

1. The accumulated complexity of IT architectures and systems inhibits business capabilities and is too cost prohibitive to maintain and support.
2. SOA can simplify and reduce the costs of integration while converting legacy IT assets into reusable services for customers (customer service), increasing quality, achieving new levels of IT productivity, and complying with regulatory compliance issues. SOA and services are viewed as ways to achieve all of these benefits incrementally over time.

A higher plateau of business value may be available through an SOA initiative, but only if an organization can get the initiative launched and cost justified to begin with. How do you get buy-in from the IT and business community for an SOA initiative based on a hypothesis of agility and flexibility? Although there are clear, concrete value metrics of an SOA initiative based on reuse and integration cost avoidances, do not forget to think strategically about the end game, about how your organization may perform when you have reached the target state of an SOA. You must remember your business goals for SOA and think broadly and strategically about how an SOA effort will impact your organization. Think about business value, but in a big way.

BIG HAIRY AUDACIOUS VALUE

While we are talking about obtaining hard ROI numbers to develop the SOA business case, we encourage you not to forget the big picture for your SOA efforts. In his book *Good to Great*, Jim Collins discusses the concept of big hairy audacious goals (BHAGs).[1] BHAGs are the big, daring strategic goals of an organization that help provide purpose for its efforts and all of its constituents.

In an SOA setting, the equivalent is shooting for big hairy audacious value, or BHAV. What we mean is that you need to create a vision for your enterprise, based on some future-state SOA goals, where you can create a new way of business for your organization, a new value plateau where your SOA efforts create and deliver cost savings, increased productivity, revenue growth, and other major value drivers.

Think about your end state as a possible value target and then work backward incrementally to the finite and achievable steps you can deliver toward those BHAVs. Think big here. Think about business agility as a goal and try to make it real for your business and IT organizations. Think about faster time to market and how your SOA efforts can achieve that goal. Consider how your SOA initiatives can impact customer satisfaction, multichannel integration, and other areas where customers are affected by information across your value chain. And do not forget about financial benefits, such as revenue growth and cost savings via your SOA efforts.

A host of potential SOA value can be captured through SOA initiatives. Two of these we've briefly mentioned: agility or flexibility, and services reuse. Along with these are a range of others, including:

- Better business alignment
- Improved customer satisfaction
- Improved ROI of existing IT assets (retrospective ROI)
- Reduced integration costs
- Reduced vendor lock-in and switching costs (IT flexibility)
- Future-proof IT solutions

There are many more that are not listed here. The bottom line is that SOA has the potential to deliver strategic business benefits as well as more focused tactical benefits at the project level. However, realizing the value of an SOA—achieving the BHAVs just discussed—is going to require commitment to SOA over a long time. That's because SOA is a process, a long-term commitment to a style of computing based on business services. SOA is not for the faint of heart. For organizations that stay the course, SOA can provide competitive advantage in a variety of dimensions that were initially planned for as well as in ways that will emerge over time.

SOA PROCESS

The important factor in delivering SOA business value is to realize that SOA is a process, an architectural strategy and vision that is realized over time through many projects implemented by distributed teams of developers and architects. SOA is not implemented enterprise-wide in a big bang fashion. It is realized through the rigorous enforcement of SOA policies that guide standards, development guidelines and best practices, processes for the services development lifecycle, and overall SOA compliance. If the SOA policies are not enforced across all the projects and project teams, SOA value is diminished, reuse benefits are lost, and interoperability is impossible. In other words, SOA becomes an IT version of the Wild Wild West. You're back to where you were when you launched your SOA initiative: silos of systems and technology that do not interoperate. Except, in a services world, the silos are more fine grained with no management framework, integration model, and without policy enforcement. SOA requires process thinking in order to achieve business value.

PROCESS APPROACH TO SOA ROI

Multiple models exist for identifying IT value to an organization. After reviewing multiple approaches, we believe that the model that best fits an SOA initiative is a process approach. Soh and Markus have created a process model of IT value.[2] In their model, three process activities in an organization determine IT value: the IT conversion process, the IT use process, and the competitive process.

The IT conversion process essentially represents the conversion of funding and labor into IT assets, such as software and systems. The IT use process is the appropriate (or potentially inappropriate) consumption or use of those IT assets to create organizational value. Asset consumption is how IT impacts the organization. In the competitive process, the impact of IT on the overall organization results in competitive advantage and better organizational performance as a result of the process of creating IT value. Exhibit 9.1 depicts the process approach to IT value.

Adapting Soh and Markus's model to the process of SOA is simple. IT expenditures convert funds and labor, and in this case existing assets, into assets called "services." These services are consumed and reused in multiple ways by many consumers to drive IT and business impact. This results in new levels of organization performance through the realization of SOA value. Exhibit 9.2 represents the SOA value process as adapted from Soh and Markus's model.

The model extends easily to fit the process of achieving SOA. The process of conversion creates SOA assets, or services, for consumption by developers, analysts, customers, suppliers, business processes, and so forth, which impacts the organization's competitive advantage. We must also add the concept of SOA governance to Soh and Markus's model, which will clearly guide and manage the processes of conversion, consumption, and to some extent the delivery of SOA value to the business.

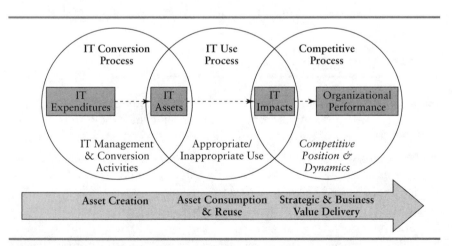

EXHIBIT 9.1   Process Approach to Creating IT Value
Source: Adapted from Soh and Markus, 1995.

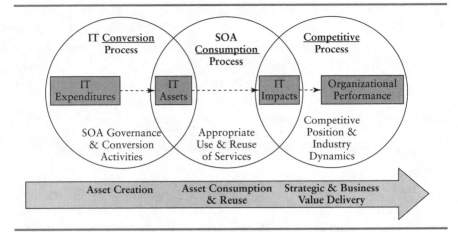

EXHIBIT 9.2 Process Approach to Creating SOA Value
Source: Adapted from Soh and Marcus, 1995.

EXPLORING THE SOA VALUE MODEL

The SOA value model shows how the process perspective helps identify the phases of SOA activities that generate value throughout the process of achieving SOA. The model provides a very useful approach to understanding the processes that generate SOA value for an organization. From these basic SOA value processes, we can begin to derive an appropriate model that describes the way that SOAs will contribute to competitive advantage for an organization.

There are three broad value-creating processes in the SOA value model: conversion value, consumption value, and competitive value.

Conversion Value

SOA conversion value is typically associated with the initial development or enablement of services within the enterprise. SOA value here revolves around developer efficiency, project cost and investment, and speed of development. Eventually, when more services are available to be leveraged and reused during the development process, developers will begin to realize even greater SOA value by virtue of working with published and proven services more than developing software from scratch. In other words, development processes will be faster because essentially the software process will begin with pretested and available services. When developers are orchestrating processes based on services more than they are writing custom code, the value of SOA will accelerate. Thus, SOA iterations will continue to drive increasing value with the increase of more services over time.

One slight difference in the conversion process is that an SOA can be realized by developing new services from scratch, by exposing or creating services from existing legacy or packages applications, or by acquiring third-party services from external service providers. The conversion process must incorporate the use case of third-party services as well as internally developed services.

Consumption Value (from Services Use and Reuse)

When services are available to be consumed, there is a wide variety of SOA value to be gained. SOA value includes services reuse, business process orchestration, and integration avoidance benefits by virtue of standards-based interoperable services. Ultimately, the collection of available services will be used as the building blocks for composite services, which are essentially services composed of other services. Even more acceleration of SOA value results as the consumption value increases. The appropriate consumption of services in an SOA is where real value begins to be harvested for an organization. Furthermore, it is during the consumption process that SOA network effects begin to take over. When enough services in an SOA are available to spur widespread internal and external services reuse and consumption, as well as the ability to orchestrate services and business processes, the value of SOA and the realized benefits will spike.

SOA network effects, or critical mass, is achieved during the SOA consumption process. But SOA critical mass is achieved only if an organization persists in developing and exposing services that will be reused and consumed by a broad audience of consumers: developers, analysts, customers, partners, suppliers, and others. If an organization hesitates or ends its SOA efforts before critical mass is achieved, tremendous SOA value will be lost.

Competitive Value (SOA Business Value)

Competitive value, or SOA business value, is the highest SOA value threshold. It is achieved after the other plateaus of SOA value are realized, including conversion value and consumption value. SOA competitive value includes the more difficult aspects of SOA to quantify, such as time to market, business agility, IT flexibility, future-proofing your IT architecture, and related strategic yet abstract SOA benefits.

Often these are the business benefits that are stated early in the SOA adoption process but cannot be quantified well enough to justify the cost in a business case. Often these benefits become the avoidance benefits that many organizations do not allow in the business case models used to cost justify a major new IT initiative.

SOA Value Model Discussion

The process model of SOA value suggests that to achieve the business value of SOA, an organization must persist in its efforts for a period of time. In other words, there must be a sustained effort to achieve SOA, and it must extend across the three processes of conversion, consumption, and competitive advantage in order to accrue the benefits at each of those stages of SOA rollout.

This *SOA value model* suggests that an SOA can increasingly deliver incremental value to an organization if and only if it persists in its efforts and achieves the multiple thresholds of SOA value that are available. An SOA must achieve critical mass, or some combination of services and consumers, such that reuse benefits are accruing, process orchestration is possible, and integration cost avoidances are realized. At this point, multiple threads of SOA value will be reinforcing one another, and the organization will be able to demonstrate tremendous SOA benefits.

SOA ROI THRESHOLD MODEL

The SOA value model demonstrates how SOA benefits are achieved over time through the sustained and iterative implementation of services projects that support the business goals of an organization. The SOA value model clearly shows that SOA is a process though which varied and compelling business benefits can be achieved. Conversion, consumption, and competitive value are harvested through a process of sustained investments in SOA over time. The fact that SOA value is achieved after some period of investment through time helps explain the difficulty many organizations experience in determining the business case for SOA. Although the oft-stated goal of business agility is first and foremost in the minds of business and IT executives, it often remains an abstract concept with little hope of being realized. It is hard to measure. It is difficult to operationalize. Yet we all know it when we have it.

Thus, reuse, as opposed to agility, becomes a convenient anchor for the SOA business case. Reuse as a concept is easy to understand, and the metrics of the value of software reuse have been broadly accepted for years. We discuss the reuse benefits of SOA later in this chapter, especially with the extended ROI that an SOA accords a reuse initiative by virtue of the large volume of potential consumers of services in an SOA.

What is clear is that *there is no single ROI model for SOA*. There is *no one* single benefit or overarching ROI approach for an SOA initiative. There are many. SOA presents many ROI opportunities based on the sustained pursuit of the benefits of SOA. And as the SOA value model suggests, the benefits are achieved through the sustained process of implementing SOA over time. SOA ROI or value is achieved in various thresholds that build on one another, all of which rely on the sustained drive toward SOA via many different projects across an enterprise. We call this the SOA ROI threshold model (see Exhibit 9.3).

The SOA ROI threshold model takes into consideration the phases of SOA adoption that clients actually undergo as well as the potential business value that can be harvested during these phases. SOA is not one big project with a single overarching ROI metric. SOA is a long-term, strategic initiative that is realized through many projects over time, that build toward the concept of having a body of

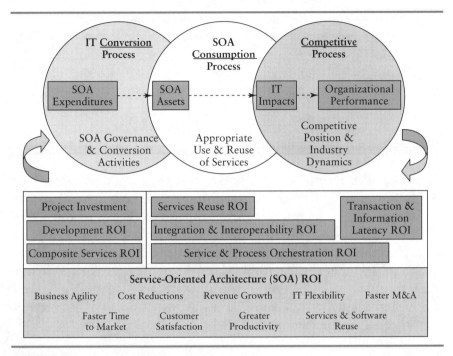

EXHIBIT 9.3   SOA ROI Threshold Model

services available for widespread consumption internally by developers and analysts as well as externally by customers and partners.

SOA is actualized at the project level where budgets are allocated and projects are approved. How do you capture an ROI at the project level and still build toward the strategic ROI of an SOA later, when it actually becomes an SOA by virtue of actually having services available for discovery, use, and reuse? The answer is that SOA is achieved through multiple distinct projects, each of which must have its own business case and contribute to the SOA business case. We call this the *SOA greater good*.

At the project level, there must be a business case for the project itself as well as an SOA greater good business case that says SOA is important. If the project is all about services, it must build toward the larger strategic SOA business case as well. For most organizations, there must be a centralized budget to encourage individual business units to work toward the SOA greater good by potentially investing more during their project to support reuse by other business units later. This typical budgeting challenge must be addressed within the SOA governance model. An exploration of the concept of SOA thresholds will explain how this model fits the reality of achieving SOA while helping manage the budgeting challenges one can also anticipate.

ROI Thresholds: Beyond Reuse

The SOA ROI threshold model addresses project-level ROI and yet still builds toward the SOA ROI, or the SOA greater good. The ROI threshold model suggests that there are multiple waves or thresholds of ROI available in an SOA initiative and that the business value that an organization can achieve will change through the course of SOA adoption. In other words, the business value of ROI is harvested in multiple phases as certain thresholds of SOA capabilities are achieved. We suggest these thresholds of SOA value, which are attained through the process of implementing SOA:

- Reuse ROI
- Integration avoidance and interoperability ROI
- Services and process orchestration ROI
- Transaction and information latency ROI
- SOA business value (cumulative ROI)

The SOA ROI threshold model builds on the SOA value model to help illustrate the various thresholds of SOA value.

Conversion Value/ROI

Conversion value is achieved at the project level during the initial SOA iterations. ROI here is focused on individual projects based on development benefits of services and SOA. Remember, though, that there may not be as compelling an ROI during conversion as there will be during downstream SOA processes of consumption and competitive advantage. In fact, some organizations may see little or even negative ROI compared to traditional project development methods because additional investment may be required to achieve reusable services and to acquire shared SOA infrastructure to operate them. Individual project budgets should not have to bear this shared infrastructure burden, but often they do. An early challenge for an SOA initiative may arise from various organizations that have a vested interest in the old way of doing things, or simply do not understand or buy into the value of SOA. To get over this political/organizational hump, business executive sponsorship is critical, including the willingness to kick in the delta dollars required to get these initial projects off the ground. This leap of faith requires business vision and calculated risk taking. If the organization does not have sufficient leadership to overcome this initial resistance, different SOA approaches may be necessary. There are many possible ROI opportunities during the conversion process, such as:

- *Project ROI,* such as reduced cost and reduced development time for a specific IT project.
- *Development ROI,* such as reduced development time and better quality of software. This benefit is expected later in SOA adoption when there are shared reusable services available to be leveraged during development. This ROI will kick in during future SOA and services iterations.
- *Composite services ROI,* such as faster development time using building block services to develop applications; this is similar to reuse ROI.
- *Reuse ROI,* which will be attained in subsequent SOA iterations once there are enough services available to be reused. Initially there may be little reuse ROI available until enough services are built to be reused.

The biggest challenge during the conversion process is achieving the reuse ROI threshold. Achieving reuse ROI requires investing in the development of reusable services and related assets in the SOA. Once an organization achieves the reuse threshold, the next thresholds of SOA ROI become possible.

Exhibit 9.4 depicts the conversion value of an SOA.

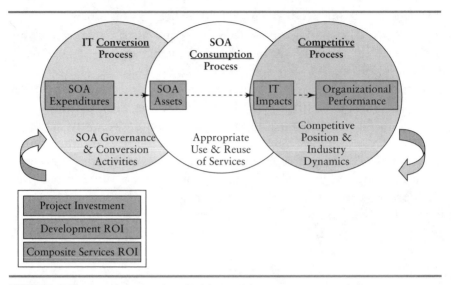

EXHIBIT 9.4   SOA ROI Threshold Model: Conversion Value

Consumption Value/ROI

Consumption value and ROI are generated through the appropriate use and reuse of services and related assets in an SOA. What defines appropriate use and reuse of services? That's the purpose of SOA governance and of clear enforceable policies. The SOA consumption process creates value based on leveraging available services. The following thresholds of SOA ROI are achieved during the consumption process:

- *Services reuse ROI,* which includes at least 80% cost avoidance savings for services every time they are reused. (Note: We believe that in an SOA, the reuse cost avoidance savings will be higher.) services reuse is the initial SOA ROI threshold to achieve, and as we've already discussed, reuse is almost always targeted as an expected ROI for SOA. Once enough services are available to achieve the reuse threshold, then the next ROI threshold, integration and interoperability, is possible.
- *Integration and interoperability ROI* includes the cost avoidance realized from implementing standards-based services rather than implementing proprietary integration strategies, buying licenses

of expensive and proprietary integration middleware, and then maintaining proprietary integrations once they have been built. This ROI is based primarily on cost avoidances and time to market for integration initiatives, as well as the avoidance of integration altogether in many scenarios. This ROI threshold is attained through more systematic use and reuse of services in an SOA to avoid traditional integration expenses and maintenance. This threshold is most often achieved after services reuse and in fact leverages reuse of prebuilt interoperable services to avoid point-to-point integrations common in the pre-SOA generation of IT. *In effect, in an SOA, services are already integrated. No incremental integration tasks are required to make them interoperate.*

■ *Services and process orchestration ROI* includes the benefits associated with orchestrating composite services and applications, as well as with orchestrating business processes within an enterprise and choreographing business processes between enterprises. These benefits include faster time to market for IT solutions and business initiatives, lower development costs and reduced development time, as well as reduced maintenance of applications due to reuse of preexisting services. Services and process orchestration ROI drives additional levels of services reuse as well, which clearly demonstrates the added value of SOA once there are enough services available to orchestrate into business processes. This ROI threshold clearly builds on the previous SOA ROI threshold of services reuse, and it enables even greater acceleration of reuse benefits by virtue of executing orchestrated processes composed of reusable building block services.

■ *Transaction and information latency ROI* includes the benefits of removing stale information from business processes or from implementing event-based services to replace traditional batch-driven business processes. Removing stale information from business processes will allow real-time processes to replace batch-centric business processes where current information is not available until the next day pending an overnight batch replication or extraction, transformation, and load (ETL) process (typical of data warehousing applications). Transaction and information latency ROI comes in the form of time value of money, customer satisfaction, and even health and safety in the case of healthcare, where a real-time view of a patient's health record can mean the difference between life and death. This ROI threshold does not rely as much on previous SOA ROI thresholds, yet it clearly builds on the ability to leverage services to implement real-time business processes and remove transactional and information latency from multiple business processes. Perhaps not as ubiquitous as the other ROI thresholds, transaction and information latency ROI will deliver significant value to an organization.

Exhibit 9.5 depicts the consumption value of the SOA ROI threshold model.

SOA Competitive Advantage Value

The competitive advantage process yields SOA ROI that represents the accrued benefits from previous SOA ROI thresholds. In fact, these SOA benefits are the *results* or outcomes of previous SOA ROI thresholds. For example, services reuse and services orchestration enable business benefits of agility and faster time to market. Integration and interoperability of services enable an organization to be agile, to reduce costs, and to be easier to do business with for customers and

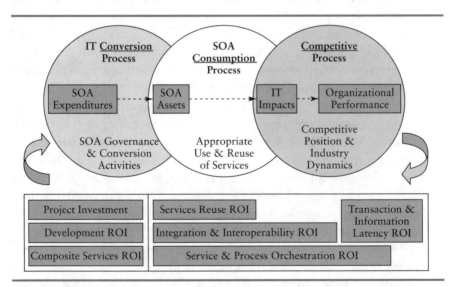

EXHIBIT 9.5   SOA ROI Threshold Model: Consumption Value

partners. In this sense, the SOA value model suggests that in the competitive advantage process, an organization is reaping the business benefits of previous SOA ROI thresholds and applying them to create competitive advantage in a number of dimensions.

Enterprise SOA business value ROI is the aggregate of all previous ROI thresholds. By the time an organization has progressed through the previous thresholds of SOA ROI value, it will have achieved many of the business benefits attributable to an SOA initiative. These can include, but are not limited to, these types of SOA business benefits: business agility, revenue gains, cost reductions, IT flexibility, faster time to market, greater productivity, improved customer satisfaction, services reuse, reduced IT maintenance costs, and improved quality. You get the picture. Many of these benefits are the softer, cost-avoidance benefits that are tough to wrap a metric around, yet everyone knows they are real.

Exhibit 9.6 depicts the competitive value, which is the aggregate of all previous SOA thresholds of value.

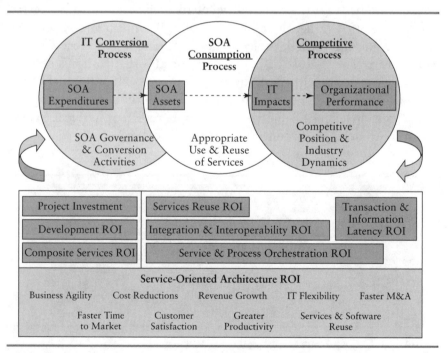

EXHIBIT 9.6   Competitive Value in the SOA ROI Threshold Model

When an organization has progressed through the various SOA value thresholds, it will achieve the enterprise benefits and business value of SOA. Exhibit 9.7 depicts the strategic business value that SOA will enable through sustained effort.

SOA Critical Mass and Network Effects

When does an organization achieve the critical mass of services with its SOA initiative? This is a common question. Eric A. Marks has written about the notion of SOA *network effects* since he coined the term in 2004.[3] This concept is adapted from Metcalf's Law. SOAs should demonstrate similar value properties. Imagine having an SOA with one service and no consumers. How much value disappears from the SOA value equation in this scenario? No reuse is possible, not to mention use. There is no integration avoidance, because one service doesn't really require an integration model. There is no possibility of process orchestration or business process management because there are not enough services to orchestrate into processes. To achieve SOA value, there must be multiple consumers of services.

Consumption-based services value is critical to the success of any SOA effort. There must be consumers for an organization's services to achieve even one threshold of organizational value: reuse. The relative value of those services will remain low until more consumption occurs, or more reuse, which will accelerate return on services (ROS). Exhibit 9.8 depicts the concept of SOA critical mass.

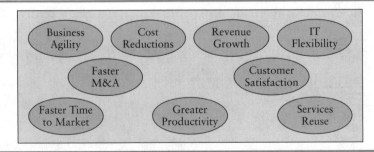

EXHIBIT 9.7 SOA Strategic Business Value

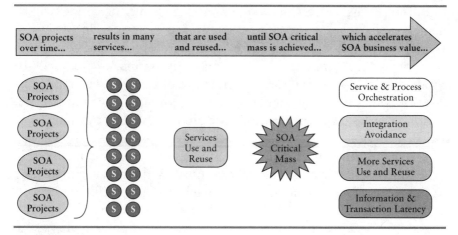

EXHIBIT 9.8 Achieving SOA Critical Mass

Exhibit 9.8 illustrates that as more services are exposed in an enterprise and used and reused in the SOA consumption process, SOA critical mass will be achieved. But when will that occur in the adoption of SOA?

Eventually, as more services become available to more consumers, the value of the SOA will increase until the point when critical mass is achieved. *Critical mass for an SOA is the point where enough services are available within a domain, or across multiple domains, such that multiple business processes can be orchestrated from them.* In other words, SOA critical mass is achieved when the SOA value reaches a threshold beyond reuse benefits only and transitions to business process benefits. How many services are required to achieve SOA critical mass? It depends on the organization, its complexity, the nature of its services, and a host of other factors. However, in general, the point of SOA critical mass is when SOA value transitions from a value proposition solely based on reuse to one based on other value drivers, in particular process orchestration.

In fact, business process orchestration presents a special case of reuse for an organization. Orchestrating business processes from services creates a new plateau of consumption of services for an organization. One reuse of a business process that is orchestrated using five services essentially represents a block reuse of those services. One question that executives often do *not* ask is when critical mass will be achieved. In other words, if an organization invests in SOA and reusable services, when will there be enough services and consumers of services such that the critical mass of business value will be attained? As Newcomer and Lomow have observed, "The real value of SOA comes from the later stages of development, when new applications can be developed entirely, or almost entirely, by composing existing services."[4]

In fact, even processes are reusable, as they may be included in other more complex processes over time as the SOA evolves and as business processes change. In this manner, the capability to orchestrate multiple business processes from a portfolio of available reusable services represents the critical mass for an SOA, where suddenly the realization of business value accelerates due to the volume of services consumption at the individual service level and at the composite service or business process level.

Achieving SOA critical mass is a challenge in many organizations. It is sometimes difficult to sell the value of investing in reusable services across business and process domains to business leaders. One of the most challenging organizational and governance issues is changing the funding model for IT initiatives and finding appropriate organizational and personal incentives to create reusable shared services in an SOA. Doing this is critical to reaching SOA critical mass. A summary of the concept of SOA critical mass follows.

- Value of an individual service is low until there are enough consumers (reuse) to accelerate return on services.
- Value of an SOA increases as the volume of services and consumers increases, and eventually hits critical mass.
- SOA network effects kick in at that time.
- SOA critical mass is the point where there are enough available reusable services such that more than one business process can be orchestrated from them.

TARGETING ROI WITH SOA INITIATIVES

One challenge for the nascent SOA adopter is selecting the appropriate ROI model for specific projects that contribute to the larger goals of the SOA. The ROI challenge is especially true given that there really is no single overarching SOA ROI model; there are many. Thus, the most appropriate way to solve the SOA ROI challenge is to refer back to the SOA drivers and SOA value drivers discussed in Chapter 5. Based on the business and IT imperatives and the subsequent SOA value drivers, certain business needs and value drivers will carry more weight than others. These high priority business requirements will help prioritize SOA initiatives as well.

If the needs of the organization are truly centered on IT productivity and services reuse, you must understand the SOA value model and the processes required to actually achieve SOA services reuse. In other words, the benefits from reuse will occur only when services are actually reused, and those benefits will be software cost avoidance as well as reduced maintenance.

Reuse is one of the most cited SOA benefits, and yet not all organizations will value services reuse the same way. And the metrics of reuse are challenging as well, especially when services reuse is based on leveraging components and legacy assets that are encapsulated in a service. In that scenario, is services reuse the proper focus, or should the reuse metrics somehow account for the original legacy assets that were exposed or encapsulated as services? And who gets reuse credit—the services group or the legacy system group that enabled the service? Services and component reuse is important in an SOA because it is more easily measured than are some of the other SOA benefits. This explains why reuse benefits are so loudly trumpeted over other SOA benefits.

However, process orchestration ROI is required for agile and flexible processes, which means once again that the ROI will be realized once that threshold can be achieved by an organization. Increased agility is another commonly cited SOA benefit. But what do people mean by agility, and when does this SOA benefit come into play? At day one or at some future point when many services are available to be orchestrated into new business processes? Measuring agility is a tougher metric to grasp as it depends on so many other factors. How do we measure agility as an SOA benefit?

Orchestration of processes requires building blocks of services to be available first, and thus an organization must expend some effort to create the reusable services before they can be leveraged in a service orchestration solution. The process of converting SOA effort into reusable services must take place before the orchestration threshold can be attained.

Exhibit 9.9 depicts how SOA value drivers may be used to help identify the appropriate target ROI model based on an organization's specific SOA requirements and business needs.

In this diagram, the SOA value drivers dictate the possible ROI paths that may satisfy those value drivers. Those ROI thresholds will deliver the target benefits that are available at that particular SOA ROI threshold.

Measuring the impact of SOA is relatively straightforward on one dimension and yet challenging on others. SOA results can be achieved from a business perspective, an IT perspective, and a services and asset reuse perspective. Implementing SOA provides many levers of ROI. Which ones are important is based on the success criteria defined by a given organization. This is where the ROI threshold model must tie back to the SOA goals, drivers, and value drivers that were identified during SOA strategy and planning.

For all targeted business goals of an SOA initiative, the goals must be operationalized such that a metric can be established. ROI targeting is a useful exercise to help focus SOA efforts on targeted thresholds of SOA value. The SOA ROI matrix will help frame the ROI for your SOA initiatives.

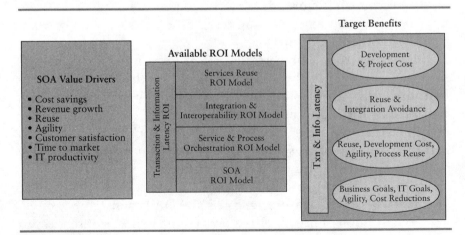

EXHIBIT 9.9   Map SOA Value Drivers to ROI Models

SOA ROI Matrix

While thinking about your SOA initiatives and the business value you seek, consider how these map to the original SOA goals, drivers, and value drivers. Do not forget about those BHAVs and the business imperatives that spurred your organization toward SOA. As you frame the business case and develop the ROI model, the SOA ROI matrix in Exhibit 9.10 may prove useful.

Exhibit 9.10 maps the SOA ROI thresholds discussed into an exhibit that examines them for their ROI focus, what type of business value can be achieved, and what ROI category can be achieved.

ROI focus identifies where and how the SOA value of a particular ROI threshold may be realized. The exhibit also identifies savings or value, indicating whether the savings are hard savings or soft

SOA ROI Model	ROI Focus	Savings or Value	ROI Category
Services ROI Tier	Developer productivity and project cost	Development cost, project cost	Cost reduction
Service-Oriented Integration & Interoperability Tier	Services reuse and integration avoidance (custom integration, packaged integration, proprietary integration, e.g., EAI)	Services reuse, cost avoidance from custom integration and commercial proprietary integration	Cost avoidance, services reuse, multichannel integration, achieve SOA critical mass
Transactional & Information Latency Tier	Cost of information latency in the value chain	Hard costs of currency, safety, accurate data	Time value of money; process speed; accurate information; better decisions
Service-Oriented Process & Service Orchestration Tier	Services reuse, process orchestration, project speed and cost reductions	Services reuse, process improvements, time to market for projects, developer productivity	Cost avoidance, reuse, process orchestration versus software development, SOA network effects
Enterprise SOA Tier	Strategic value, customer satifactions, time to market, competitive advantage	Reuse, process efficiency, cost reductions, revenue enhancement	Revenue growth, cost reductions, IT productivity, business agility

EXHIBIT 9.10   SOA ROI Matrix

savings. Of course, often this determination varies from organization to organization. The ROI category for each threshold is also described. This exhibit should help focus SOA initiatives on the ROI thresholds that map to specific organizational goals.

SOA AND SERVICES REUSE

Most of the SOA ROI models for SOA are targeted at the reuse of software, components, and services. Reuse benefits of an SOA are easier to document and validate than some of the other more compelling and strategic benefits, such as agility, flexibility, and time to market. Reuse provides a common sense and intuitive basis for justifying investments in SOA, and it allows an organization to develop some preliminary cost savings around processes that are usually fairly well known.

While software reuse in an SOA context provides a very useful ROI anchor point, we must remember all of the entities that are reusable in an SOA. Some of the artifacts that may be reused in an SOA include:

- Schemas
- Code
- Components
- Legacy assets
- Services
- Processes

There may be other assets as well, and we do not even go to the level of shared infrastructure, networks, or hardware. In other words, there are more things to reuse in an SOA than services, although in an SOA, services are the fundamental asset of concern.

Measuring reuse in an SOA is a matter of extending existing software reuse metrics to services. Dr. Jeffrey Poulin identifies three fundamental metrics that are useful in measuring software reuse:[5]

1. *Relative cost of writing for reuse (RCWR)*. Developing software that is intended to be reused requires incremental effort. In fact,

Poulin estimates that it requires 50% more effort to write a component for reuse. This is due to the extra effort to:

1. Generalize for additional requirements.
2. Add more detailed documentation.
3. Test to increase trust.
4. Test for additional potential uses.
5. Prepare the component for distribution.

In a services world, we would expect that effort to be less because services are interfaces to the business logic functionality. However, for the sake of our model, let us adopt the 50% incremental effort for now.

2. *Relative cost to reuse (RCR).* Reusing components that are designed for reuse does not eliminate 100% of the effort. There is a cost of 20% assigned to reusing preexisting components. As Poulin states, "Reuse does not come for free." Reuse effort involves tasks such as locating the component, understanding it by reading documentation, and technical effort relating to integration, unit testing, and system testing. There may be others. However, reusing an existing component typically requires only 20% of the effort required to write the same component from scratch. If the RCR of a component is 20%, or 0.2, that means an organization will save 80% of the development effort. That is a significant cost avoidance for any organization.

3. *Software reuse payoff.* Using these simple metrics, software reuse achieves breakeven within one reuse of a component. That is, using an RCWR of 1.5 and an RCR of 0.20, breakeven is achieved at one use and one reuse of a component. The assumptions with this model are twofold: You are investing in a software component that you would have written anyway, and you have identified a second user of the component.

Translating Software Reuse into Services Reuse

From this discussion, it becomes clear that applying software reuse metrics will form a reasonable baseline from which to justify services reuse in an SOA. Assuming the same baseline metrics of 50% incremental effort to create a reusable service and a 20%

penalty to reuse an existing service, let's explore the dynamics of services reuse.

First, business services are generally more coarse-grained than components are. Often they are composed of existing components, legacy transactions, and other business logic. In other words, services encapsulate more business logic and expose it using a standard interface. Modern tool sets facilitate the process of examining existing components and legacy assets and of exposing that business logic as reusable services. Under this scenario, services may well require less incremental effort and cost to develop as reusable assets. They may be faster to develop as well, assuming tools continue to evolve to support exposing of various legacy systems using composite application development tools, metadata-driven development models, and ultimately service orchestration approaches to services design and development. The implication here is that services are faster to develop and are potentially less expensive to write as reusable services than as components. It may be that the 50% percent premium to develop reusable services is a high estimate.

Second, the process of consuming and reusing existing services is different from consuming or reusing software components. In an SOA, services will be reused in multiple ways. They will be reused as is or simply be invoked. They will be leveraged by orchestrated processes using business process management applications. And potentially they will be leveraged by composite applications or composite services (services composed of other existing services). And business processes can potentially be reused as well. In these scenarios, the services are simply reused without a cost penalty to make use of them. In other words, there is not a 20% cost penalty to reuse services. While the cost to reuse a service may be less than reusing a component, consumers still must invest time to understand the semantics of a service and to apply those semantics to the process consuming the service. Doing this will result in some cost beyond simply invoking the service.

Third, updating or modifying services can be either a simple process that extends the functionality of a service without breaking the service contract for its current users, or it can result in a completely new service. However, service modifications may result in a necessarily incompatible change to an existing service, probably with some grace period for consumers to move off the deprecated version of the service interface. It is this third case that introduces complexity into the services development and deployment lifecycles, and therefore more costs. If a new service results from a major modification of an existing service, then perhaps the RCWR and RCR estimates are close. If a service is extended to new consumers by expanding its capabilities without disrupting the functionality of the original service, then the reuse benefit is even greater.

Finally, in an SOA, services have different consumption patterns from software components. Services will not be exposed or developed unless there are known consumers of a service. In fact, we advocate developing or exposing services that have clear reuse and broad consumption opportunities for the organization. If this is not true, the service should not be developed unless there is some clear critical requirement that makes it an exception. For example, some initial SOA projects that attempt to implement reusable services may not have organizational share support and requirements for reuse of a given set of services. In this case, the project team has no choice but to implement these services, even though they may have only one consumer. The project team may have to make a best estimate on building out the service to be reusable and trust that good services design will facilitate enhancing service functionality to address a broader functional and consumption spectrum when they eventually agree to reuse those services. Services also have consumers beyond the IT organization whereas components or traditional software reuse is restricted to the IT developer community.

In an SOA, the community of potential consumers is very diverse and represents a tremendous volume of service reusers. It includes the IT development community, but it can also include business analysts, business process analysts, and external consumers such as customers, suppliers, and other trading partners. Thus, the actual consumption value of services extends far beyond the original software reuse metrics posited by Poulin. Those metrics are great, and perhaps they underestimate the true business value of services in an SOA given its diverse community of consumers.

Finally, for services, there are clearly the intended users (and reusers) that were originally planned when a service was published to a registry. However, an SOA should also plan for the emergent reuse of services. In other words, business units may discover that some existing services may be useful for them, and thus the consumption for an already-developed service increases simply because it is available. This "unintended" emergent reuse pattern, which is good reuse, should also be encouraged when building reusable services.

Reuse benefits in an SOA setting are significant for an organization. Using Poulin's metrics, which are proven and accepted industry-wide, you can begin to establish the ROI foundation for your SOA initiatives as the first threshold of SOA value to achieve. Once you begin to achieve reuse benefits of services, it allows these incremental ROI to be achieved as well:

- Faster time to market
- Lower development costs
- Lower maintenance costs
- Elimination of one-time integrations, point-to-point integration
- Elimination of proprietary integration, replaced with standards-based integration

However, do not reduce or limit your targeted SOA value only to reuse. As we have seen, services are different from software components. You should consider tuning Poulin's reuse metrics in an SOA and services context, using empirical data, and then expand the scope of the business value to accommodate the much larger consumption of services in an SOA.

Reuse and Retrospective ROI

An interesting feature of services reuse is the fact that they can be created based on legacy IT systems, mainframe applications, and other dated or "heritage" applications. When services are created from legacy mainframe applications, for example, additional value can be harvested from IT assets that are more than likely already fully depreciated, or "off the books." In other words, they are fully paid for, written off, and in maintenance mode. However, when they can be further leveraged by exposing their business logic as reusable services in an SOA, additional incremental ROI or business benefit can be harvested from these legacy IT assets. This "retrospective ROI" is essentially gleaned from dated assets that are bought and paid for. This approach may free up additional IT budget to potentially refactor such legacy assets over time. Look for opportunities to extract additional incremental value from legacy assets. Retrospective ROI is no less valid than other ROI elements derived from an SOA.

Service Reuse and Time-to-Market Impact

A recent client visit elicited the observation that any effort to achieve more reuse slows time to market for the project. After some thought and discussion with many colleagues, we suggest this approach to resolving the time-to-market challenge for services reuse. Recognize that reuse of services must be established at the business level first and foremost. Get broad agreement that a conceptual business service has applicability across multiple business processes, divisions, business units, or corporate entities. You can achieve this through existing cross-domain collaboration processes or as a dual effort. If the reuse opportunity is within one business unit, the reuse decision can be made through the normal IT governance and project budgeting and approval process. The time-to-market reuse challenge is best overcome by approaching service reuse from a top-down business perspective first, similar to our tenets around services identification, modeling, and design. The next three steps establish a process for ensuring maximum reuse while avoiding time-to-market delays:

1. Determine business reuse during business modeling process
2. Determine functional reuse during business requirements process
3. Determine technical reuse during services design and development

Our premise is that if you have established the business demand for a reusable service, top-down first from a business needs perspective, then the requirements vetting process will be faster and smoother than a bottom-up process that begins with technical requirements. This will help establish the business urgency for such a reusable shared business service.

Once business reuse has been established, functional reuse must be determined. By functional reuse, we mean the business functionality that is encapsulated by the service. If the functionality of the service is such that the functional reuse enables business reuse, there will be fewer obstacles to reusing a given service.

SOA and Operationalizing Agility

In Chapter 1 we set the stage for service-oriented agility. As we stated, SOA holds promise to finally make the word "agility" real for organizations.

What does "agility" mean? How does it differ from "flexibility"? Are they the same? Here is *Webster's* definition of "agile":

> *Agile – adjective: 1. Characterized by quickness, lightness, and ease of movement; nimble. 2. Mentally quick or alert: an agile mind.*

Now, let's explore the definition of "flexible," also from *Webster's:*

> *Flexible – adjective:*
> 1. *a. Capable of being bent or flexed; pliable.*
>   *b. Capable of being bent repeatedly without injury or damage.*
> 2. *Susceptible to influence or persuasion; tractable.*
> 3. *Responsive to change; adaptable: a flexible schedule.*

Two broad themes can be gleaned from these definitions: speed of response and ease of movement in the agile sense, and the ability to bend or adapt. Now, as we stated, the challenge with these words is to operationalize them, or make them real in a business sense, and then to find a way to measure them. Once such abstractions are operationalized and measurable, they are tangible.

Measuring agility is difficult. However, as agility depends on so many other factors, how do we measure agility as an SOA benefit? Some aspects of SOA agility include:

- Speed of response to a stimulus, external or internal.
- Degree of business change introduced without changing the SOA or IT architecture (tolerance to business change).
- Range of business and IT response options available to a given organization. Agility and flexibility will increase the range of options or increase strategic degrees of freedom.

In order to operationalize agility, we have to be able to define it so we can measure it. We can operationalize "agility" in this way:

Agility: The ability to respond quickly to an external change or new business requirement. "Quickly" means the total elapsed time required by the business or IT organization to react to an external threat or business change with an appropriate response. "Quickly" in this scenario means faster than you could respond previously. A benchmark or baseline metric is required for this metric.

Operationalizing SOA Goals, Drivers, and Metrics

Agility, flexibility, and other targeted SOA business goals must be converted into measurable entities that can be tracked to monitor progress and ultimately develop the ROI models. Doing this requires operationalizing the goals into statements that relate to metrics, and then defining metrics that can be measured. We advocate a three-step process for operationalizing SOA business goals:

1. *Define the SOA goal, driver, or value driver.* Be as specific as possible, ascribe qualitative value to it and a target to shoot for (e.g., reduce development costs by 20% and improve time to market by 30%).
2. *Operationalize the goal, driver, or value driver.* Clearly define what the goal is and make it real. In the example we used in Chapter 3, we operationalized agility as:

   SOA Value Driver: Improve business agility.

   Operational Definition: Increase time to market for business initiatives that rely on IT systems development, enhancements, or modifications. "Agility" is defined as the relative speed in which IT can provide support for business initiatives.

   Measurement: Time difference between an established baseline metric based on past projects and services-based projects, based on total elapsed calendar time.

3. *Define the measurement.* Be clear about how you plan to measure the goal, how to collect the data, and what baseline data may be required to prove it. Do not be afraid to test hypotheses. To test a hypothesis, you must state what the anticipated results will be and then find ways to prove that the results happened.

Determining the ROI for IT investments, or any investment for that matter, is a useful way to clarify the organizational value and business impact of investments. SOA, as we have discussed, has a clear business value when the ROI model is based on services reuse. However, as we have suggested, focusing solely on reuse leaves more SOA potential value on the table. Expand your value equation to include the entire spectrum of available SOA benefits, including soft benefits. Set big hairy audacious goals for your SOA, determine the metrics and process for attaining them, and then execute. Operationalize your SOA goals. Make them clear, assign ownership to their success, and define a metrics framework to track progress. SOA metrics are crucial for tracking success and monitoring organizational progress toward stated goals.

SOA METRICS AND SOA SCORECARDS

Metrics are crucial for the success of an SOA. Not just any metrics; we advocate a comprehensive metrics model called an SOA scorecard. The SOA scorecard is a metrics model that unites all SOA constituents to help manage the many facets of an SOA: financial metrics, business process metrics, architectural conformance metrics, service-level agreement (SLA) metrics, and operations metrics. This is a federated metrics model.

We use the example of the Mach number to drive the importance of SOA metrics. The term "Mach" comes from Ernst Mach, a great nineteenth-century scientist from Austria. Mach is the ratio between the speed of an object and the speed of sound in the medium in which the object is traveling. For example, Mach 1 is the speed of sound. An airplane that has the velocity of Mach 3.0 is traveling at three times the speed of sound as measured in the prevailing atmospheric conditions. Mach's revolutionary paper, "Photographische Fixierung der durch Projektile in der Luft eingeleiten Vorgange," was presented to the Academy of Sciences in Vienna in 1887. The term "Mach number" was first used in public in 1929 by Swiss engineer Jakob Ackeret. It first appeared in English publications in 1932. And it took until 1947 for Chuck Yeager to break the sound barrier, or achieve and surpass Mach 1, in his historic supersonic flight.

Until we had a way to measure the performance of high-speed air flight, we couldn't develop the solutions (fast planes) to achieve and surpass that performance goal (breaking the sound barrier). We needed the metric before we could achieve the performance goal. SOAs need metrics before they can achieve their performance goals. An organization needs an "SOA Mach number" to set the performance bar for its SOA initiative.

An SOA scorecard will provide a metrics framework for desired SOA and services performance. This framework should be created during SOA strategy and planning. The specific metrics will vary by organization. Taken together, these metrics comprise an "SOA steering wheel" that not only guides SOA and Web services to their destination (business goals) but also serves as a baseline to which all future performance improvements can be compared. An SOA scorecard puts a steering wheel on your SOA.

The SOA scorecard metrics model will accomplish a few important goals given this context:

- It ensures that all participants have a stake in SOA success.
- It ensures that all facets of the organization are involved: executives, business process owners, IT management, architects, developers, and support teams.
- It operationalizes and contextualizes the SOA (e.g., financial and ROI metrics, business process metrics, SLA metrics, operations metrics) for all stakeholders.
- It federates the metrics for all organizational stakeholders into a single management model.
- It can be implemented using common tools, such as dashboards, to make SOA metrics part of the management fabric of your organization.
- It defines the new level of performance that SOA will deliver. SOA scorecards can help achieve your SOA Mach number.

Defining SOA Metrics

SOA metrics must be identified to support the clear business outcomes defined from the business and IT imperatives, SOA drivers, and SOA value drivers. A clear business outcome might be "Achieve 30% Faster Time to Market for New Products." In order to make this clear business outcome measurable, a number of metrics must be devised to support it. One metric would be measuring the time to market for life insurance products, which would require measuring the total elapsed time from some trigger event until an ending event and then finding appropriate ways to track the metric. SOA metrics can be defined as the necessary measurements to determine progress toward a business goal. SOA metrics must be measurable, or able to be compared to a standard, and must measure the SOA contribution toward achievement of the business goal(s).

To make something measurable, it must be quantifiable according to numerical measures that can be compared. Examples of SOA metrics could include:

- *Business metrics.* Market share, time to market, cost savings, revenue growth, and customer satisfaction
- *Process metrics.* Process cycle time, process durations, process failures, number of process occurrences
- *Financial metrics.* ROI, cost savings, revenue growth, IT budgets, project costs
- *Usage metrics.* Number of Web services or services used; number of uses for a Web service or service; number of consumers; number of services or assets used or reused
- *Performance metrics.* How well a process or system is running (e.g., SLA, contract terms, uptime and downtime metrics, system outages, system failures, total cycle time)
- *IT efficiency metrics.* Asset reuse, services reuse, application development time, application quality, integration savings
- *SOA optimization metrics.* Number of services in production, number of services being reused, services utilization
- *SOA governance metrics.* Compliance metrics, governance exceptions, standards conformance

A metrics model that builds the desired business performance into the SOA strategy and implementation plans upfront is essential to SOA success. The model guides SOA progress, provides feedback, and ensures that everyone involved has visibility into the SOA success. A metrics model will help make your SOA journey more successful.

SOA Business Case Strategy

Developing the business case for SOA will involve all the ROI models we've presented in this chapter. The most important thing to take away from this chapter is that SOA is a process. Achieving the strategic business benefits of SOA requires commitment to your SOA strategy. It is a lifestyle change. Achieving the ROI thresholds of SOA value we identified requires sustained implementation of many projects over time.

The real question is one of expectations and ultimate objectives. What are you seeking with your SOA efforts? ROI? Business value? Business impact? Strategic business enablement of new capabilities? Revenue? Cost reductions? Depending on what your goals are and how your organization manages investments in technology and business challenges, your SOA goals may vary. That said, understand that SOA offers significant business value, ROI, and strategic enablement benefits. But you must stay the course. You must continue on the SOA path over time to reach SOA critical mass, where the business value accelerates.

This SOA business case approach may be helpful. However, do not forgo the BHAV approach to SOA value. Think big with your SOA strategy, and implement services to solve real business challenges. Finally, do not limit your SOA value to services reuse. There are bigger value levers available to you if you can get beyond reuse to the business benefits of SOA. Think about a possible SOA Mach number for your organization that maps to BHAV. Do not constrain your SOA value by current IT performance benchmarks. Think big.

Consider these next points as you develop your SOA business case. These are merely suggestions, but they may prove useful to your efforts.

- *Address known pain.* Match target SOA projects to known and documented business pain. (It is easier to justify a project that addresses known pain points.)

- *Find hard savings.* Find all areas where there are high-impact hard savings to the organization. Focus on reuse savings initially, but do not leave out other potential hard savings.
- *Identify customer benefits.* Find customer-facing benefits from the project that may increase revenue or improve customer experience.
- *Capture strategic benefits.* Tie them back to enabling capabilities.
- *Identify all the soft savings,* cost avoidances, and other SOA benefits.
- *Tie your SOA business case, ROI, and metrics to the business imperatives,* SOA drivers, and value drivers identified during your SOA strategy and planning sessions. Show how SOA addresses or resolves those issues.

SUMMARY

SOA is a relatively new discipline and is still quite misunderstood. One of the challenges to SOA is defining the business case and ROI for it. We have developed an SOA ROI threshold model to more accurately reflect the process by which SOA value can be achieved by an organization. This model is a very solid approach for understanding what investment will be needed to create a portfolio of reusable services in an SOA. Do not let your SOA be reduced to reuse metrics. There is bigger value to be had. Do not let your SOA be constrained by conventional metrics of IT value. Those are anchors to the past, not performance metrics that reflect where you want to be with your SOA efforts in a few years. That's why the SOA Mach number concept rings so true. Think about a metric that reflects the performance that you desire, not the performance of past capabilities. Find your SOA Mach number, use metrics to measure your progress, and think big. Go for the big hairy audacious goal that is possible.

NOTES

1. Jim Collins, *Good to Great* (New York: HarperCollins, 2001), pp. 197–204.
2. C. Soh and M. L. Markus, "How IT Creates Business Value: A Process Theory Synthesis," in *Proceedings of the 16th*

International Conference on Information Systems, ed. G. Ariav et al., December 10-13, Amsterdam, Netherlands.

3. Eric A. Marks, "The SOA Network Effect: Technical and Cultural Issues Drive Value," ComputerWorld Online, August 16, 2004.
4. Eric Newcomer and Greg Lomow, *Understanding SOA with Web Services* (New York: Addison-Wesley,), p. 16.
5. Jeffrey Poulin, *Measuring Software Reuse: Principles, Practices, and Economic Models* (New York: Addison-Wesley, 1996).

Index